JOHN DE KAY. Photograph from a bust by AUGUSTE RODIN. — 1908

Women
and the
New Social State

by
John de Kay.

The rights to reprint or translate this book belong exclusively to the author, but he is prepared by arrangement, to give these rights without compensation to himself, for any country under terms which will assure the most general circulation of the book and on condition that all sums usually payable to an author, will be paid to the international toilers' organizations.

To My dear Brother William

John de Kay.

8 May '19.

I dedicate these pages in recognition of the sacred influence of women in my own life and of a debt to them which I can never hope to pay.

JOHN DE KAY.

Steinhof Castle, Lucerne,
20th July 1918.

BY THE SAME AUTHOR:

LONGINGS	1907
THE WEAVER	1908
JUDAS (A DRAMA)	1910
THOUGHTS	1911
BROWN LEAVES	1911
THE PEOPLE'S MONEY	1912
DICTATORS OF MEXICO	1914
LOVE AND OTHER SONGS	1916
IMMORTALITY	1916
THE WORLD ALLIES	1917

PREFACE.

Notwithstanding the inevitable preoccupations involved in the direct control of a great business I have during the past fifteen years written many hundreds of pages upon the subjects treated in the present volume. Through the fortunes of war the manuscript is in one of the belligerent capitals and the inscrutable intelligence of those who govern in the name of Liberty does not permit me to obtain these writings during the war.

It is not difficult to understand this as it will be gathered from these pages I am not especially enthusiastic about war and am optimist enough to dare to hope that humanity might occupy its time more profitably than in a destruction of itself and in the shameless murder and folly which now disgrace mankind. As a new basis of social conflict is surely being laid throughout the world one must view with increasing alarm the long train of horror which has passed and that longer train which is to come as the most senseless, the most shameful and the most monstrous which history can ever record.

Were it not for the uncertainty as to when I may again come into the possession of my manuscript and the conviction I have that the problems discussed in these pages are of the most general and pressing importance, I would not subject myself to the criticism which may arise from the fact that this volume has been written in a few months, amid interruptions and preoccupations which have prevented the consecutive and tranquil consideration demanded for subjects of the highest moment. This book has been written in trams and trains, and on the margins of newspapers, but fortunately also through the whole of some quiet nights and in early morning hours when the world about me was asleep.

As it deals with the problem of saving life and beautifying the earth, rather than with the destruction of life and the spreading of ruin and havoc among men, some will consider it of no use or interest. I do not hope it will be immediately popular but I am persuaded that the principles announced are sound and indicate the lines along which generations of the future are destined to create a well-ordered social state. Whether this result may come soon or late I have discharged a duty I owed to myself and which consisted in adding one more stone to the foundation of what I have conceived as possible for a new commonwealth.

It began with my book "*The People's Money*" published in 1912. To this I added "*The World Allies*" in 1917. Other volumes are in progress and I hope will in due course be published.

In these pages I deal with the psychological and physical differences most pronounced between men and women and seek to indicate to what extent their mental and moral traits arise from their sex and how far they may be influenced by environment, by the difference in their occupations, and by the social customs which have created a system as monstrously wrong and degrading to women as it is unfair to men.

The principles of education and some of its present grave defects are outlined and a more sound, rational and moral system is suggested, together with practical illustrations of its application to men, women and children.

I show in what respects women are and must remain

permanently different from men, in what ways they are man's superiors and why it is that the most important achievements of the greatest women are not comparable to those of the greatest men, also how women may be honourably protected from man's gross abuse of social liberty and in what way men and women should be made responsible for their conduct.

I deal with the economic position of women and demonstrate that if they are now induced to enter into a competitive wage struggle with men, as a result of the shameless war waged in the interest of international plutocracy, they will generally enslave both themselves and men. Also the economic reasons why the exploiting classes are interested in the extension of such a movement, and how it may be stopped. Also the reasons why any extension of government ownership or centralization of the power and functions of governments, as they are now constituted, is contrary to the interests of mankind and a menace to its liberty.

In chapters eight and nine these questions are closely examined and the practical steps are indicated as to how the means of production may pass from its present proprietorship through the hands of those whose manual and intellectual labour now creates all material, intellectual and spiritual wealth and how it may be universally socialized.

The measures I suggest are practical and yet fundamental and are adapted for immediate application in the world of realities, rather than in some vague world of unrealities which does not exist and will never exist. They lead by sure and peaceful steps to a universal social commonwealth and constitute the remedy for the existing world-exploitation, economic anarchy and social injustice.

I show why industrial toil should be performed exclusively by men and machines and the social and economic measures essential to accomplish this result. I indicate how

VIII

women may be free from industrial slavery of every sort and enabled to devote their lives to their natural careers, to the end that millions of women would not be homeless and childless and other millions living either by arduous unnatural toil or through prostitution in its ordinary or in its hundreds of hidden forms.

The academic and practical basis of political rights and the principles of government are considered with the view of showing why democracies are not democratic, also as to what should constitute the right of one man to exercise any form of control over another and why an abstract right to power does not exist. Also why all hereditary political power is wrong in principle and harmful in practice and why it must be abolished, together with its train of so-called dignities and titles which make practical autocrats of a few men and snobs of all the rest.

I have considered the curious psychology of the mass which sees safety in numbers and does not recognize the danger involved in an unorganized or badly advised multitude and the practical effect of man's general tendency to accept and defend everything inherited from the past, also the claims which institutions of great authority and antiquity put forward for the continuation of their control of mankind and the extent to which such authority should be repudiated and set aside.

The basis of education for children and the only principles upon which they may be taught self-control and equipped for the realities of life are examined and illustrations are given as to how these principles may be applied.

I show why the League of Nations idea in the form in which it is conceived by the actual rulers of mankind is only an imposing phantom; also in whose interest such a league will be formed and run; why the suggestion is now put forward and why it will not be of the slightest use as an effective safeguard against future wars. Only such an organization of PEOPLES as that outlined in "*The World Allies*" and in these pages can bring security and peace to the masses.

The oppressed and patient millions in all lands have always had and will always have common interests one with the other. They are national in nothing but name and prejudice, while the plutocracy which exploits and destroys them is an organized international force which gives effect to its designs through governments and these governments cannot be brought under the trangible control of the toilers until millions of labouring men and socialists are effectively organized throughout the world. It is the solemn duty of these men to reach without delay an international basis of accord and a definite plan of action in order that they may put an immediate end to the shameless murder which disgraces humanity and which is ruining the world.

They represent the only force which can bring order out of the chaotic horror into which mankind has been plunged by the ambitions, greed and tyranny of international high finance and they owe it to themselves and to posterity to take immediate steps to this end. The steps which they can and should now take are indicated with precision in Chapter IX. of this book. They have borne too long and patiently the abuse of power by a few men who have assumed dictatorship throughout the world and who are now engaged in carrying out a policy of international murder on a scale which threatens to bring irretrievable ruin to all belligerent peoples and which may be followed by a general social catastrophe unless the toilers and socialists form a world alliance for the peaceful solution of their common problems.

The avidity with which the masses cling to all the phantoms created to perpetuate their own oppression is an indication of how desperately mankind stands in need of real leadership and how little likely it is to follow anything which may be truly effective in the attainment of a proper commonwealth. If all these tendencies were not so melancholy in their display of the almost unbelievable blindness of humanity, they might be regarded with less misgiving by those who have no illusions as to the actual social order or as to the steps which must now be taken for the genuine service of mankind.

I show how the hold of political parties over the choice of candidates may be abolished, together with the baneful control exercised by a few over all administrative and legislative actions of governments, and how it may be rendered forever impossible for nominal rulers, cabinets or parliaments to murder millions of men without their consent and convert the world into a hideous ruin in the exclusive interests of national exploitation and international imperialism—or upon any other pretext whatsoever.

The polygamy of men, involving as at present none of the honourable obligations which should be inseparable from all acts of such social importance, is brought under review and stern measures are suggested to meet an evil which has always been one of the tragedies of civilization and which will develop in ways fatal to the material and spiritual life of great peoples and a menace to all social order.

One chapter is devoted to the definite outlines of a new system of marriage, sound in its principles and morals and in strict accord with the nature and practice of men who are at present able to have all the advantages of relations with several women at one or another period of their lives, without incurring any of the responsibilities which should be inseparable from their conduct. This new system would not in the least interfere with the noble and ideal happiness which is sometimes realized by men and women in the existing order. It would tend to discourage the polygamous conduct of men, because of its stern justice and the responsibilities which it would impose upon men.

It is the last chapter of the book and I would wish that it be read last in order that it may occupy (in the minds of those who do me the honour to read these pages) its relative place in the work as a whole and therefore be more clearly seen in its true perspective.

I have no doubt, when the matter is viewed in its world tendencies and covering great periods of time, it will be seen that promiscuous sexual relations and plural marriages may altogether disappear. All local, national, international and co-operative organizations of men and women who labour with their brains and hands are steps whose remote end will be universal monogamy, because these steps are all leading to a universal socialization of property and labour and that would put an end to exploitation and war. It would put an end also to idleness and want, which are the extreme and immediate cause of so much social disorder and evil.

As Nature sacrifices the present for the sake of the future, so it sacrifices the parent to its offspring—in the interest of the future. As this is applied to mankind it must tend towards perfection in the moral, as in the physical realm.

There can be no two opinions upon the question, that the interests of the children are best protected through a continuous union of both parents with the offspring. This means that the perfection of the individual, and consequently universal human perfection, will one day rest solidly upon a foundation in which the union of one man and one woman, as a social unit, will be the universal base.

I hope that a few who read these pages may find in them something more universal than measures designed to meet the needs of our age in the great questions relating to education, economics and the social state. Important as those issues undoubtedly are there is something still more essential to mankind as it concerns the relation of the individual to the universal Nature and his place in Society.

I have endeavoured to define the general principles which may be applied by the individual to his conduct and followed by him in all that concerns his present and most remote aims and through the understanding of which he may attain not only the social ideals which should attend the ordered evolution of man, but those more personal and higher ideals of the individual with respect to his possible place in the universal order.

To those who are able to regard these pages in their true significance, there will be revealed not only a sound policy for society but a comprehensive philosophy of life, through which man may find his destined place and understand his true relation to his fellow men. There is in this philosophy something which shows how man may progress in harmony with the universal Nature towards a great destiny to be conceived only in universal terms, and raised above any limitations which man may himself prescribe.

JOHN DE KAY.

CONTENTS.

Chapter I

THE INSTINCTS AND CHARACTER OF WOMEN. Page 1.

The problem of woman and her place in the world. Man's errors regarding woman. Women as competitors of men. This contrary to nature. Dangers for women in present industrial system. Some moral and physical peculiarities of the two sexes and their relation to the economic problem. Women sacrifice themselves and men toil for their own children not for the race. This is instinct not ethics. Ethical aspect of the masses. Lowness of ethical standard of this age. No equality between men and women. Various differences. Nature's way of attaining its ends. Women the conservative element in society. Not creative. Guardians of the home and children. Women regard each other as competitors all engaged in the same task. Men more impersonal (even in competition). Men jealous of each other's achievements; women of beauty and qualities attractive to men. Possible influence of education on woman's creative faculty. Culture and woman. Reasons why women study. Importance of sex and motherhood in woman's life. Care and education of children. Children should be made responsible for their acts: free and self-reliant. Examples of method to attain these ends. Importance of punctuality, truthfulness, a healthy body. Present untruthfulness between men and women, children and parents. Those people best governed who are least controlled by laws. Further principles for the upbringing of children. Relations between children and parents. Highest development of men and women expressed in founding home and rearing children. Importance of mental cultivation for women as equipment for life. Woman as inspiration of man. Examples of Mill and Nelson. Women alone appreciate contemporary great men. Woman's position towards ethics morals and conduct. Deception as a fine art. The sexes complementary, not equal. Most potent force in man's achievement is woman's approval. Woman's tendency to exaggerate importance of sex and undervalue other considerations. Women must respond to and carry out nature's designs even though they may never know or understand why.

Chapter II.
WOMAN'S MORAL POSITION AND HER PLACE IN HUMAN ACHIEVEMENTS. Page 39.

Clearly defined differences between men and women to be taken into account in order to solve existing economic problems. Women both superior and inferior to men. Progress to be measured by good of all. Women to be neither ignorant nor slaves. Woman has not been taught anything of real value. Woman's weakness is her strength and greated charm. All competition between men and women is wrong. Man's exploitation of and unfairness towards women. Woman should not duplicate man's work but enter upon her own career: motherhood. All professions should be freely open to women. Women good physicians and actresses. Rational basis for medical and legal professions as a whole. How far will the gulf between the creative achievements of men and women be narrowed in the future? Woman's nature and functions are obstacles to highest attainments in this field. Stupidity and inefficiency of majority of both sexes. Comparison of average man and woman. Immortal artistic and scientific creations have come from men even if largely inspired by women. Exceptional women and their achievements. Rarity and importance of genius. Importance of birth and education of children. Lack of freedom of both men and women. Unimportance of ballot under existing conditions. All surplus of toil passes to unproductive class. Woman's highest sphere the home. Harmfulness to her and the race of forcing her into industrial competition. This only of advantage to exploiter who profits from greatest possible competition among toilers. Some striking characteristics of women. Their attitude towards morality, sex and suffering. Contrasted to men. Religions created by men. Man's vanity and egoism. Only by recognizing and respecting differences between men and women can highest powers of both be realized. Spiritual similarity of average type. Brevity of individual life and its relation to designs of nature. Importance and difficulty of scepticism and originality. The present status of Liberty. Tenacity of adherence to tradition and accepted religions. Spiritual side of science and true religion. Limits of man's possible knowledge. The wise investigate what the foolish worship. Differences between scientists, philosophers and priests. Evil in present relations of men and women. Inadequacy of divorce as a solution. Historic point of view: similarity of ancient and modern exploitation. Ruling castes changed from personal to impersonal tyranny. Present horrible conditions the creations of men wherefore they may be remedied. The effect of the war upon the present system.

Chapter III.

THE GENERIC INFLUENCE OF ETHICS AND SENTIMENT. Page 70.

Existing hope that the recent world-calamity may make possible a new social structure. Natural laws should no longer be set aside, for this results in ruin and disaster. Relations of men and women towards one another beautiful and important only in proportion as founded upon sentiment and personal understanding rather than creeds, customs or laws. Hypocrisy of ruling classes. Low ethic of present era. Masses unaware of their enslavement. Mockery of

XVI

religious professions in face of the war. Necessity of facing problems as they are and of solving them in accord with human nature. Difficulty of helping mankind. Some differences in attitude of men and women towards legislation, property and the struggle for existence. Origin of legislation a feeling of self-defence. Woman's instinct of self-defence strong; her feeling for justice weak; her prejudice decided and unreasonable. Only exceptional women view great questions impersonally. Women and violence. Deception as a weapon. Male and female animals and self-defence. Women in law-courts. Attitude of women in business transactions; not graceful losers nor qualified gamblers. Influence of economic dependence and drudgery upon women. This would be altered under my system of marriage. As women take up the work of men they tend to lose their characteristic traits and become more like men in various ways. Lack of punctuality and rigorous discipline in life of women and its result. Attitude towards property and comparative honesty of men and women. Systems of checking. Stimulus to morals of employees in making them feel they are trusted and conscious of their personal dignity. Toilers should be made to feel they are not working for anonymous company which merely makes them machines, but for themselves and society. How and why present industrial system is an injurious moral influence. Individual independence in Switzerland. Freedom of masses traceable to economic independence in a really democratic nation of small farmers rather than of industrial wage-slaves. Economic independence always the preliminary of political freedom. Secret ballot a decisive power for the masses only when toilers formulate a definite program and unite solidly in defence of their proper interests. Example of practical value of secret ballot. Lack of genuine democracy in other so-called democracies. The masses are employed on a basis preventing their rise above the level of an ordinary product whose selling-price is determined not by value but by the necessity of the toilers. Employed by machines they become part of the machinery and slaves of the economically organized machines. Present vital importance of organization nationally and internationally if freedom is to be attained by the masses.

Chapter IV.
MAN'S ABUSE OF SOCIAL LIBERTY.   Page 87.

Man by nature polygamist. His polygamy however carries no legally binding social obligations tending to abolish a system inflicting injustice on millions of women and ruinous to humanity. Ideal of happiness to be found in the relation of one man and one woman. Intolerable present position of woman and its causes. Indignation against war and possible civil strife. The toilers' effort to rule or wreck industrialism. Only general ruin would follow violence. Problem of the millions of women whose natural protectors have been murdered. Evils of lack of responsibility placed on man's promiscuous relations. Hypocrisy of mankind. Tragedy of woman's position. Man's nature. Essential that men and women bear consequences of their conduct. Difference of man's and woman's point of view. Importance of man's acts to society, and society's duty to surround such acts with safeguards. How far has society the right to regulate personal conduct? Present restrictions of divorce and their cause. Highest interest of toilers the withdrawal of women from competition by giving them homes. Relation of men and women outside of marriage and legal age of assent. These relations rendered impossible and unnecessary by the system set out in last chapter of this book. Enormous surplus of women over men. Altered status of woman since the war. Her present course and its disastrous consequences. A word about the clergy. The masses and a social commonwealth. Obedience to authority. The courage of doubt. Tyranny of public opinion and general tyranny: by whom and how it is exercised. Possibility of progress.

XVIII

Chapter V.

THE PSYCHOLOGICAL IMPORTANCE OF PREJUDICE AND TRADITIONS. Page 101.

Obstacles in the way of development of humanity. Conflict of personal happiness of individual and larger issues. Nature's sacrifice of present to future; man's sacrifice of future to present. Harmonization of laws of nature and man. What is progress; how to judge of it and how to attain it. Inability of ideal reformers to realize ideas and selfishness of really practical organizers. Present primitivity of instincts. Philanthropy, its status and motives. Relation to public opinion. Sacred authority of customs and institutions and resulting evils. General ignorance of actual conditions. Uselessness of dividing wealth and other reforms, unless man learns that his personal ends are truly to be realized only through the general good. Essential that masses have an open mind towards criticism of all that is man-made. Danger of unorganized numbers. Power of and need for organization. Past and present attitude of rabble towards opinion of others. The Inquisition—war. Fickleness of masses. Fashion and social intercourse. Following the crowd Unsoundness of our social structure. Nature, not man is just. Nature however not ethical in man's sense. Possibility of presence in nature of an ethical aim. No limit to possibility of man's moral attainments. "The meek shall inherit the earth." Passing of brute force. Morality of man and its place in evolution. Force of the ideal. Man's goal. Harmony with nature lies in man attaining impersonal justice and universal sympathy. Comparison of man's moral attitude towards his parents or children. General tendency to regard what has been long sanctioned as right. Influence of prejudice even on greatest minds. Custom and public opinion among Sioux Indians. Man should seek greatest good of greatest number and harmony with nature's justice, which makes no attempt at equality but lets each individual reap as he sows. Moral basis of man's laws. Individual and collective murder. In how far is human conduct ethical? Solution of human problem by morals. Only minority to be governed by purely moral considerations. Philosophers and dreamers, indifferent to public opinion, set up standards of true morals. The economically independent seem to act ethically by giving to others. Reason why the ethical value of such charity is small.

Chapter VI.

THE PRINCIPLES OF EDUCATION AND POLITICAL RIGHTS. Page 120.

Defects in educational system due to devices of ruling classes. Position of clergy, autocrats and plutocrats. More attention should be paid to microscope, telescope and economics. Narrow conception of present education. Inadequate both for poor and rich. Poor should know laws of hygiene, mechanics and nature. Education too restricted and mechanical. Importance of learning principles underlying facts. Illustrations of insufficient teaching in cases of history, reading, writing. Of erroneous teaching as to authority, religion and government. No enquiry made. Defects in education of women. Omissions, overemphasis of emotional side and resulting lack of counterpoise. Why the best educated are the daughters of some artisans. Causes and results of differences between education of poor and rich. Women now marching towards enslavement. Wrong basis of suffrage. Demand for the ballot with reference to existing relations between men and women. Illustration in case of Switzerland. Reasons why co-operation between men and women is right and why competition is wrong. Evils of industrial exploitation of women. Danger of impending economic enslavement. Substitution of labour of women for labour of millions of men killed in the war. Resulting benefit for plutocracy. Solution lies in economic freedom and ability of men to support women. Ineffectuality of ballot

XX

Numbers of no importance. Sex is no basis for right to vote; this should be political and historical education, regardless of sex. Ignorance of history of institutions and consequent attitude towards actual wrongs. Cause of slow progress of humanity. Inability of masses to discern connection between exploiters and governing institutions. All toilers are brothers—this may be understood by all. This is the basis on which men must unite and act. Sentiment as a factor in mass-action. Women who vote should cast off prejudice, nationalism and cease to fight in an industrial competitive war. Democracy an illusion. Masses have no real voice or understanding of conditions. Vote not of primary importance so long as man's instincts are unsocial. Political power of employers; coercion of employees. Interests of toilers cannot be protected through political institutions, except after organization on a world scale. Evil of violence and civil war and resulting disaster. By organization and peaceful pressure only, may the masses become the rulers of the world. Real property and war-profit. Latter should be cancelled. Arms should no longer be manufactured. Natural and peaceful measures for toilers to attain their rights. Governments as instruments. Organizers outside of politics. Plutocrats' employment of politicians to run governments. Despots who rule democracies. Eloquence of politicians and effects on the masses. Misconstituted parliaments. Masses wish to remain under illusion of their sovereignty. This wish taken advantage of. Resulting powerlessness of the masses.

Chapter VII.

A SOUND BASIS FOR POLITICAL POWER AND THE SCOPE OF A LEAGUE OF NATIONS. Page 147.

The right to power, who has it and the criminal use to which it is put. Functions of governments. Right basis for political power. Ecclesiastical power

XXI

and place of religion in the state. Position of Jews. Their international importance. Evolution of democracies. Powerlessness of the masses. Difference between legal and moral rights to power. Hereditary power as check to progress. Some evils of this system. Aristocracies of war, of wealth and of intellect. Our grotesque institutions. Dangers of armament and present system. Readjustment of political power essential. True and false "Majesty." Undemocratic character of so-called democracies. Present control of governments. Politicians and their masters. What should be basis of power. Right of decision regarding lives of men. Position of masses towards war. Power and duty of press. Prevention of war: necessity of a world-organization of toilers, not of a league of the governments of nations. True causes of the war. Movement towards internationalism and the attitude of plutocracy towards it. Need for immediate action; for leadership. Stupidity of man. Immediate dangers invisible to blind humanity. Betrayal of humanity and possible results. Tragedy of the war. The League of Nations. Not even a step towards abolishing wars. No governments—only the common man can make war impossible. How and why the League of Nations will not carry out what is required and will not abolish wars. The prejudice of nationality. The importance of castes which are international. Abuse of common man. Decisions of a court of League of Nations and obstacles in way of their enforcement save by war. The Swiss Confederation. Peace a result of rule by the people. Indivisible world-interest of toilers. The new tyranny and feudalism. The place of the United States in the present system. War will be so long as nations are equipped for war. Necessity for toilers' international organization to enforce complete disarmament as the only road to peace. Laws of compensation and values. Oneness of the world. Senselessness of hatred. Russia and her future. International armies and the suppression of Liberty. Dangers of nationalism. Impotence of League of Nations of this sort. Humanity's need for peace and

XXII

only means of attaining it. Destruction a violation of law of life. Scepticism not directed against League of Nations in principle, but against this particular league which would not be a League of Peoples. Basis for real League of Nations. Dangers arising from having taught men to murder their brothers. The "Allies" and the so-called peace. Comparisons of scope of the government and of the positions of soldiers and clergy in various lands. Progress depends on elevation of masses. Lesson of unified variety of races in America. Prohibition. Germany and paternal government. Germany's road to freedom; her intellectual achievements. Contrast with United States. Importance of philosophers. Individual self-control. Slowness of reforms. Essential conditions unaltered by war. More wealth for plutocracy. The ensnaring of woman into the old system. Proposal to curtail right of inheritance and resulting benefit to labour; effect on the money-makers. Progress and the minority to which it is due. Parliaments and a remedy for their inertia. The initiative and referendum. Transfer of government into the hands of the people. Methods of election. Power and function of press. Religion and politics. A long road before man will arrive at ideal state. The regrettable power of tradition. Inability of masses to think for themselves. Juxtaposition of castes. Need of a sense of dignity. Human life is everywhere for sale—nowhere sacred. Man should be master, not slave of the machine. Political role of the philosopher now and in the future. Necessity of experts in government.

Chapter VIII.
INDUSTRIALIZATION OF WOMEN AND NATIONALIZATION OF INDUSTRY. Page 216.

Effect of industrial exploitation seen in rapidly altering status of women. Evolution of master and slave in feudalism and in industrialism. Rise of tenants to proprietorship of land but no definable world-

XXIII

tendency in land question. In proper commonwealth industrial toilers must be proprietors of their homes. Principles of industrial centralization not applicable to farming. World-importance of small farmer. Power of employer in industrial community. Freedom proportional to economic independence. Material and moral advantages of farmers. Inadequacy of measures and theory of trades unions. New competition of millions of women added to other evils of toilers. Why this is merely an aggravation of labour problem. Conditions previous to the war and participation of the toilers in what they produced, compared to profits of plutocrats. Why these wish to force women to enter all spheres of labour. A warning: the results of industrial enslavement of women. Remedy: a fair distribution of all production. Complete disarmament essential. Perfection of machinery and use of inventions. How industry could be organized to do away with present abuses and injustices. Purpose of giving votes to women. — Why government ownership is a fictitious remedy. Harmfulness of nationalizing means of production and distribution. This as means of increasing the tyranny of bureaucracy. Political and economic dangers of government ownership. A check to individual development. Aggravates evil of centralization of power. Narrow line between paternalism and despotism. Would destroy independence, responsibility, initiative, progress. Effort necessary to prevent individuals and nations from degenerating. Importance of feeling of personal dignity. Difficulty of peacefully transferring power from one class to another. Controlling power of government exercised by the best organized. Why it is fatal for government to be also industrial master. Lesson to be drawn from actual conditions in belligerent countries. An exception where temporary government participation might be efficacious. Institutions will never be perfect or permanent. Tendencies along which civilization is to move for several generations are clearly indicated and can be foreseen. Melancholy aspect displayed by inertia and helplessness of masses.

Chapter IX.

THE PRACTICAL STEPS TOWARDS SOCIALIZATION.
Page 235.

The practical steps which can be immediately taken and which will lead by sure and peaceful ways to the complete socialization of capital and labour without transferring either to the ownership or control of governments. Registration of property. Conditions and purpose of registration of bank-notes and other securities. War debts to be paid through war profits. Gradual capital tax. Progressively rising inheritance tax. Land taxed upon basis of productive capacity. Organization of scientific agriculture and a co-operative system of collection and distribution. Avoidance of waste, loss, underproduction and unsalable surpluses. Chance for millions to become small farmers with benefit of own production or profit in agricultural enterprises. My system of payment which must apply to communal and state undertakings as well as private capitalism until private capitalism has disappeared. Compensation to labour to be established on basis of productive value and human rights. Establishment of minimum return for capital; all surplus to be divided between capital and labour and society as a whole. Capital to be appraised. Establishment of basis of minimum return, minimum wage for labour and socialization of capital, labour and agricultural production. Shares of capital stock to be issued to actual owners and outstanding securities to be cancelled by public trustee. Obliteration of fictitious capital. Distribution of profit of enterprise between toilers therein engaged, registered holders of certificates of stock and national fund for socializing enterprise; of this fund part should be devoted to educational purposes, determined by federalized organizations of labour. Means for carrying out socialization of all enterprises concurrently. Right of employees to representation on board. All meetings of share-holders open to public.

XXV

Advantage of toilers to invest in stock. Government auditors. End of strikes. The World Parliament of Labour. Its importance, organization and powers. Decrease of payments by public trustee and addition to socializing fund. End of private ownership of all industries. Disappearance of slums. Decentralization of population. Combination of industrial employment with work on land. Buildings rented for shops, apartments or tenements to be appraised similarly to land and industries in order to establish rent on basis of minimum return to capital. Method of dealing with landlordism. Abolishment of small shopkeeping. Public markets. Evils of present retail distribution. Closing of stock-exchanges. End of financial speculation. Gold a commodity not a god. Insurance organizations socialized. The sense in which high finance is international and yet creates wars. Danger of creating backward states under present system. Proper League of Nations would put international finance on different basis. Means to this end. Money of the future an international currency. The socialization of people. The new universal co-operative commonwealth. Mastery to those who toil with hands and brains. Transition gradual, but a beginning can be immediate. Importance of ethical evolution. General conclusions. Benefits of my system tending to establish and maintain a genuine social state.

Chapter X.

THOUGHTS CONCERNING PHILOSOPHY AND CHRISTIANITY. Page 253.

Human longing for Immortality. Poets and philosophers and their part in human progress. Enduring and transient fame. Great men persecuted by their own and worshipped by subsequent generations. Inadequacy of religions and institutions. Man's speculation and its necessary limitation. Man's hope of an ethical aim in Nature. Scientists and philosophers have found justice in nature but as

XXVI

yet no moral aims. Faith versus Philosophy. Sources of inequality among men. Basis for system of morals. Boundaries to man's possible knowledge. Inability to establish any system eliminating all assumption. What man can know about Life. Importance of the great river of Life aside from individual life. Spiritual happiness. The highest meaning of Immortality. The infinite progression from man's striving towards the Unknowable and towards his highest possibility. Achievement ever in direction of hope. True significance of hope. Man's moral progress. Evils of material or spiritual paternalism. Present tyranny and how exercised. If Christianity had ethical significance for those who profess it, there would be no war. In how far Christ's teachings are adaptable to our own or any other society of men. Christ's ideal state a spiritual kingdom. Man's error in attempting to apply this materially and literally. Christ's teaching of obedience to all authority. Criticism of this and other teachings based on the lower moral standard of the Old Testament. Evils of gospel of rewards and punishments and of "Thou shalt not." Most exalted teachings come from those who reject Christianity. The church a check to human progress. True meaning of the Divine Love for man. Inability of mankind to comprehend or follow the Christ. Misinterpretation of high spirituality of Christianity. Possibility that humanity may rise to a plane where laws are no longer necessary; at present it is only at the beginning of its development. Immortality only possible as evolution to a higher state of being. Man's dignity. Evils of pretention, superstition and submission. Why man must cast these off to attain his highest spiritual development.

Chapter XI.

THE NEW MARRIAGE SYSTEM. Page 272.

Human desire for happiness. Increasing complexity of relations between men and women and resulting

XXVII

unhappiness. Moral failure in whole range of human relations. Solution of present economic and social problems of women. Flattery of women and its results. Danger in their industrial employment. Cheapness of women as an industrial commodity. Results of industrial "equalization" of men and women. Calamity of competition. The generations of fatherless children. Need for change in basis of payment of toil and for a new marriage system. Women now largely dependent on generosity of men. Necessity for contracts. Unique character of marriage contract. Present unfairness; hypocrisy; insufficiency of present legal protection for women. Injustice of present moral standard. Not polygamy itself but injustice connected with present form of polygamy is reprehensible. How women can attain greatest economic and social rights. Efforts of men and women should be united. Woman in the home and her real economic independence. Legally women under no disadvantage except sometimes in case of divorce. Man's natural polygamy and the form it takes at present. Sacred influence of love. Rarity of ideal relations between men and women. Unnecessary compromise existing in all human affairs. Highest social relation is monogamy; ethically and biologically most sound principle. Difference between polygamy and promiscuousness. Moral superiority of the former. Advantage to children through care and love of both parents. Decrease of over-centralization and of vice. Man's development away from need for restraint put upon him by public opinion. Immediate measures ultimately to lead to establishment of monogamous social life. Protection of women essential to their real emancipation and social freedom. Evils for women of promiscuous sexual intercourse and of competition with men. Results of universal socialization of which one will be a real monogamy. Position of man and woman in the home. Comparison with business partnership. Women's place in the activities of men. Influence of mothers. Importance of education and necessity of altering education of girls. Happiness of mankind is in the

XXVIII

keeping of women. Reasons for actual conditions. No short or easy road to highest ends. Need for a new marriage system paramount. Such a system outlined, in harmony with human nature. Present fear of public opinion and its effect on morality. Necessity for same rule of conduct for all classes of society. Senseless and compromising divorce laws now existant and the evils they cause. Necessity for altering basis of payment of toilers and marriage based on resulting conditions free from competition between men and women. Essential provisions of the new system. How and on what basis marriages should be contracted; how terminated. Legislation to ensure support of women and children; impossibility of sexual relations without marriage and all marriages to be equally legal and binding. Plural marriages for men because of surplus of women. Position of women in their first and subsequent marriages. Advantages of this system. End of pretence and injustice towards women; no need for industrial competition between men and women; abolition of prostitution and decrease of disease; no tendency to lessen actual monogamy, on the contrary; only takes conditions into account thereby eliminating unfairness to women and injuries to society. Greater freedom of choice for women and resulting benefit to the race. A hopeful look into the future and the goal man may attain.

CHAPTER I.

THE INSTINCTS AND CHARACTER OF WOMEN.

During the last hundred years a great many books have been written as to the nature and qualities of woman and the place she should occupy in the life of the world.

Of all who deal with this subject it is the poets who best understand the nature and province of women, perhaps because it is only to the poet that women most clearly appear in their natural role.

It is to the imagination that the charms of women make the strongest appeal. The most important relations which men establish with women are founded entirely upon a sentiment in which reason does not exercise any considerable influence. This sentiment is for the poet what fragrance is to a flower.

The philosopher approaches women from the point of view of one who would find a reason for the most important acts of life whereas so far as women are concerned their most important acts have no reference to reason. They spring from the hidden fountain of primitive instincts which unconsciously operate within a closely restricted circle for the primary purpose of perpetuating the human species.

The poet's conception of women is the true conception

but as only a few men are poets, the ones who are able to see woman as she is are an exceedingly small minority and women never see themselves as they are. Of all the problems man has tried to solve, he has made the poorest showing in his dealing with the problem of women. He has mismanaged everything but he has recorded his most egregious mistakes in his mismanagement and misunderstanding of women. In theory he has exalted her to a superior place, while in practice she has been degraded and enslaved. A great part of this anomaly may be accounted for by the charm, tenderness and affection which she shows toward man and his feeling that as she places her life in his hands, he is bound to her by special ties of deference, respect and tenderness. At the same time his economic institutions and irrational system of marriage have forced an ever increasing number of women to enter the competitive struggle for existence against men who by sympathy and nature do not wish to compete with them.

Underneath the surface politeness shown to women there is the stern consciousness that, through no fault of their own, they are forcing the hands of men in all professions and also in an ever increasing degree in trade and industry. The situation created by the industrial exploitation of the masses is becoming constantly more serious for both sexes. It cannot pursue its present tendency without consequences of the most general and destructive character in all industrial nations.

In considering the most important aspects of this problem it is essential briefly to examine some phases of nature as expressed in the moral and physical peculiarities of the two sexes, and the measures necessary to the adjustment of their lives to the new conditions created by the exploitation and other crimes of plutocracy.

I am unable to agree with any of the propositions which have been the most generally upheld by philosophers as to the ethical attitude of woman towards society or as to her moral position and I am entirely opposed to all existing notions as to what should be her economic status.

The contention of philosophers has been that the attitude of woman toward the future is dominated by an ethical consideration for the race, rather than by any personal regard for herself or for those with whom her life is spent. I reject this theory and all conclusions which are inevitably drawn from it. Neither men nor women regard the race as more important than the individual and in particular a woman's interest in the race is limited to her own offspring. She is not prepared to sacrifice the present for the future except as regards her own children and her instinctive readiness to make this sacrifice is entirely unethical. It is the most general and primitive of all instincts and applies to nearly all the higher types of animal life and to the males as well as females of nearly all the more important species in their natural surroundings.

The greater part of the life-toil of nearly every man is devoted to the support and protection of others. When his resources are meagre they are almost wholly spent for those who have a claim upon his affections. To realize how unethical is this attitude it is only necessary to observe that nearly all individuals recognize no claims whatsoever of anyone outside the strictly limited circle of their own families. This is one of the most general as well as the least ethical of animal propensities. When we witness the drudgery and economy of the toilers and realize that, by depriving themselves of many things to which they are entitled, they accumulate a small fund of insurance, we say in profound admiration that life insurance is love's tribute to death, for "what hath man of all his labour" and vexation of spirit?

It is because men and women will make these sacrifices solely for their own offspring rather than for our common humanity that we must disassociate these purely instinctive measures for the protection of offspring from all ethical considerations. We observe that animals in general, to which we deny all capacity for ethics or even for speculative reasoning, sacrifice themselves until their offspring is self-supporting. The uncertainty of life and the keen struggle rendered essential through competitive industry, have impelled men and women to endeavour to assure the protection of their offspring through the accumulation and bequest of property. This property is never bequeathed to their neighbour's children but always to their own, because the nature of men and women is such as to make them incapable of considering the race except in so far as it is represented by their own offspring. All this is outside the bounds of ethics. It is for the perpetuation of personal offspring and is a general characteristic of all the more important animals except the males among domestic species. These do nothing for their offspring. The instance of dogs is typical. The male does not in any way concern itself with its offspring and does not appear to recognize them, whereas the female not only feeds them but when she no longer has milk and they must all live upon what they are given, if there is an insufficient amount she refrains from eating more than will barely suffice and leaves the remainder for the puppies. She cannot be induced to eat while they are hungry unless she is fed in a separate place, where she is momentarily withdrawn from the sight of the distress of her offspring. If one of the puppies is weaker than the rest she gives her protection to the weakest with a solicitude which is touching to witness, as I have had occasion personally to observe with the wolf-dogs in Switzerland.

It may also be observed in some of its most marvelous

manifestations among insects which show that as regards their offspring they act with great solicitude and prudence. The care with which some butterflies and beetles prepare for descendants whom they will never see is an illustration that throughout the animal world there runs a mysterious thread of sentiment and foresight which cannot be ascribed to experience, tradition or external education. It is a deep-seated and all prevailing instinct of reproduction, but it is personal, not racial; it is material, not ethical and it appears as a part of the development of the individual whether it is applied to men and women or to animals in general—including many insects.

It is due to the fact that some men and women were able to bequeath not only sound bodies but substantial fortunes to their offspring that the world is indebted for its oldest, though not for its greatest names. The most exalted greatness amounts to genius. This is rarely transmitted and can never be explained.

The attitude of men and women toward the present and the future is not dominated by ethical considerations. If it were we would not witness the shameless exploitation and misery of the masses and we would not mortgage the future in order to avoid the payment of debts contracted in the present. Never in the history of man has there been such a tragic demonstration of the truth of these statements as may be seen in every phase of modern life.

In so far as there is a noble and generous sentiment amounting to an ideal on the part of the masses who are fighting one another for reasons and under a system they do not understand, it may be said that we have a stupendous example of the willingness of men and women to sacrifice the present to what they regard the future welfare. The unfortunate part of this is that only those who are sacrificing all, are in any degree dominated by ethics and in this they are only partly so dominated; because a great part of the present sacrifice is made under the pressure of public opinion created by unethical orators and editors. It is offered in the mass under a sentiment of contagious and collective enthusiasm and is for the most part quite an unthinking acceptance of what is vaguely called duty and for these considerations, while the sacrifice is not to be minimized, its ethical importance is not too high and will be entirely lost and turned to hatred and regrets when the issues appear in their true light after the passing of years.

Following the exploitation of the common men upon a scale so stupendous as to be unimaginable in past generations, the exploiters have destroyed these poor men to the number of millions which appal mankind and which no honest historian, writing of this age, will be able to record without unfeigned horror, indignation and shame. The ethical standard of the present age will suffer by comparison with the most mournful pages in the long and gloomy history of man. We have so high a regard for ethics that we permit a strictly limited class to make fortunes of thousands of millions through destroying the common men and to hoard these fortunes, while we issue at the same time a greater amount of mortgages against future generations and thus pass on to hundreds of years of posterity a burden of debt whose creation represents the crowning shame of the world. Posterity will not have a high regard for our boasted ethics but it will marvel at our audacity in the realms of destruction and at the genius displayed in selling so many mortgages against people who are yet unborn. It may well be wondered if these pledges are ever to be redeemed.

If present indications of the regard which man has for the future do not warrant any hope of a successful appeal to his ethics, it is because in his most consequential acts toward those outside his family he is not an ethical being. As women are more religious, but less spiritual than men they are also less ethical. A woman sacrifices herself for her children but without the slightest regard for the anonymous posterity called the human race. Her attitude toward the race is devoid of the application of the higher principles of morality to conduct. Her relation to the present and her outlook upon the future are neither ethical nor spiritual. Her inspiring devotion to her children is a natural female instinct not confined to women alone and is totally devoid of ethics.

It should be an unfailing principle with those who seek truth to bear an open mind toward all that may be said upon either side of any question concerning which the truth is sought and it is in this spirit that one must give all consideration to opinions with which he may be quite unable to agree. To close the door to any view which may be put forward in good faith is possibly to lose some evidence which might have a bearing either upon the final decision or upon the manner in which it is stated. With this principle always in mind and notwithstanding the high value which I place upon the noble influence of women in my own life, and through which I am under obligations that I can never hope to discharge, I cannot accept that there is the slightest equality between men and women. There is a sense in which women are superior to men. They bring to life its greatest charm. They are our mothers, our consolation in childhood, our refuge in manhood and our only companions in death. They exercise a most benign and noble influence and hold a control over man's most intimate sentiments which few men realize or would care to admit.

Most women may be conscious of their subtle powers but few would be able to trace them to their source. The facility with which women disregard important and general principles as applied to conduct and the satisfaction they derive from temporary trifles are incomprehensible to most men and that is one of the reasons why women are incomprehensible.

In the next chapter the difference in the attitude of men and women as regards the dominant motives governing conduct is entered upon in some of its most general and consequential manifestations and I do not therefore now touch upon the subject beyond saying that the general acts of mankind are not governed by any conscious principle and that they are controlled almost entirely by environment and expediency. How far men understand and apply principles to conduct in ways which are foreign to the nature of women, is dealt with under the same heading. Women are always children—they never grow up. That is one reason why they understand children as men rarely ever do and why they can spend entire days playing the games of childhood—which few serious men can play for an hour. They appear to lose this characteristic in proportion as they depart from the normal tendency of women and take up the studies and occupations peculiar to men, which indicates that as they gain something which normally pertains only to men, they lose something which was exclusively their own. It may be seriously doubted whether this is an advantage either to women or to the race.

A woman's point of view may be that if she dedicates her time in this way it is evidence only of an unselfish devotion to someone who commands her sympathy and tenderness and that it is for the good of the child her time is so spent. Even if this were quite true it is equally true that men would be incapable of performing a like service howsoever great the inducement might be. Also it may be said that man can and does constantly devote all or the greater part of his time in the unselfish service of those dependent upon him and perhaps as the founding of homes and rearing of children are indispensable to the complete development of both men and women, the lot of each in this work amounts to the most natural and effective expression of themselves — which would of itself be an all-sufficient reason.

The influence which a woman exercises over a man through their children may be taken as a typical proof of her intuitive faculties as well as an evidence of her abilities of observation, from which she has come to know that men are most happy when they are worshipping themselves. Perhaps she has learned this from all the religions devised by men, since they consist in worshipping some God whose attributes represent man in his most noble and terrible aspects. The use which a woman makes of this sentiment may be quite unconscious but it is none the less effective.

A woman sees in her children the most enduring element in her relation to the father and as a rule the more points of resemblance which she finds between the father and the child the more she is able to minister to the vanity of the man and he has no greater weakness than vanity. In one form or another man's vanity is responsible for some of his most illustrious achievements and to it may also be traced some of his most pathetic mistakes and nearly all his real and imaginary troubles.

It would be interesting to trace this sentiment of human vanity as it is further expressed in the relation of men and women towards their own and the opposite sex and from which it appears that although both sexes may be equally susceptible to flattery there is an important difference in the qualities or talents which each would desire to possess and which it is supposed to be a credit to exemplify. In this difference will be found a partial explanation of the importance involved in the occupation of each and in what is considered to be worthy as ultimate standards of attainment. Women will be vain of their beauty, the charm of their manner and a soft voice. Also of those secondary attainments such as music and art, but least of all will they regard general culture and philosophy —since it is in the strictly feminine qualities that they find the source of their most effective power. Men on the contrary who are worthy of serious consideration will not be flattered if told they are beautiful but would highly esteem being regarded as strong, brave, chivalrous, gentle and intelligent. That these appear to be more dignified and worthy objects of attainment is of only a strictly relative importance because what each sex seeks to exemplify are those attributes most naturally, generally and strongly attractive to the opposite sex and they have been defined above. If it can be said that the qualities essential to excite the admiration of a woman are higher than those requisite to attract a man and that therefore as woman is more surely reached through her ears and man through his eyes and that the woman demands intelligence, whereas the man will be quite satisfied with beauty, that women display in this respect superior qualities, the fact appears to be rather that nature has implanted certain permanent tendencies to serve its own impersonal ends. The first requisite to great and sustained work and therefore to large achievement is a sound body and when nature has caused an attractive and well made animal to offer the highest appeal to a similar animal of the opposite sex it has taken the first and most essential step in the accomplishment of its larger designs. A good brain in a poor body is of little use and a good body is more likely to have a good brain than a poor one. It is then, only through what appears to be a natural selection upon physical grounds in the line of first importance and intellectual grounds secondarily, that the species may not pass to lower but to higher planes, because as all evolution upwards is in any event slow, there would be no time for important progress in a race propagated upon a basis of attraction contrary to what I have outlined because it would become extinct before its goal was remotely in sight.

Women are the great conservative element in society chiefly because they understand only what is tangible and near at hand. They are not constructive but on the contrary are conservative and reactionary. They prefer to stand on the ground they know and cultivate a small spot of earth while they leave the contemplation of the heavens to men. Women always prefer gold coin to paper money and they never like cheques. This is not to be regarded as a trivial incident because it has a deep significance as illustrating a phase of woman's character and of her habit of thought which has an important bearing upon her general attitude towards life. I have never known a woman who would not spend from two to five times as much money when her servants did the ordering by telephone and she paid the bills by cheque, than she spent when she came directly into the matter and paid with bank notes—especially of small denomination. They spend still less when they pay in gold. The average woman who has had no experience in business and who acts according to her natural instincts would convert her fortune into gold and keep it in a safe in her bed-room. It would never occur to her that money should be employed the same as men, that every dollar represents a day's toil for someone. She would never build enterprises in strange lands, but would keep her ships near the shore, forgetting that they are useful only on the sea. Her provisions are sometimes safe —not because she can look into the future as men are constantly doing—but rather because she is by nature opposed to taking risks. Nearly all men are gamblers, while most women are not.

In practical life this means that women do not wish to take risks alone howsoever they may be willing to take them with men. They are conscious of their inability to fight the world on equal terms with men and they are reluctant to risk even moderate comforts for the chance of luxury which is associated with doubts and in an enterprise which may fail.

While there is no human limit to a woman's courage, if she is called upon to risk all things for a man she loves, she is nevertheless consistently opposed to those hazardous enterprises which appeal to the imagination of men, while they excite only feelings of doubt and fear in the minds of women. She is moreover, the guardian of what she calls home and her children and the appeals they make to her are such as constantly to impress her with the helplessness of human nature and a strong reluctance to put it under any unnecessary stress.

It may be taken as a general rule that women lack the courage which comes from taking risks and accrues to man through the great conquests which he has made over the most potent forces of nature. Women lack the high creative imagination belonging exclusively to genius, which is confined entirely to men. If these great gifts have been denied to her by Nature she has an indefinable intuition which is not only an important but an essential attribute of a being who is generally incapable of logic or speculative reason.

In so far as woman is able to share in man's desire to

attain speculative ends and to arrive at definite and sound conclusions, she generally arrives sooner than the man and by shorter routes. While the man struggles up the winding paths and marks each step from the bottom to the top of a mountain, a woman reaches the summit by a short cut which she cannot explain and would be unable to retrace. In its bearing upon attaining tangible and practical objects this method is of first rate importance and can be used by individual women with great success, although it has no strictly logical value and as it cannot be explained either by men or women, and is not in fact understood by either, it can not be raised to a principle or passed on in any logical, intellectual or social scheme. Women are on the whole not creative and by nature are qualified for only one occupation which is to care for a home and children, and this occupation is usually undertaken without any definite or systematic preparation and without any adequate appreciation of the great responsibilities involved.

It is because the natural occupation of all normal women is the same that they stand toward each other in the relation of actual or potential competitors and regard each other, not with the generosity born of a division of labour, but with the hostility of personal antagonists who are all engaged at the same task.

It is due primarily to the fact that what constitutes the whole of the life of a woman is only a part of the life of a man and that man's interests are so great and varied that he is able to regard the majority of men with sympathy or complete indifference.

It is significant also that in proportion as the occupation of man is diminished in importance and his competition with other men is correspondingly increased, his attitude is one of interested hostility toward his own class, while he is capable of taking a totally different view of the class with which he has no competitive relation.

In the higher realms of human endeavour this principle is most noticeable. At no time are there more than a few philosophers on earth. They are never in relations of competition with mankind and are consequently able to survey the activities and analyze the motives of men from a purely impersonal point of view, realizing that they stand upon their own ground, that their number is strictly limited and that there can be no boundaries prescribed for the speculative attainment of the human intellect.

The greatest of these men whose lives are exclusively devoted to the development of their own philosophy, are not infrequently antagonistic to all or part of the theories of each other and in that sense may be said to come within the general principle, that a similarity of occupation necessarily engenders a tendency to natural antagonism, but there is an important difference: that it is not the antagonism of one man for another, or the refusal of one to find anything of merit in the other, but rather an attempt to clarify or extend the principles previously announced by others, while paying full tribute to such part of all reasoning as is not deemed to be incompatible with an elevation of human understanding. A philosopher's principles are to him the children of his highest being and when he puts them forward it is in a sense more exalted than any parental pride in offspring which he is prepared to defend. If he is jealous at all it is that his principles may not be lost upon a humanity in whose interest they have been patiently brought into the world.

When we pass through the various phases of philosophy to music, we have an illustration of the truth of the principle governing conduct which I have applied to the attitude of women toward each other. Even the great achievements and the noble genius of the ones whose music has filled the earth with song, were not exempt from this weakness. Wagner could find nothing to commend in the music of the illustrious Meyerbeer, he did not like Mozart and would not listen to contemporary composers who are now regarded with affection. Most of Wagner's great contemporaries could see nothing of special merit in "Lohengrin" or "Tannhäuser", and it may be asserted in all confidence that without the affectionate devotion of Liszt, who was so conscious of his own value as not to be jealous of the genius of his friend, the story of Wagner's fame might not have been recorded even until this day.

As we ascend the scale of intelligence and character we find that men are more jealous of the attainments of others than of their wealth, family, rank or public power. Whereas it is precisely these which are the secondary objects of woman's jealousy; while her first object is beauty and those other qualities which are regarded as the most attractive to men and she is only a little jealous of those high mental attainments which some women may possess and which most women do not even remotely understand and even then only regard in proportion as they are able to observe how they affect men.

The masses regard wealth, rank and power as the accidents of birth or as arising from the injustice of man's institutions. A poor man may not be jealous of the riches and power of another man because he attributes his humble lot to causes beyond his personal control. He was born humble and poor in a world where it is difficult for his class to rise and he accepts his fate with amazing resignation. If this humble man happens, as he usually does, to be also stupid he will feel an almost unbelievable dislike of men who are vastly superior to him in physical or mental endowments. He will distrust everything amounting to genius and will generally pay no distinct homage to individual greatness until long after the man to be worshipped is dead. The greatest benefactors of the human race were not idols so long as they mingled among men. It is only when generations to which they did not personally belong were able to regard their work as distinguished from its creators that anything approximating fair estimates was possible. If this attitude of the masses were based upon a keen realization of their personal deficiency it might be made the basis of great and general progress, but it does not spring from sentiments so helpful or just. It arises from the vanity, the self-satisfaction and the stupidity of the masses who do not realize their own inferiority and who suspect and distrust everything which they are too ignorant to understand—little realizing that their descendants will worship what they have rejected, and not knowing that this is the universal experience of mankind. They also do not know that in this distrust they are exemplifying the most primitive of all animal instincts, since animals are afraid of everything new, and only lose their fear through education.

The attitude of women toward each other displays the same tendencies. Women who may not be jealous of the riches or good fortune of others are rarely ever fond of those who are more beautiful than themselves. They will talk *to* other plain women but they only talk *about* women who are more beautiful. I knew one woman who deliberately disfigured herself because she was too beautiful to obtain employment as a governess and was not educated for anything else. A plain girl, be she rich or poor, will have friendships among her own sex, which it is quite beyond the power of a beautiful girl to establish. These will remain some of the permanent tendencies of humanity, but the apparent necessity to express them, as they are now expressed, would be in a great measure abolished through the acceptance of the principles set out in succeeding chapters of this book and in "*The World Allies.*"

There is an important phase of woman's development which is worthy of greater consideration than it receives and that is with reference to the effect which education has upon her creative faculties.

There is a great defect in the attitude of women in general toward all culture because they usually pursue learning not for itself, but as a means of making them attractive. Culture is not the object sought by them for its own sake, but rather in order that it may be used for a brief time in securing their natural position in life, which is to have a home and children and also from a feeling that unless they are so trained in the same courses pursued by their acquaintances they will have an incomplete or deficient education. Their training may begin at an age when they can have no realization as to the reasons why they pursue certain studies to the exclusion of others but the routine of life is accepted, as children accept a religion, without knowing why they believe or disbelieve in anything. This may appear to be a critical attitude toward women, who in youth pursue the study of literature, music and painting, but if closely examined it will be found to be correct and verified by history and general observation. If they had cultivated their minds because of an inherent love of culture for its own sake they would not abandon music, literature or painting almost immediately after marriage. This is not due to the lack of time in which to continue their studies because the classes in society in which the studies of the so-called cultured women are most generally neglected after marriage are those in which the women have the greatest freedom from care and the largest opportunities for leisure.

It is because they studied as a means to the end I have described that they gave up their studies as soon as they had served the purpose indicated, namely of increasing their attraction for a brief period when it is important for them to be attractive. Also for the further reason that motherhood and all it implies has a more important natural claim upon a woman than the pursuit of any form of personal culture to be derived from literature, music or painting. Woman finds the fulfillment of her life not in books and music, but in life. If this were not so she would not endure the suffering and incur the dangers involved in bearing children, or support the trouble and vexation of caring for them. It is because the normal woman is a potential mother that she attaches the highest importance to the relation which involves motherhood and it is partly because this relation involves not only suffering and pain, which men do not share—but also sentiments of tenderness which men cannot understand, that it has for woman an importance and significance which men do not appreciate and are quite unable to feel.

This sentiment on the part of woman is intensified and enlarged in proportion to the personal care she bestows upon her children and the sacrifices she must in consequence make of her personal freedom, comfort and ordinary pleasures. The women who do not nurse their children, who do not bathe and care for them, from infancy deprive themselves of the greatest happiness involved in motherhood, and they also withhold from their children the most important and often the most benign influence. The servant to whom a child is entrusted instinctively sacrifices the future to the present, whereas in the care of children this policy should be reversed. The servant gratifies the whims of childhood and thereby wins the temporary affection of the child, whereas the intelligent mother will impose a reasonable and fair discipline which takes into account the large and permanent interest of the child. The parent is not concerned so much with doing what is agreeable to his offspring as in doing what is for its highest good and what is calculated to promote the qualities of patience, truthfulness and self-control.

Children should be taught the importance of observing things for themselves. It is the basis of all true education and of all important subsequent success in life and without it nothing can be understood in its true proportions.

Only in the earliest childhood should people be controlled by prohibitions of any sort and threats are always wrong. Beginning at two years of age children should have their liberty with its complement, which is that they must respond for their acts. They will make the same mistakes over and over again but if this is always followed by its own results, as in nature it is, the children learn that within themselves lie all the consequences of their acts. It is only such an understanding, which is self-acquired, that is of the slightest moral importance either to children or men and women. Progress of true importance is only recorded as children and adults rise above prizes and punishments. The lack of achievement must of itself be a sufficient punishment both in and out of schools, and only in so far as this becomes in fact the attitude of humanity towards all attainments can we feel justified in ascribing any high value to man's attempted instruction.

All education among a free people from infancy to maturity should be conceived with the object of creating free, self-governing, self-reliant, reasonable and truthful men and women. These qualities which are so essential to any large and useful achievement can only be acquired through rational and loving guidance during the early years of life. The one who enters upon the serious business of life whithout such a solid foundation of character is most grievously handicapped and will suffer in failure and anguish from the great defects for which he is only partly responsible. The world is not only uncharitable, it is unjust and it applies stern measures in dealing with defects which are so general that one would think they might be more leniently regarded and mercifully pardoned. The greater a man's range of observation among all classes of society, the more he will realize the unpardonable waste of talent—which sometimes amounts to genius— through defects in character arising solely from lack of restraining and intelligent discipline in youth. The only discipline which will be of unfailing service in mature life is that which arises from self-imposed discipline in youth. All restraint imposed from without is useless beyond the age when it can be imposed from within and this age is from one to three years, as a beginning, among normally intelligent children. Many people who have the care of children may not understand the application of the principles here outlined and which may therefore be more obvious if specific instances are cited.

I adopted among many other similar methods the following policy with my three children and have been able to observe its effect upon my son now nineteen and my two daughters now seventeen and eighteen years of age.

At the age of three they had access to a safe in which there were always a few dollars in small coins. I explained to them that one dollar represented a day's toil for some man or woman. That ten cents was the value of an hour's work and that every time they spent ten cents they spent an hour of somebody's life. On occasions we worked together in the garden when they were only three years old until they were tired. I kept an exact account of the time and when their work was finished each one was paid ten cents per hour. When enough was earned they went with me to a shop in Chicago and each purchased a pair of white boots. The next day one wore her white boots in the mud. Ordinarily their boots were cleaned by a servant. At this point I suggested that the child should clean her boots. She was not forbidden to play in the mud or scolded for having done so. In cleaning the boots she soiled her dress and this I asked her to wash—not by way of punishment but as someone must do the cleaning and she had acted without foresight it should be done by her. She regarded this as natural and quite just but the next time she played in the mud she asked for old clothes and black boots.

This experience was not lost on her or on the other children. I made it a point that there should always be a quantity of sweets in their nursery. All children like sweets and most adults require them if they do not drink wine or spirits. When the sweets were first put at their unrestricted disposal at the age of three they all ate too much and were ill. Nothing was said of the incident but it never happened again and they had learned a valuable and self-imposed lesson in restraint.

It is impossible to attach too great an importance to punctuality and to a faithful compliance with any promise that may be made. I state it upon my experience as an employer of thousands of men that no other single quality except truthfulness is of greater moment to a successful business career.

Again and again I have promoted men of inferior ability over the heads of others who had far greater talents and business capacity but who at a critical time might be two minutes late. Of all defects this is the most difficult to remedy even in youth. When one of my children was not ready to start at the precise time arranged for any excursion he was left behind. There was no scolding or punishment and the child realized that it had only suffered the natural consequence of its own act. I explained that trains and ships do not wait for careless passengers and that an engagement taken with me was more important than one taken with a train or ship.

At the age of six my son had a silver watch which he took care not to break. His sister had a music-box which played the Russian anthem. My son found this much too sombre and his solution was to throw the music-box into lake Michigan. Instead of punishing him in the way children are usually punished we sold his watch and with the proceeds he bought another music-box which played the same tunes. He did not get another watch until he had earned it by manual labour at ten cents an hour although he had constant access to money in the safe. It was a long time before anything else was destroyed. The same method was applied when toys were recklessly broken.

Similar methods were adopted with regard to studies and play.

There was observed the most strict care that all tasks would be reasonable but the principle applied was that only those who worked were entitled to play. These methods have never been changed and with respect to the matter of using money, when my son left home for school he was given liberty to sign at the bank on the understanding that he should present me at the end of each term an itemized account of his disbursements. I placed no limit upon what he was to draw but he never spent half the amount which I would have given him as a reasonable allowance.

It must not be overlooked that the natural instinct of humanity is to attain its ends by the easiest available means and that in the early years of childhood the natural conduct is devoid of ethical considerations. One of my children who was fond of flowers gathered a bouquet for his mother when he was two years old. When he presented the flowers she gave him a bonbon. After he had eaten the sweet he asked for the flowers. He then gave her the flowers in exchange for another sweet. This operation was repeated four times. That it was quite unfair and unethical did not occur to the child, but the only remedy against a repetition, which would have been morally bad, was to accept future bouquets because they had been gathered by the hands of childhood and were beautiful and the act of thoughtfulness was rewarded by a kiss. This incident was never repeated.

There was another matter to which I attached the greatest importance and that was that the children should never be unduly fatigued and that they should not be expected to work with their brains when their bodies were tired. It is clear that the most pressing demand of nature is the one to be the first satisfied, and that it is of more immediate importance that the tissues destroyed by bodily toil should be repaired than that the vitality should be at the disposal of the brain. It therefore follows that the brain cannot do its best work when the body is tired. A few minutes interval for play between studies does not retard mental activity unless it wearies the body.

After long walks or hard manual labour, continued for some hours, I have found it almost impossible to write. Prolonged experience has convinced me that the most sustained and the best mental activity is to be realized early in the morning when the body is completely rested after some hours sleep. My best mental work is done between four in the morning and noon.

It is easy therefore to understand that men whose bodies are always overworked have no ambition to study and if they read at all they usually read senseless rubbish —such as newspapers; and that is also one reason why the worst and most sensational newspapers are patronized chiefly by labourers. That is also one more reason why there can be no widely diffused and useful instruction among the masses so long as they are physically overworked.

It is useless to hold before the people our pretensions as to the importance of education while they are in an economic slavery which renders education impossible. It is also senseless to preach to them regarding the sacredness of life while we murder millions of men for imperialism and high finance.

Our pretensions and preaching are slowly being set in their true light by a deluded humanity, which is gradually realizing that as men see the senseless destruction of life, it is natural they should hold other lives at a slight value, and that to this sentiment may be traced all exploitation and nearly all injustice.

It is due to the mistaken policy of parents and the comparative weakness of the children that most children are afraid to tell the truth when they have done anything which they feel will be punished by the parent. As a measure of temporary self-defence and escape from immediate consequences children become untruthful, resort to deceptions and invent all sorts of devices in order to obviate the necessity of answering for the infraction of some senseless law prescribed by a thoughtless parent. The deception is discovered and the parent is grieved to find that the child has been untruthful, while failing to realize that the parent more than the child is the actual author of the deception, because he made it impossible for the child to be natural and also truthful and truth was sacrificed to nature as it always will be under similar circumstances. The same principle holds true among adults when one is in a position of dependence upon the other. The greater part of the countless deceptions which men and women practice in their relations with each other arises from the impossibility of telling the truth. Both prefer to bury their heads in the sand and hear only what is agreeable or that which does not wound their vanity or lessen the sense of proprietorship which each wishes to feel toward the other. As this whole attitude is wrong in principle and a violation of the most personal rights of individuality it cannot fail to be disastrous in practice in all the relations of life. It begins in childhood through lack of moral understanding between parents and children and is continued to the end of life through the formation of ties arising from the expression of one's nature which may be quite contrary to one's professions.

In the interests of a nobler humanity the whole of this shameful structure of falsehood and deception should be swept away and men and women should be able to pass their lives from childhood to age in an environment of freedom from all pretence.

It is impossible to imagine the great heights of beauty and moral grandeur which mankind might attain under a system of life which would enable men, women and children to be truthful, brave, self-reliant and free. As life is in any event brief and filled with tribulation and disappointment the time has come when it must be more free from the self-imposed shackles which hold men and women to a level that is as unsatisfying to their nature as it is insulting to their intelligence and degrading to their morals. What have they to gain by continuing the existing makeshifts and pretence and what do they not lose by failing to assert their intellectual and moral independence and integrity?

No laws were made in dealing with my children if they could be avoided but when they were made they were inflexibly enforced. It was carefully and simply explained that some things might not be done, that if they were done they carried an invariable consequence, that this was a universal principle of nature and that we must not sow what we do not wish to reap. That if you put your hand in the fire you would be burned the first time, the second time and every time—and that you must not put your hand in the fire unless you wish it burned. Most parents are constantly threatening their children with punishments which they never inflict or if sometimes inflicted it is done without consideration and usually in anger. They are constantly making laws which they only occasionally enforce and then in the same ill-advised manner. The result is that the children know nothing as to conduct based upon the principles of justice, reason or self-control and have the further moral disadvantage of finally losing all respect for rules or laws—even those which are essential, natural and just.

If the fire had not burned and the child had been punished by the parent it would not have understood the reason and would have resented the punishment, whereas it does not resent, but on the contrary understands the natural consequences which invariably follow its acts. In proportion as these are understood by the child the indiscretion is not repeated, whereas all restraint which is imposed as an external and arbitrary act has only a passing importance of no value, and does not instill any lesson in self-control.

In the home as in the state, the people are best governed whose acts are the least controlled by laws or rules. The fewer the regulations in the state and in the home, the better the government and its effects upon the development of the governed. The principle in both instances is that people who are to become free and responsible men and women should be subject to the minimum of rules and laws. They should be taught that the self-control voluntarily and logically imposed by the individual over his own acts is the most important safeguard for himself and for any society which seeks to establish the institutions of justice and liberty by the assent and under the sovereignty of the people.

I have considered that the illustrations here given might be useful to an understanding of the principles involved and that nothing is too trivial in the life of a child and no detail is unimportant when it relates to the principles of conduct and to their application to the ordinary affairs of life. A great deal of generalization is indulged in by people who have done nothing towards reducing their generalities to practical experience and who would be quite unable to indicate what is meant by teaching self-government to children.

I am also opposed in principle to any system of education which prematurely separates children from their parents. I have no doubt that France, England and to a lesser degree America, have suffered from the general practice among the so-called upper classes of sending their children away from home at an early age, because it tends to sever those intimate and natural ties between parents and children which are so important to children and which impose upon both the parents and the children certain great and useful lessons of mutual respect and self-restraint.

The feeling of reciprocal duty toward one another will be a more potent and higher rule of conduct than any which can be imposed by considerations of general public utility or morals. The independence which is supposed to result from the present system is not independence in its true sense and may not instil any of the great and important lessons in genuine self-government. It leaves the child dependent upon the parents for the means by which the ties of home are to be severed and the parents pay a fixed annual sum to maintain a system which gradually makes them strangers to their children and leaves them at their most susceptible age to the intellectual and moral guidance of those who are generally inferior beings, because they are ill-equipped and poorly paid.

The effect of this policy in the education of children may be quite as considerable in its results upon parents as it is upon the children. Men and women as a rule do not get more than the minimum of happiness or self-improvement that may be derived from their position as fathers and mothers. Usually the men take little or no interest in the education and training of their children and are content to leave to servants and to paid instructors the moral and intellectual supervision of the ones for whose lives they are responsible. Among those who are the most independent financially the men consider that they have no time for what they call trifles, that the education and discipline of children is not their proper concern and that it is a duty which devolves entirely upon the women and in this class of society the women pass this duty on to the servants for similar reasons. The result is that neither the parents nor the children receive from each other the important lessons of self-sacrifice, self-control and breadth of sympathy which all may acquire from a relation holding such large possibilities of emotional and ethical value.

Man shares with woman the pleasures of having children but woman alone bears the pain. It may be said that among the toilers the men assume the burden of supporting the children and that this is a counter compensation, but those who have been able closely to observe the life of the poor will be almost unanimous in saying that the lot of the toiler's wife is as unenviable as his own, that her burdens are not less than his and that her work is never done.

Among people who are financially independent the advantages are all with the man, except the great spiritual importance which suffering brings to life and in this the advantage rests with the woman. I am convinced that the most complete and natural development of both men and women and the expression of their highest qualities of service and generosity can be achieved only in the founding of a home and the rearing of children.

The distractions which necessarily attend the material side of this relation may not be conducive to the most sustained and profound mental work for the man, but there is no doubt that the philosophy and music which have most permanently influenced mankind would not have been written by men who had never known the love of women and the caress of a little child. It may well be that the noblest work of man is due partly to the fact that he has had such relations. Young men and women picture a state of supreme happiness in marriage and the home. They drink their cup of earthly and of spiritual joy. Their children reach maturity and leave home. The parents are once again alone. They are thrown back upon themselves, where they must find all the interest of life. The man turns to his philosophy, his music or his art if he is fortunate enough to be able to do so, while the woman, if she has no large interests, turns to various fads which arise either from the restlessness of women who have been mothers and whose occupation is at an end or from those who have never been mothers and who have in consequence never fulfilled the natural functions of women. If these women had in youth laid the solid foundations of a liberal and rational education—if they had pursued their studies as an end and not as a means to quite a different end, they would not in their age be destitute of the great personal resources in which alone enduring pleasure and peace may be found.

I do not minimize the value of the studies women pursue or the importance of mental cultivation for women but it should be approached from a point of view different from the present attitude of women towards culture. It should be a systematic and serious cultivation of the mind, not in order that it may superficially shine for a brief period, but that it may be well grounded in the principles of a genuine education which is undertaken as an essential part of a woman's equipment for life. When the material incidents and the emotional sentiments involved in having and rearing children pass with the lapse of years, the only solid foundation of happiness or contentment between a man and woman is an intellectual understanding. This is all the more important and enduring if it exists independently of any community of material interests. The majority of mankind never have an intellectual life of any importance at any time, but I am convinced that this does not arise from their incapacity for such a development but rather from their lack of any opportunity or sufficiently strong inducement for the cultivation of their highest faculties, traceable partly to economic pressure, overwork, oppression and the evils which must always attend such wrongs. It may be difficult for cultivated people to understand that any inducements are needed to cause men and women to seek culture for its own sake and yet such is the case even among those who have leisure and it must be even more true among those to whom all leisure is denied.

As the men who are to continue to direct the thought of the world will always associate with the women who represent the culture or the attraction of their time, it is to the highest interest of mankind that the culture of woman should attain a different standard and be acquired for its own sake. The defects of woman's education and the erroneous motive from which it is acquired may to a greater degree than is generally regarded, account for the fact that woman remains permanently uncreative in any intellectual or artistic sense.

Women study poetry more generally and assiduously than men but they never write a great poem and what is perhaps more extraordinary, they usually discontinue reading poetry soon after marriage, whereas people who study poetry as an end in itself, rather than as a means to an end, never cease to read and enjoy it and their regret is that they cannot find time enough for the continuation of those intellectual pursuits, which are the source of ever increasing harmony and charm.

The study of music occupies an important place for some years in the life of nearly every girl whose parents are able to afford it. Millions of young women play the music written by men and yet no woman has written any music which can be regarded as great or important. They are able to play symphonies, but man alone is the creator of symphonies. Women are the constant and principal patrons of the drama and opera, but they have never written either a great drama or opera. Women are the theme of the illusions, the passions, the despair and the noble dreams of men and it is to them and about them that the most illustrious poets and inspired musicians have sung their immortal songs. These objects of so much of the high genius of men have not responded either in verse or symphonies, but with appreciation and affection which are the highest incentives and the greatest sanction that men prize as tributes to genius. I doubt if the affection and sympathy of women would be less if they were genuinely educated. The more intelligent and cultivated the woman the better she may understand and appreciate the intellectual achievements of others. No poet or musician will sing his songs to a statue or to a fool if he can sing them to a cultivated, intelligent and spiritual woman.

Man may sing his noblest songs to a woman as he would sing them to a wild flower or to the sky and if she is unable to respond to them with her intellect, she may still be his source of inspiration through a spiritual sympathy which is unspoiled by a senseless or superficial education.

In the vast and varied range of human greatness, the philosophers, poets, artists, musicians and warriors have recorded their obligation to the devotion and sympathy of women and have inscribed forever the names of the ones to whom they and through them mankind are indebted. Taking from the long list only two men who stand at the extremes of human temperament, who were as unlike as men can well be, we find John Stuart Mill and Lord Nelson paying their tributes to women who were probably as completely different as women ever are. Mill thus dedicates his famous treatise on "Liberty":

"To the beloved and deplored memory of her who

was the inspirer and in part the author, of all that is best in my writings—the friend and wife whose exalted sense of truth and right was my strongest incitement, and whose approbation was my chief reward — I dedicate this volume. Like all that I have written for many years, it belongs as much to her as to me; but the work as it stands has had, in a very insufficient degree, the inestimable advantage of her revision; some of the most important portions having been reserved for a more careful re-examination, which they are now never destined to receive. Were I but capable of interpreting to the world one half the great thoughts and noble feelings which are buried in her grave, I should be the medium of a greater benefit to it, than is ever likely to arise from anything that I can write, unprompted and unassisted by her all but unrivalled wisdom."

As Nelson's fleet was moving into action at the battle of Trafalgar and this great man felt he was entering his last struggle and that death was at hand, he commended Lady Hamilton to the protection of his country; and after recounting her important services to the nation he said:

"Could I have rewarded these services, I would not now call upon my country; but as that has not been in my power, I leave Emma Lady Hamilton, therefore, a legacy to my king and country, that they will give her an ample provision to maintain her rank in life.

"I also leave to the beneficence of my country my adopted daughter, Horatia Nelson Thompson; and I desire that she will use in future the name Nelson only.

"These are the only favours I ask of my king and country at this moment when I am going to fight their battle. May God bless my king and country, and all those I hold dear."[1]

He spent his last hours in England praying over his child as she lay sleeping and almost his last words as he was dying in the battle were: "Remember that I leave Lady Hamilton and my daughter Horatia as a legacy to my country. Take care of poor Lady Hamilton."

She was the inspiration of his most illustrious achievements and was regarded by him with a tenderness and a passion which are as touching as they are rare among men and yet his noble appeal fell upon deaf ears. The beautiful association of Nelson and his friend was not conventional and as hypocrisy was in England—what it still remains —a religion, those who did not hesitate to do what they were not sufficiently courageous to avow, did nothing to comply with the last wishes of their immortal countryman.

It is not by accident that great men are rarely understood or truly valued except by women. The jealousy with which the ordinary men regard great men, is not exceeded even by the jealousy with which plain and insipid women regard those who are beautiful and talented. It is due to this and also partly to the fact that women are not competitors with men in the realms involving creative ability, in the noblest forms of art, literature, music and philosophy, that men find in the sympathy of women the eternal inspiration which arises from the capacity of human nature to admire what it cannot aspire to emulate and what in fact it is not supposed to emulate.

Women who may be most strict in matters of personal conduct may have no clear notion of ethics or understand that morals may be only remotely related to con-

---

[1] From Nelson's last request, 21st October 1805. Original in British Museum A 34—992 ff 1618.

duct. They will not fight their way out of a difficulty if they can possibly lie their way out. They have been forced, as a consequence of man's attitude to reduce deception to a fine art, because in general the attitude of men dissuades women from telling the truth if it happens to be unpleasant. Women therefore are only partially responsible for one of their greatest defects. It may also be taken that this applies to men as regards the extent to which they are truthful to women. If the principle applies to both, its effect upon man is less general and important because his relation to woman is one of greater economic, personal and moral independence. The same observation may be applied to children who, in general, will only tell the truth if they feel by instinct or know by experience, that it may be told without undue criticism or unpleasant consequences. That is one of the reasons why men make a sorry farce of their attempts to deceive women, who are able instantly to detect deceptions, because an important part of their own lives is made up of effects, produced by temporary and articifial means.

Also there enters into woman's understanding of man a sentiment which men are too vain and self-absorbed to indulge and that is a feeling of entire love and devotion which penetrates where man's logic cannot find its way. A woman finds her way to the inmost secret of a man's heart because she loves the man more than she loves herself and a man fails in this respect because he loves nothing and nobody more than himself. This does not prevent men from making the most complete sacrifice for others and from freely giving their lives for others, but in the constant and routine relations of men and women the man gives his time and the woman gives herself—and there is a great difference in this distinction.

This is only one more indication of the difficulty which

arises in any attempt to estimate the relative equality of the sexes. Happily for mankind they can never be other than complementary and in no sense equal, and they are only in their places of highest usefulness when they occupy their natural spheres in the co-operative relations which unite them in life through distinct and separate employments. Notwithstanding she is not man's equal, the most potent force in his highest achievement is the approval of woman. Her admiration which sometimes amounts to worship, is his greatest incentive to do what is beautiful, heroic or sublime. Her pardon is ample excuse for all defects and a sanction for all conduct. She is nevertheless incapable of forming any proper conception as to abstract justice and in principle her highest test of morals is the conduct of sex toward sex. Notwithstanding this and also woman's restricted range of vision, men are so vain and stand so much in the need of an audience for their philosophy if they are great and of a confessor for their follies if they are small, that they go for consolation where they can and therefore they go to women.

It is to women that the greatest and most noble messages of men have been first spoken and it is from women that man has sought and found understanding and sanction for his most mournful defects. Women are able, as men never are, to regard with compassion nearly all that is frail in human nature, and to love and reverence all that is sublime. In the little village of Bethany to the east of Jerusalem there lived a woman named Martha:

... "and she had a sister called Mary, which also sat at Jesus' feet, and heard his word. But Martha was cumbered about much serving, and came to him, and said, Lord, dost thou not care that my sister hath left me to serve alone? bid her therefore that she help me. And Jesus answered and said unto her, Martha, Martha, thou art careful and troubled about many things: but one thing is needful and Mary has chosen that good part, which shall not be taken away from her."(1)

Most women are nevertheless unable to realize that what they regard as almost the totality of morals may be nothing more than a matter of age, temperament, position and climate, whereas the most important moral considerations are quite unconnected with any such issues and only remotely concerned with any relation of the sexes.

The attitude of women toward the principles of morality arises partly from the fact that in general they are neither logical nor spiritual and also because sex has for them the great and essential importance which nature attaches to the highest form of self-expression for the individual.

It is because the nature and interests of men are so radically different from those of women, that men cannot accord the highest importance to what may be for them one of the minor interests of life. It is far from my purpose to underestimate the significance of a relation which holds so high a place in the most beautiful associations of life, but it is impossible to hope that the attitude of women toward this relation can ever be fully understood or equally shared by men, howsoever ideal the result might be both for women and for men. It is important to observe that the attitude of both is not of recent or accidental origin, but is inherent in nature and responds to a definite design of that mysterious force, which is responsible for life and which displays the same tendencies in the peculiarities of countless species in the animal world.

The same reason which appears to induce nature to alter the attitude and to lessen the attractiveness of women after marriage seems to operate among animals

---
(1) Luke X 39—42.

in general in so far as it can serve the interest of the various species.

A further illustration of this principle may be found in the fact that among certain flying ants, as soon as the female begins to propagate she loses her wings. This tends to reduce the risks of accidents and to keep her at home, which may not be more pleasing to the ant than the similar fate is agreeable to women, but the utility and practical sense in both instances cannot be ignored. Both must respond to the general and impersonal designs of a force which they cannot understand and which uses them as the means towards an end which they can never know.

CHAPTER II.

WOMAN'S MORAL POSITION AND HER PLACE IN HUMAN ACHIEVEMENTS.

In order successfully to deal with a problem which has increased in gravity in proportion to the industrial development of nations, it is essential to clarify the vague conceptions now so generally held as to the equality of men and women and with impartial equity to indicate their true position and the measures which may put an end to the senseless rivalry and discord now so general among them.

The social and economic problems involved in the exploitation of women demand a straightforward solution. This can be realized only upon the basis of taking into account the clearly defined difference which exists between man and woman as regards their natural endowments, which determine the part that can be most effectively taken by each in the life of the world.

It may be gratifying to a certain type of woman to read the nonsense written by men as to the equality of the sexes and as to the homage with which women are supposed to be regarded by men, but it will be more useful to enquire as to how far this homage is actually shown by men and in what respects women are both superior and inferior to men. Upon this basis it may be possible to indicate in what ways men and women may establish relations of the greatest mutual value, freed from useless competition and dedicated to the realization of the highest personal aims which are forever inseparable from the general social welfare.

The failure of men to realize that there can be no true progress which is not measured by the good of all and their more lamentable failure to understand that there can be no isolation of either sex in any great and useful human evolution, are responsible for all the wrongs which castes have inflicted upon humanity and which men have imposed upon women.

So long as women are either beasts of burden or pampered dolls they are unfitted for their natural career of motherhood. A stream does not rise higher than its source and what man sows in the suppression of the intellect and liberties of women, he reaps in the stupidity and license of his children. The generosity which is born of intelligence, independence and self-control and the noble aspirations which alone can raise mankind above the present level of savage brutality do not thrive either in ignorance or slavery.

The attitude of man towards woman has been wrong, not because she has not been taught to compete with men, but because she has not been taught anything of the least importance or value, while she has at the same time been made to feel that she was not sufficiently intelligent to enter with men upon the great subjects of moral and scientific enquiry which stand as the most noble records of human progress. The extent to which man has carried his worship of brute force and to which he personally exemplifies it, has its counterpart in his vain and arrogant attitude towards woman, who may be in one sense a weaker being, but whose weakness is in fact the greatest charm of human existence. It is fortunate for humanity that women are naturally inclined to accept the protection of strength, even when they stand superior to their protectors in all those beautiful qualities which are the adornment, the stability and joy of life.

For reasons which will be clearly exposed and which contemplate the highest good for both women and men, I am completely opposed to all competition between them and I do not in the least share man's unjust prejudices as regards the capacities, the duties and the destiny of women. Let there be no illusion about man's actual attitude towards women as it is generally exemplified in the so-called pretension of equality, in the giving of votes to women and in the vast designs now being carried out to reduce them to an industrial slavery more pathetic than any which has existed since the world began. Man's real feeling upon the subject of sex equality should be measured, not by his platitudes which flatter women's vanity, but by his shameless industrial exploitation of their vital necessities, by his scandalous abuse of their emotional sense of duty, by the tyranny established over them through priests, at whom he scoffs and by his hypocritical system of one-sided polygamy and his abominable degradation of the fairest of all the beings of earth.

It is not possible to predict what may be the achievements of woman when she is freed from the prejudices and the tyranny which have always attended her, but it is not to her interest to attempt to duplicate the only work which men are able to do and which would automatically bar her from her most important and natural career.

Women should be educated, not for industry, but for motherhood and when the industrial slavery of men is abolished they will be able to so protect and surround women and children, that motherhood will lose most of the terrors with which it is now regarded by the masses among the poor. When also it will no longer be an honour for some women to spend their time in idleness and dissipation and when deliberately childless marriages among the rich are regarded as legalized prostitution, there will be fewer women who will prefer industry and the professions to homes and motherhood. All professions should be open to women upon equal terms and in some professions women will excel. The great intuitive faculty possessed almost exclusively by women might be put to a vast and noble use in healing mankind. Contrary to the contention of physicians I hold that the impersonal attitude of doctors towards their patients leaves untouched the most important of all resources for healing and that is spiritual suggestion. The lack of sympathy and spiritual understanding shown by the average man and particulary exemplified by doctors, prevents the attainment of the highest powers of healing.

In these great qualities women naturally excel men and they should be able to attain a high rank in the medical profession. As a matter of simple justice no obstacles or prejudices should be allowed to retard this phase of woman's evolution for the few who are qualified and who might prefer it to marriage. There are also many women and especially girls who cannot be induced to speak frankly with a physician and it is one of the beautiful qualities of their sex that they will confide only to a woman what may be information essential to an understanding of their case. In this respect there is a great sphere for women who desire seriously to enter the medical profession, although only very exceptional women would be qualified for surgery.

The whole basis of medical practice is wrong in principle because it is degraded to a money-making occupation and the interests of the doctor can be served only through the illness of his patient.

As matters now stand, the most studious and generous-minded men who have no independent income, are deterred from the study of medicine because of the difficulties of establishing an income through their profession by methods which accord with their sense of duty and professional service. The result is that perhaps the best of all talent is not attracted to this profession and when men rise to great eminence as physicians they are not infrequently so occupied with money-making that they neglect all study and are consequently not in touch with much that is essential to their highest usefulness.

The medical profession will never be upon a rational footing until it becomes a department of public service scientifically organized and maintained. It should be open to men and women upon equal terms which should include a rigid and comprehensive education in natural science, and higher standards of general and special instruction than now prevail and requiring years of training in hospitals, under strict supervision of superior men or women.

The number allowed to enter upon this career could be effectively controlled by the austerity of its qualifications. From the commencement of the study the student should be independent of all financial considerations. The state should bear the cost of education so long as the courses prescribed were mastered and when the student was qualified to practice he should be assigned his sphere of activities and adequately paid by the state. Pensions against disability and age should be provided and no physician should be allowed to accept other fees, gratuities or payments of any sort from his patients or the public. This would attract women and men whose ambition led them to a truly scientific career and would dissuade those scheming business doctors from embarking upon a career which would offer no opportunities to exploit the misfortunes, credulity or vanity of their fellow-men. My system would put an end to the temptations to profit from the illness of the rich and neglect the poor and would also insure to the poor the best medical attendance. The life of one man would not be saved by an operation for which he paid a doctor five thousand francs for an hour's work, while many other men were dying at the same time because they could not afford medical aid.

A similar system should be applied to the legal profession which would put an end to nearly all litigation and force hundreds of thousands of meddlesome lawyers to earn an honest living by useful employment, instead of creating and fostering strife which benefits no one but themselves and which is contrary to every public interest.

These two professions when raised to their proper dignity would be attractive not only to a higher type of intelligence and character than they now engage, but they would also offer inducements to exceptional women who now quite properly look upon medicine and the law with horror.

To what extent the great gulf existing between the creative achievements of men and women in the highest form of speculative thought, literature, art, music and science may in the distant future be narrowed, it is difficult to predict. It must constantly be borne in mind that the natural inclinations and functions of women, which are inseparable from their sex, and which arise precisely through the meaning of their sex, have stood and may always stand as obstacles in the way of the highest attainment, of which a man has been and will be capable.

What must frankly be faced is that nearly all men and women stand upon the same level of stupidity. From an intellectual point of view there is nothing to choose between them in the mass. Both are ignorant, vain, selfish and inefficient and if women are not more efficient than men, they are less selfish. The lives of both are a ceaseless grind for the meagre means by which they may live and as regards the mass, neither the one nor the other has had the social surroundings which reasonable beings should create and in which degradation, ignorance and poverty would be unknown. On the whole men are more debased than women, but this may be traced in great part to the surroundings in which their days are spent, to the nature of their drudgery in the factory and mine, and to the absence of those gentle and ennobling influences which are at all hours making their appeal to women through the tender helplessness of children. The greatest curse to humanity is alcohol, and men, more than women are addicted to it as a vice. The stupidity of most men is such that the only form of sociability of which they are capable is to offer drinks to each other and such is their absorbing vanity that they offer and accept more than they can afford to pay for, and more than they should consume. Happily for humanity the average woman is protected against this particular vice by the restrictions of her home and infrequency of visitors. Among the rich, where the women pass their days in idleness, in gossip or flirtation, there is nothing to choose between them and the men of their own class. The men may employ their days making money and their nights in spending it and the one may not be more creditable than the other.

It is outside all these realms, both in their depths of poverty and ignorance and in their senseless luxury, vanity and idleness, that we must look to find the ones whose intellectual and moral achievements stand as monuments to the glory of mankind. And there we find that what is most imperishable on all the pages of time has come from the hands of men. The philosophy, poetry, music, art and science which have immortalized the struggles and hopes of humanity through the ages are the work of men. These may be taken as indicating a great and permanent superiority of some men over other men and over all women.

To what extent these great achievements have been inspired, or even rendered possible by the intimate influence of women in the lives of the most illustrious men, cannot be truly measured, but the story of the greatest lives is woven in all its parts with the threads of woman's devotion, faith, sacrifice and love and who shall say, if these threads could be traced, they would not lead to the source of all human inspiration and account for all human genius.

What we definitely know is that those men who have cast the greatest lustre over the world, have been almost unanimous in their recognition of the noble and inspiring influence of women in their own lives and with the most humble as well as the greatest man, the sweetest word in any land is "Mother."

How far the intellectual and social restrictions imposed upon these mothers may account for their apparent lack of creative faculties it is of the highest importance to enquire, but to what extent our enquiry may be rewarded by an approximate approach to the truth, must be a matter of widely divergent opinion. It is to be observed at once that as women depart from their career as wives and mothers, or as they do not marry or have children, their tastes, occupations, and general attitude toward society are unlike the majority of their sex. They become more like men and are in consequence less feminine. As they evolve in these tendencies they pass from their natural relations with men into lines of activity which can be usefully followed by only a few exceptional women. The majority of all men and women can work only with their hands.

That is their misfortune because as society now stands such work is poorly rewarded and even in the most ideal commonwealth it would never be highly paid. It therefore follows that if vast numbers of women are employed outside their homes it must be in competition with men and what is worse, the greater part of this competition will be among the classes where man's labour is the most poorly paid, because it will be the hardest or the most unskilled classes of labour.

Nothing can be worse for humanity than such a shameless degradation of women. Quite apart from the great economic and social dangers involved in the industrial employment of women there are considerations of the highest importance to women which they will be well advised to heed and which should dissuade them from becoming industrial wage-slaves.

Both from nature and experience it should be clear that nothing is to be gained by humanity as a result of the masses of women attempting to compete with men and that in all competition where endurance and physical strength are involved women's achievements will remain inferior to men's and therefore they will be paid less than the unfortunate poorly paid men.

Some women may aspire to excel in what have generally been regarded as the occupations of men, but in proportion as they hope to approach the standards already set by men, they must abandon their normal occupation as women. When this is abandoned, as it has been by great numbers of women, either from necessity or choice they have not in a single instance achieved anything which can rank with the greatest achievements of men. Those who do not admit that there is any natural difference of great physical and intellectual importance between men and women, traceable directly to their sexual differences, will encounter difficulties at each step in illustrating their contention. I believe that the greater part of the physical, mental and spiritual differences between men and women may be ascribed to an origin more profound than the unwise and tyrannical laws of man. Nature appears to have prescribed for both sexes what is to be their normal and highest form of development, and as they depart from the co-operation of home life and enter the competition of industrialism, they will fail to attain the industrial independence which is the chief object of their toil and they will destroy those natural relations upon which alone society can securely rest.

When we consider the highest achievements of humanity we are contemplating the genius of a comparatively few men and women and are in a realm from which the great majority of mankind is and will always be excluded. Notwithstanding the vast changes which future generations will witness in the surroundings and intelligence of the masses, there will arise in those remote days men of such towering genius as the world has never seen and whose achievements we cannot now even vaguely imagine. Then as now, there will be the impassable gulfs of human inequality and the great differences in the endowments, capacity and natural spheres of action between men and women. The boundaries of human understanding and sympathy will be extended into regions whose existence is as yet unimagined except by a few lofty souls, now unknown to humanity and who would not be heeded even if they were known.

Too much importance has been attached to the so-called economic dependence of women and to the repressive influence which it is supposed to have exercised over her creative faculties. In the highest sense of the word women are not creative and in the realms where man's creative faculty expresses its most inspiring power it has risen serene above all the incidents and trials of life. The most oppressive material surroundings have never been able to destroy the genius, or humble the creative faculties of man, notwithstanding that the dependence of genius upon the petty whims of wealthy or influential men has been more oppressively felt than any like dependence which could conceivably be imposed upon a woman by a man with whom she was closely associated.

Man not only rises above all outside oppression but he has further often to contend against as great a lack of sympathy and understanding on part of those most closely associated with him as could well fall to the lot of any woman. In spite of all adverse circumstances of dependence upon others and the burden and distractions involved in the more intimate relations of life, man reaches a moral and intellectual plane which belongs exclusively to himself.

There is a great and varied range of action in which men are able to attain results of so high an order that there is no measure of comparison between the sexes and their dissimilarity is further emphasized through the achievements of women in lines of activity in which men are wholly incapable. In singing and acting the emotional nature of woman has carried her to the highest pinnacle of success where she has shown a genius and artistic capacity not excelled by any man.

As nurses and as those who are to minister to the ones in distress women are unique and supreme. Their patience, devotion and sympathy towards the ones who are ill, are the outward expression of a profound spiritual intuition. They instinctively know what men can never understand and that is that in gentleness, resignation and sorrow there is something divine.

If we believe that human life can justify its existence

because through the struggles, the hopes and the despair of man, he is slowly rising toward a goal which is as yet too lofty and remote for him to define, we will attach the highest importance to the duties involved in the birth and education of children rather than regard them with our present indifference. In this most important realm, so far as it concerns the birth and the greater part of all education, man's place is incidental and insignificant compared to that of woman. Not only do the health and future welfare of the child depend largely upon the conduct and attitude of the mother before the child is born, but from its earliest infancy the mother exercises an influence from which no child is ever free and which may determine the whole course of life, especially of everyone whose privilege it is to look back to childhood in love and veneration for his mother.

Nature does not bestow all her gifts upon one of her children or upon one sex. It does not make woman superior to man in all which she alone is qualified to do—and also make her the equal of man in everything he may be able to do. The greatest differences in the powers and achievements of men and women may be traced, not to the laws of man, but to those of Nature. They may be traced to the sexual difference between men and women and the great, but separate work which is consequently natural to each in the life of the world.

During the past three hundred fifty years in the most advanced societies in which great numbers of women have had time and opportunity for the cultivation of their powers, and where the resources of general culture were increasingly at their disposal they have not produced anything of highest importance in philosophy, science, and the arts, while within the same period man has attained a more remarkable development in nearly all these great expressions of human genius, than the total previous achievements of humanity since the world began.

There remain also to his credit the gigantic achievements in realms of invention, exploration and mechanics, which have all but completed his conquest of earth.

In man's imposing intellectual and material conquests women have taken the place of spectators and inspirers rather than creative equals.

There are exceptional women who are superior to nearly all men, but there is no instance in which a woman has achieved anything approximating the equal of the greatest man. Men and women are not to be regarded from the basis either of equality or inequality, but as complementary and mutually interdependent beings. All discussion upon any other basis becomes mere contention which obscures the great issues arising from the inherent difference between men and women and which must inevitably be displayed in their life-work and evolution.

It is due partly to the spread of fallacious teaching as to the supposed equality of men and women and partly to a mendacious system of industrial exploitation, that an ever increasing number of women are struggling against men and are consequently deprived of the natural surroundings of women in the life of the world. It is only when women are in their normal sphere that they can realize the fulfillment of their own nature, inspire the highest achievements of man and avoid the calamity which will follow the industrial enslavement of men and women through a general extension of competitive employment of women under the plea of necessity, or the false illusion of a supposed equality.

It is not an improvement in woman's position or a

high tribute to the value of her so-called equality with men, when the result is to transfer her activities from the natural occupations of the home to the degrading and destructive grind of the factory. It is one of the most melancholy signs of our times, that millions of young girls are forced into the army of wage-slaves before they are fifteen and continue until they are seventy if unfortunately they attain so great an age.

The struggle for existence into which women have been drawn in ever increasing numbers would have no place in a well regulated society. This competition between men and women for their daily bread is unnatural and in every sense detrimental to the race. It can be terminated only through the economic emancipation of men and a radical alteration of existing social relations between men and women. Men imagine they have attained freedom through democracy, but there never existed less true liberty than in 1918. The so-called free men in the great industrial nations are the dupes of petty politicians and the slaves of imperialism and high finance, while their women are being given the ballot, called the equals of men and forced by millions into industrialism in order that the grist of plutocracy may be ground for the smallest toll at which its grinders can live and rear more slaves. The ballot is not likely to be more important to labouring women than it has been to labouring men. If the use to which it has been put by men may be taken as an indication of what is to be the effect of increased suffrage, there is no reason to regard it as in any sense a usable means by which the masses may attain economic freedom.

The slow progress made by the toilers in industrial nations has been realized chiefly through economic organization. In my books dealing with capital, labour and industrialism, these questions are closely examined and sound remedies put forward to abolish the greatest evils which now beset mankind.[1]

It is shown in my books why a new system of political economy and a new definition of values must replace the existing order and why man's attempts to establish an ideal commonwealth have always failed and may never be realized. They are books in which practical measures are defined for application in a world of realities—not in some vague world of fancy which does not exist and which is not to be brought into being through dreams — howsoever noble they might be.

There is only one position in which nearly all women may express their highest faculties and render to humanity the most important service within their gifts, and that is in the home. They are not intended by nature to be competitors of men and they should not be forced into an unnatural and destructive industrial warfare, against their own interests and those of humanity, and for the exclusive profit of exploiters. I have shown in my books how the products of toil pass from their creators to those who do not toil or spin and the interest which plutocracy has in causing two or ten people to work for an aggregate wage which one should receive. As the surplus of all toil, above the amount required to maintain the life of the toilers, passes directly to unproductive classes, it is the policy of these classes to extend to the utmost the industrial and competitive labour of everyone who is able to work.

The ideal state for plutocrary would be one in which every man and woman and all children over nine years of age would be compelled to struggle against one another in productive industry, because the greater part of all production passes from its producers to their exploiters. The commonwealth which the toilers have the power to

---
[1] *"The People's Money"* and *"The World Allies."*

establish would be free from competition between men and women and there would be no child-labour or industrial exploitation.

It would be a state in which every man would be paid according to his production, rather than upon the basis of his most essential and competitive needs. It would result in the obliteration of milliards of fictitious values, prevent the future creation of similar paper and terminate forever wage-slavery and war. This is not an ideal to be reached through any ethical appeal to the strong, or through the destruction or division of existing property, but through a general adoption by labour of the peaceful methods which capital has employed to dominate and enslave mankind.

In the realization of a proper Social state the part to be played by women will be great and decisive. In a larger measure than is generally realized, their future and that of humanity depends upon the decisions taken within the next few years. Unless the fatal defects of civilization which have brought mankind within sight of irretrievable ruin, are fundamentally remedied, there is no hope for the ordered progress or the peace, happiness, and genuine liberty of the race.[1]

In considering the position and natural life of women it is essential to examine some of their most striking characteristics. The conclusions of the average woman do not bear any relation to reason or to anything outside her own experience and aims. Her decisions are generally based upon the most primitive motives. She is only interested in illusions when they are entertained respecting herself. Men listen to her words, not because they are wise, but because they are gentle and sometimes prudent. She has

---

[1] *"The World Allies"* explains the origin and extent of the industrial evils and shows in what way they may be peacefully remedied. Also the origin of this war and only in what way future wars may be avoided.

her feet on the earth and judges by results which she can see in a tangible form. She favours only such projects as are on the surface likely to succeed and is not greatly concerned with hopes that are long deferred. Woman must worship something to which she can give a definite form, and this she finds in symbolic religious rites. Most women will sacrifice everything to appearances but in this they are closely followed by most men. It may be said that society has forced upon woman her attitude toward what is stupidly termed the "social problem" whereas in fact it is an attitude confined almost entirely to women and arises from their instinctive wish for the exclusive possession of what they may love or admire. As they have little inclination to regard matters abstractly, women naturally hold most restricted views as to morality, and are consequently prone to regard conduct—not from the point of view natural to the persons involved—but rather in the light of its significance if applied personally to themselves. They are generally unable to distinguish between conduct and morals or to realize that they may be only remotely related one to the other. Most women who are what is termed "faithful," consider themselves moral, even though they tell twenty lies a day, and ride on a railway without paying their fare when overlooked by the ticket-collectors. A woman may also be engaged in the exploitation of her sex at bargain-counters, or in her own home or through industrialism, where her security rests upon the degradation and ruin of her sisters and she may see nothing immoral in her conduct because she is what is vulgarly called "respectable." This applies with even greater significance to men who exemplify the same exalted notions of morality.

The difference is that while the men engaged in similar exploitations are not influenced by any moral considerations, they understand that what they do is in fact immoral and this is what most women do not understand. Perhaps men who deliberately practice what they know to be immoral are more reprehensible than women who do not know that what they practice is immoral but even such men would possess an intellectual advantage in their capacity to form judgments and in their understanding of the relation of morals to conduct—even though they would not apply them.

It may be justly urged that there is little encouragement to be derived from the knowledge of what is immoral when it is not accompanied by ethical principles which put this discrimination to any noble use. I have known women who, after understanding this principle, would thereafter be sentimentally affected by it, but when it came to a choice between boycotting stores whose low wages and bargain-counters were responsible for the ruin of thousands of girls the "respectable" women nearly all closed their eyes to the moral considerations involved, and still patronized the shops which sold bargains to women and drove girls into the streets. As an editor of a daily newspaper I had a melancholy experience in testing this question when I published the stories of poor girls and urged all honest men and women to boycott the stores. The only effect of this campaign was that the stores (and exploiters of women in general) boycotted my newspapers and I was obliged to make good the financial losses thus sustained. Among the great numbers of women who were horrified at my disclosures, not one offered to render any practical assistance and the only ones whom I know to have shed tears were the girls who read the galley proofs.

Nature has implanted in women an impressive regard for sex because they are the mothers of mankind. It is an attitude which man's nature does not share; principally because he is only an incident in propagation and that which is connected with it is consequently of more significance to women than it can ever be to men.

It would be fortunate for humanity if woman's sentiment as to this relation could be fully and generally shared by men, but this is the case only in exceptional instances and then it rests upon sentimental grounds, rather than arising from the inherent physical considerations which are of such natural importance to women.

Women are superior to men in the resignation and patience with which they bear pain, and in the inspiring personal devotion to those they love. These are beautiful and essential gifts of nature to those whose suffering makes them the mothers of mankind.

The natural life of woman is to bear children and to care for them. They are the tokens of her suffering and her noble dreams.

Coupled with their physical pain women have endured enough anguish to drown the world in tears but they have not been able to write, paint, carve, sing or pray this anguish into any exalted ideal of religion, or any system of morals or philosophy. This may be accounted for partly by the fact that women are not greatly interested in constructive pursuits and still less in an attempt to create an ethical system which may answer to the suffering and hopes of the world. They are chiefly concerned with what is more tangibly related to themselves and their offspring. As women accept suffering as the natural lot of life they do not seek for the solution of its mystery as man constantly does through his more impersonal sentiments and philosophy, and through those feelings which poets and dreamers have been able to immortalize in song. Man's place in speculation and ethics belongs exclusively to him. In his highest achievements he has no competitor, howsoever much he may need to sing his songs and his prayers to women.

Man creates and worships his own divinity, while woman worships either a man or a religious symbol which man has invented.

It must be confessed that a more horrid and dismal collection of gods could not be imagined than the ones which men have successively created and destroyed through the ages. It may well be hoped that women will enter into this special realm of creation in which they cannot do worse than man has done. There is a scope for improvement so vast that they might find an image higher and more divine than man has been able to conceive, because man in his vanity can conceive nothing higher than himself; whereas women are always seeking an ideal of perfection which they are never likely to find.

In his creative imagination and vanity man finds in himself the reason for the existence of all things, whereas the natural woman finds the reason for her existence in her relation to some man and in the interests which grow out of that relation.

It is because nature has so endowed men and women with their own and personal attributes, which establish a well defined difference of intellect and diversity of interest between them, that men alone have been able to inscribe their genius upon all the pages of time, while women have created an atmosphere and a charm which have in some of man's most notable achievements played an important part.

It is only through a clear recognition of the physical, intellectual and spiritual differences between men and women and a stern respect for these differences that the highest powers of both may unite in the freedom and elevation of mankind. The great majority of both sexes are not spiritual. They are merely religious, which is quite a different matter. If no woman has recorded anything which may rank with the great intellectual achievements of men, it will be attested by experience that under similar circumstances nearly all men and women act similarly and as regards mankind in general there is little to choose between the masses of men and women upon spiritual grounds. The men are more brutal and the women more hysterical and timid in their attitude towards life, particularly where sentiment is concerned and this arises essentially from their difference in temperament, outlook, interest and occupation.

From the lives of nearly all men and women and of all animals and plants it is difficult to assume that there are ethical considerations controlling the vast and manifold aspects of nature or entering into the means it employs to attain what appear to be its ends. This may be accounted for by the brevity of life and our limited capacity to observe nature and by the evident fact that we cannot do more than guess as to what might be its possible purpose, if we assume that such purpose must logically exist. We cannot do more than traverse the limited space which lies between the mystery of birth and death. We know that neither our reason howsoever great, nor any other faculty, howsoever exalted it may be, can take us back to the beginning or carry us onward to the end of life. There is a strictly prescribed circle within which the mind of man is confined by limitations which appear to be insurmountable in this phase of existence. We can trace nothing to its ultimate source or destiny and can offer no explanation sufficient to account for the vast and wonderful phenomena which are displayed upon the earth and throughout the unmeasured heavens.

In their discussions of the principles of human knowledge most philosophers, not only in ancient but in modern times, have laid it down as fundamental that what is doubtful must be regarded as false—whereas it would appear more reasonable to say that what is doubtful must be regarded only as unproved. It is sufficient in this connection to contemplate the immense range of absolute knowledge which now completely disproves some of the most ancient as well as the most harmful views long held by mankind. This has arisen through discoveries by which some of the most important principles have been established. The altered aspect of the heavens, and a partial explanation of some of the wonders of earth, stand to the credit of a small number of men whose scepticism and enquiry, once so generally distasteful, are now regarded with gratitude, veneration and wonder. The whole of man's useful knowledge has resulted from his investigations, his doubts and his speculations with reference to what is recorded in the great book of nature, which would have remained forever closed if exceptional men had been content blindly to accept traditions and follow the advice of priests.

It may be asserted with the most general sanction of history that all human progress has resulted from the criticism, and destruction of customs and institutions and the abandonment of opinions which, through long usage and almost general acceptance, were formerly held to be sacred. The intellectual and political progress and the meagre religious toleration now attained by mankind have all arisen through the infidelity of brave, thoughtful and original minds, who were prepared to say that institutions which had been worshipped, deserved only to be torn down and that beliefs long held to be sacred were wrong.

Upon the ugly ruins of what man once regarded as

holy temples, erected in the name of liberty or of God,
he has successively built and burned what he believed to
be temples more sacred. This is a tendency which will
continue so long as men doubt, dream and speculate,
which is to say that it will be a permanent tendency, because
the mystery of life will remain unsolved and true
liberty, general culture and economic justice for humanity
are a goal to be attained only through the passing of thousands
of years, if in fact they are ever attainable.

All this tends to illustrate that man's attitude toward
everything new, so long as it is peaceful, should be one
of open-minded enquiry and of readiness to accept as a
principle that no institutions or customs are permanent
among men and that the most hopeful tendency is that
all things constantly change. It is the problem of humanity
in these incessant changes to guard those tendencies
which lead toward general enlightenment, freedom and
peace and to discard and reject everything that tends to
discrimination, race prejudice, hatred and violence.

In my analysis of the theory of liberty and the limited
extent to which it has been established there are set out
with precision the reasons why liberty, in its truest and
most important sense is still only the dream of mankind
and why its realization is so painfully slow.[1]

It is true that Socrates would not now be poisoned for
his opinions. Milton, Savonarola and Spinoza would not
be imprisoned, tortured or burned at the stake, except
in belligerent nations during this war, but it still remains
to be recorded with regret and humilation, that now, as
in the past, all who announce social or ethical views,
contrary to those which the masses profess to hold, are
subjected to a new form of punishment and torture.

The punishments which autocracy once decreed through

---
[1] "*The World Allies*" pp. 31—65.

the Sanhedrin, the Tribune and the Popes of Rome, is now inflicted through the clergy, the press and a dull and stupid middle class, which have together elevated the appearance of respectability and justice into institutions claiming to be more sacred than religion, liberty or life itself and in none of which is there justice, liberty or a noble and spiritual religion.

The present generation has within its recollection the vulgar abuse which an ignorant and bigoted clergy, with the aid of an equally unintelligent press, hurled at Darwin, Spencer and Huxley, whose patient labours directed by independent, great and luminous minds, have bequeathed to man a store of knowledge so precious that they will receive the gratitude of all thoughtful and enlightened men until the end of time. The capital crime of these noble benefactors of humanity was, that great and important principles, which they proved beyond the point of controversy to be scientifically sound, were a contradiction of the teachings of priests who pretended to speak with the authority and in the name of God, whom they contended ought to know more about the origin of man than any scientist or philosopher. Perhaps this may be so, but in that event the information has not, so far as we are aware, been confided to the clergy, neither in this nor in any other age. It still remains engraved on the rocks and fossils and is illustrated by the plants and animals of earth and through the pageantry of the sky, and it has fallen exclusively to the lot of scientists to read or attempt to explain what has not been written by the hand of man.

The more a man is interested in an investigation of nature and the more wonders he is able to see as he turns his microscope towards the marvels of earth, and his telescope towards the gorgeous splendour of the infinite sky, the more truly spiritual he becomes and in its largest sense he is more religious than other men, because he better understands how vast and superhuman is the overruling Power. He is the most sincere worshipper of the mystery of creation because he is not content merely to mumble meaningless prayers or eulogies to a Creator without taking the trouble to look at the never ending wonders displayed in the most minute, as well as in the gigantic objects of creation.

There is more true religion involved in spending an hour studying the marvels of the brown dust, which one takes from a mountain flower and finds that under the microscope it is a great cluster of delicate and beautiful eggs containing future generations of flowers, than there is in babbling pages of ignorant and meaningless praise to the Author of the Holy Book of Creation, without having so much as opened the book.

We would have only feelings of contempt for those who spent their time addressing eulogies to some philosopher, whose books they had never read and whom they worshipped merely because other people did the same, and yet that is precisely the occupation of priests and their followers as distinguished from men of science and it is the priests who claim a monopoly of religious feelings.

Some day the scientist will be looked upon as the only true worshipper of the Creator, because he alone is able to understand the boundary beyond which man cannot go in his knowledge and conception of the ultimate Cause, from which flow the vast and endless rivers of life. It is only when we know the marvels which Nature reveals to man through science, that we can realize man's limitations and therefore appreciate how impenetrable is the mystery of life.

The critics of all men who are in advance of their time do not trouble to reason as to whether these men may be right. It is sufficient that what they teach is new and solely for this reason it is to be condemned. When one reads the stories of the persecutions which for thousands of years have been inflicted upon illustrious and immortal men he cannot refrain from wondering at the restricted horizon of humanity and that it learns nothing from what is recorded on the pages of time. The scientists and philosophers regard the limited knowledge of man as they might regard the possessions of children on the sea-shore. They know that if one has a hundred grains of sand and another a thousand there are millions of other grains which await the coming of other men. It is in this light that superior men must regard all pretentions to a knowledge of the mystery of life, which is not only unknown but probably unknowable, even though man may pass through an endless succession of lives in which the mystery remains with only its aspect altered.

The wise men investigate what they cannot understand, while the foolish worship it. When men of science differ —not in their established facts, but in the deductions they draw from their facts—they do not regard each other as enemies. They know that both may be wrong but both are seeking the same end—which is to know the truth, whereas in matters of religion, if one differs from the theologian he is considered not only an enemy of the church but also an enemy of truth. This difference in the attitude of scientists and priests toward all enquiry is not flattering to the priests, but is a characteristic and inevitable difference between men who seek the truth and require definite evidence, by way of proof, and other men who pretend to possess the truth without being able to explain or demonstrate if or why it is true. Both the philosopher and the scientist seek a solution of the same mystery. The scientist searches for what he believes may never be found. He and the true philosopher have open minds and weigh all evidence, whereas the clergyman searches for nothing, explains nothing, and knows nothing as to the mystery which he assumes to have solved. It is evident that to attempt to impose upon mankind for centuries a moral control based upon prohibitions and to hold before humanity a standard of conduct to be determined by the hope of rewards and the fear of punishments could have no other effect than the establishment of deep-seated wrongs which inevitably lead to the downfall of the hideous institutions from which they arise.

As one regards the grotesque position of men and women in their most intimate relations, the causes and extent of the evils involved in their present economic position and the baneful effects of an unsound, unnatural and immoral social order, one is bound to express astonishment that these evils have been so little criticized and so long suffered to endure, and that the teaching from which they naturally and logically flow should be still seriously put forward and blindly accepted as if it were right or true.

Following the custom of humanity, which is to attempt to cure a small part of the ills which it deliberately or blindly creates, the solution of the marriage problem is sought in the divorce courts, whereas the institution should be brought into harmony with the nature and practice of mankind.

In considering the economic position of men and women and the influence of environment over social customs, I confine my observations exclusively to the so-called Christian nations.

When we regard the influence which women have exercised in the rise and fall of the most ancient and powerful states and the part they have taken in the more recent and also in the current history of nations, it is at once apparent that it is only possible to form approximately accurate conclusions of contemporary history by close observation of the various classes of society in their own lands. As regards our generation this personal study is more essential than a knowledge of any written history, although the conclusions reached must be based upon the general experience and the relation which our generation necessarily bears to the past.

It is upon this principle that my present observations do not extend to the far East although I look with keen anticipation to the time when they may be supplemented by impressions of similar problems, which I hope more closely to study in the great oriental nations.

In the history of nations a most striking similarity between ancient and modern economic exploitation and social compromise is everywhere manifest and may be said to have undergone changes only in degree and practice, but no radical change in principle. There are introduced into the modern civilizations certain elements unknown before the age of industrial trusts, but the tendency to distribute the vast surplus created by toil, to those who do not toil, remains as it has always been. The ruling castes have changed from personal tyrannies of men to an impersonal tyranny of stocks and bonds. The only practicable way to put an end to this latter tyranny without restoring the former is explained in my books.

It is essential to regard present world tendencies in the light of the philosophy of history, which does not mean an examination of battles, or of certain apparently decisive events, but rather an investigation of the origin and trend of movements which have culminated in the events. It is only as these tendencies are weighed in their true perspective that the outstanding events in history display their ordered significance and that their logical relation to the present may be traced.

Only those who have had a direct part in the great conflict of world forces and who have also been able impartially to observe their operation from a vantage ground far above the conflict, can fully realize that the ghastly state of society is the inevitable result of man's general and habitual disregard for the rights of the weak; of his gross abuse of a new power accruing to the few through industrialism and of his contempt for true and impersonal justice and for general and solid freedom. The horror now spread over the earth is the exclusive creation of men and is in no sense accidental; neither does it represent anything approximating what stupid people term divine vengeance. Man is reaping only what he has sown and it is a harvest which our descendants will reap again and again so long as they live under the existing or similar terms of injustice, violence, exploitation, oppression and hypocrisy.

In *"The World Allies"* I show why man's exploitation and injustice necessarily led to the present war and demonstrate that the only hopeful sign in all this horror is that it is exclusively the creation of men and therefore may be remedied by men, whereas if this were not so, humanity would be without hope. Happily for man the sentiment of revenge can have no origin higher than man himself and as it is his own ugly creation it may be outgrown.

I have observed the social and economic problems at close range through association with nearly all classes in the principal western nations. I know the struggles of the poor, how they toil and what they sometimes dare to hope. I know their qualities and defects and why it is that they bear the hardships and the burdens of mankind.

Also in what ways only they may make solid progress and why they can never attain and hold political power.

I am equally familiar with the most intimate life of the classes which rule the world and place the load of their arrogant power upon the backs of the common men — also with the precise means employed to perpetuate their mastery of the world. From these remote extremes of life, in positions of great personal power and of no power, I have been able to weigh the problems and regard the hopes of nearly every class of society and in my books I give what appear to me the only effective, honourable and peaceful remedies for existing economic and social evils. The solution of the economic problem cannot longer be deferred if the masses are to escape indefinite bondage or be saved from a general and disastrous world violence.

What I have written is put forward in the conviction that it advocates the only tangible measures which may now be employed to remedy the general and grave evils involved in our outrageous industrial, political and social institutions and now aggravated beyond all believable bounds by a horrible and avoidable war. What I believe will be the verdict of posterity, is set forth in my books.

The opposition to the views expressed will not arise from the most intelligent or moral elements of society but from the most pretentious and also from those whose interests are opposed to the withdrawal of women from industrial slavery, solely upon economic grounds which they seek to conceal.

It may be recorded in all confidence that the latter category includes the ones who temporarily wield the most power and who enjoy the most complete liberty from the restrictions which they impose upon the masses.

Even before the war man's outrageous exploitation was dragging an ever increasing number of women and children into the industrial machines and the future of women and children was menaced. This terrible evil has been almost unbelievably accentuated through the murder of millions of men and unless it is now remedied by fundamental measures, the future holds nothing but economic slavery for men, women and children and in this state there is also moral ruin for women. In subsequent chapters I show why women must not follow the present tendency and why they must decline to fall into the trap now set for them by the ones who wish to consolidate their exploitation and increase their own fortunes and powers through the toil of underpaid men and struggling and deluded women and children.

In another chapter I examine the anomaly shown in the fact that those in whose hands large and arbitrary powers have been most abused are precisely the ones to whom more power is constantly accorded and whose professed opinions as to the duties and rights of the masses are accepted as true and final and followed in slavish obedience. These pretentions are exposed to a clear definition and set in their true bearing because they must one day be dealt with by an exploited and groping humanity in the only way which offers the slightest hope to the masses and which can save the world from an indefinite perpetuation of the existing wrongs.

Those who control public opinion and impose their rule upon supposedly free people will always oppose, upon what they piously call "moral grounds" any measures calculated to abolish their tyrannical and immoral institutions, designed for the exclusive benefit of the few and subversive of every honourable principle of political and social justice for the masses.

CHAPTER III.

THE GENERIC INFLUENCE OF ETHICS AND SENTIMENT.

One of the most difficult phases of man's apathy and thoughtlessness with which all reforms have to deal is the general attitude of mind that whatever is must be right. Slowly through the ascendancy of the intellect over the imagination and through the application of great principles discovered by science, some of the chief barriers so long on the path of human progress are being thrown aside, but the goal of genuine economic, social, intellectual and ethical freedom is buried in the remote future. It may be that the present calamity which has all but destroyed our so-called civilization will make possible the erection of a new structure rather than an attempted repair of the old ruins, whose hideous incongruities can no longer be concealed. They should not be allowed to serve as the basis of a new patch-work to perpetuate the old superstitions and social wrongs.

In the new economic and social order which must be established before man can attain true freedom and find his place in nature, there must be no attempt longer to set aside the natural laws or to perpetuate man's unnatural injustice.

The relations of men and women towards one another will be beautiful only in proportion as they are founded upon sentiment rather than guided by necessity or any form of appearances and they will have a moral importance only in so far as they are controlled by feelings of personal understanding and sympathy and are not concerned with customs, creeds or laws.

It is because the ruling classes are able to live in hypocrisy, that large numbers of otherwise honourable people pretend to exemplify ideals in which they do not believe and compared to which their actual lives are nothing more than the sombre shadows of a beautiful image which will remain beyond their reach. The existing economic and social institutions are founded upon violence, exploitation and hypocrisy and should not be permitted longer to enslave and destroy the masses.

As we look across the centuries we read with indignation and horror the laws which rulers and priests imposed upon mankind in the name of God and we marvel that men could ever have submitted to such a shameless abuse of power, to such odious measures of oppression and to such outrages against their pride, dignity and honour and yet the future will regard the present atrocious era as the most melancholy chapter in the history of man.

It exceeds in exploitation, oppression, barbarity and shameless pretence the most dismal experience of the human race and the extent to which this destruction and outrage have been carried are beyond all that could have been conceived possible by any man in any other age.

This is not in the least understood by the masses who have no opinions except those obtained from parliaments, the press and the priests, whose only occupation is to uphold the existing order of society because their present authority could not exist in a properly constituted state. The control exercised by the few is established by means so gradual, indirect and subtle that the masses are never aware of the extent to which they are enslaved. It may be that even their destruction by millions in a senseless and avoidable war, waged by plutocracy for its exclusive benefit and against the most sacred rights of mankind, will not be sufficient to convince them that while they may have the fiction of liberty they are in fact slaves. The institutions which have kept men in social and intellectual slavery are being dissolved through their own defects. Their ruins cover the earth. They were founded upon the sands of pretension, violence, injustice and tyranny and from these man had no possible chance to achieve any permanent good. If the old fragments are put together under the old system or under any system maintaining the old principles, there is nothing but ruin in store for this and succeeding generations. If the religious pretensions of the past had been anything more than the hollow mockery of men professing what they did not understand and could not therefore believe, the ghastly murder of so-called Christians by one another would have been impossible and even unthinkable.

Those who seek emancipation from industrial slavery and social degradation should face the problems as they are and realise that they can be solved only through measures which conform to the practical needs of society and which do not attempt to meet injustice with violence or rely upon the ethical conduct of the strong, or confide to unorganized and untrained masses the direction of a world which they are not able to direct, except through the use upon a social basis, of the brains which now dominate capitalism.

Were it not for the impressive lessons of history one would express amazement that it should now be necessary to contend for the recognition of principles so elemental to the well-being of mankind and so essential to an ordered world and yet it is probable that the social state I have outlined will not become a reality for many generations, not because it is so far beyond the reach of humanity, but because humanity does not understand the value or importance of organization, in order to grasp what is within its reach. This will remain one of the great misfortunes of mankind for which I entertain no illusions. Man will pass from one form of oppression to another, from one injustice to another, from an old superstition to a new one, from the tyranny of one to the tyranny of many, from feudal slavery to industrial bondage and perhaps through communal disorganization back to slavery. A better way is simple and is precisely indicated in my books, but it is the misfortune of men that they do not look beyond the immediate present and that they condemn themselves to the most devious, difficult and doubtful paths which do not lead them towards high and permanent social ideals.

In considering the measures most effective for the realization of a new social order, founded upon justice and following what appears to be the design of Nature, it is useful to examine some of the most pronounced differences in the attitude of men and women as regards legislation, property and the struggle for existence.

It may be stated generally that legislation designed to protect society from violence, especially as regards persons, has its origin in the primary sentiments of self-defence and sympathy. A woman's instinct of self-defence is strongly developed, while as regards sympathy, except in a restricted personal sense, she is generally deficient and only with great difficulty is she able to understand the principle of abstract and impersonal justice. Her prejudices are so decided and so unconnected with reason that they are with difficulty overcome by reason. Only exceptional women will view great questions impersonally. In the mind of a woman a thing is so because it is so and that is the end of the matter.

In times of social disorder, if women take part in the

actual violence they are more violent than men, probably due partly to the fact that they are less generous in their moral judgments and are less able than men to control their deepest feelings. They also retain more of the primitive instincts of the female which, in a state of savagery among people and animals, is left to guard the young and when aroused in defence is more ferocious than the male. The difference between the male and the female when aroused to action may also be attributed in part to the fact that the male is engaged in a constant fight for the means of life. He must battle for his daily food and he enters a contest more as a part of the routine of life, whereas the position of the female is such that when she must fight, it is a defensive struggle in which she must win, or perish together with her young. It is one of the most interesting of all the subjects which can come under one's personal observation to note the actual operation of these instincts among animals and people in savage countries and in the law courts of great cities.

If the female animal is conscious of her inability successfully to defend her young her first move is to conceal the existence of her offspring and attract the assailant to herself. The birds, the deer and many other of the weaker animals adopt these as first tactics and only in the event of failure do they attempt a defense by force, whereas the female wolf, lion and bear stand their ground and await with an apparently sure confidence and smouldering rage the near approach of an enemy. They express a consciousness of strength. These natural differences in tactics, so generally displayed among animals, may be seen to operate with men and women, not only in the more primitive phases of existence, but in life as a whole, whenever they encounter personal difficulties or come into conflict with powerful institutions. The first instinct of the woman is to escape the difficulty through the use of her most effective weapon which is deception. She will not stand her ground except as a last resort, whereas man stands his ground. If a woman is attacked in the courts she loses restraint and if she loses her case she can never be convinced that there is any justice in the courts. She takes a decision against her as a personal insult and injury. It will never occur to her that she might have been wrong. The reasons she gives to herself she considers should have been sufficient for others.

In matters of business where transactions involve large sums, the attitude of women, who are otherwise the most honourable, deserves to be noted. In all great cities, millions of money or bank credits change hands daily on the verbal orders of men. In stock exchange transactions a man telephones his broker to buy or sell securities to the value of a million and the order is executed without question and without written confirmation. When the contract note arrives next morning, the man may have lost twenty per cent of the sum, but it never occurs to him to say that the order was an error, or that it was not given; whereas in dealing with women such orders involving important sums are rarely executed on their verbal word.

This is due to two primary reasons: first because women are not graceful losers — in business as distinguished from love — and therefore do not like to stand by a bad bargain and second because they do not respect their word as men respect it. They do not realise that the whole structure of modern life rests upon confidence and that among men, when a man repudiates his word, all transactions are impossible and business is at an end. That women do not realize this, is due to their limited experience in large affairs and to the deficiency of their education. Also to the fact that they are by nature not qualified for or intended to gamble on the exchange.

Environment and occupation are the most potent factors in determining conduct and a long continued habit becomes almost as binding upon conduct as the most distinctive traits, arising through inherited qualities. The characteristics peculiar to women and in which they differ most from men are readily traceable. Their lives are spent in economic dependence upon men. Under my system of marriage this would be altered. So long as they remain in their places of highest usefulness to the world they have a most restricted choice of occupation, since as wives and mothers they all have the same occupation. Society is so improperly constituted that even in their homes the life of women involves only varying degrees of drudgery. As women move out of their natural sphere of employment and take up man's work they gradually lose some of the most conspicuous of their own personal traits and begin slowly to express those displayed by men in similar occupations. In proportion as their work bears less resemblance to the natural work of women, they express less and less those distinguishing traits which belong to them exclusively in their natural surroundings.

The precision of statement and punctuality of conduct required in the great and responsible work of men are not essential to the natural work of women. This has an important and injurious effect upon their character. Also the lack of all rigorous discipline in the life of women tends to a carelessness in thought and expression from which men are by choice or necessity more free.

The exactitude and care which are forced upon all men employed in important and responsible work are traits which the greatest employers naturally display as a result of their character. Without these essential qualifications men never attain positions of commanding importance or great power, and women never attain them. When they occasionally inherit important positions they employ men to discharge their responsibilites. There is little or no occasion for the display of these qualities in the natural sphere of women because there is no special necessity for punctuality and precision. If they begin a thing today they may finish it in an hour or in a week and as they are constantly going from one thing to another they cannot understand or impose discipline upon themselves or upon others. Man's occupations subject him to method, discipline and precision. When the wheels of industry are set in motion on the stroke of the clock every man must be at his post. It is one of the inevitable results of an age of machinery that men should become the slaves of their machines and the basis of wage-exploitation through which industrialism has been developed, is such as most effectively makes the man subsidiary to the machine.

The tendency of women to become more like men in proportion as they follow men in their occupation and environment is forcibly illustrated in a diversity of ways. Not only do their dress, manners and habits of thought undergo radical changes, but in matters of conduct women become more like men. I have observed in the Western States of America that one rarely finds a woman undergoing sentence of imprisonment for a crime against property, while it is a frequent occurrence in the industrial States, among women who otherwise belong to the same class and who are neither better nor worse than their sisters in the West. In the case of the former there are only a few women engaged in any occupations outside the home and they are therefore not brought into contact with life as employees upon the basis of competition with men and consequently do not share their temptations with respect to the property of others.

In proportion as women compete industrially or otherwise with men and as they are forced to assume the responsibility for the support and protection of others, they yield to the same temptations, exhibit the same defects and commit the same crimes. This tendency will increase in an exact ratio to their obligations and to the opportunities afforded them to commit offenses against the property of others. The fact that women are never on trial for the misappropriation of millions, while men constantly are, is not to be attributed to any moral superiority of women over men, but to the more solid reason that almost no women are ever in a position to misappropriate millions, whereas great numbers of men always occupy such positions.

I state it as a matter of experience, as an employer of men to whom great sums were constantly confided, that it would not be possible to conduct our immense financial and industrial institutions on the present basis of underpaying employees, without the most exact and effective precautions being constantly observed against the temptations placed in their way. So perfect is the system of checking and counter-signatures, that money to the amount of millions passes daily through the hands of underpaid clerks in great concerns without the loss of a penny in a year. To the outside observer and also to the employees themselves, this system is all but invisible and never in any manner obtrusive except in continental shops where nobody appears to be trusted. Without a scientific accounting system modern institutions could not exist. It is a part of the extensive machinery set up by industrialism to cope with the impersonal nature of modern employers.

to whom the employees are unknown even by name and are generally regarded as so many units in a great and complicated machine.

It is the duty of those who control great enterprises to safeguard men from temptations in such ways that they will not be aware of the existence of any direct or potential restraint, because of the moral effect upon the men employed. If they do not attempt to abuse their trust, because they know that the abuse would either be impossible or immediately discovered, their fidelity is without any moral importance to themselves, whereas if they can be made to feel that they are trusted, it has the most beneficial influence upon their moral natures and inspires a devotion and sense of dignity which are of the highest importance to the individual and of inestimable value to his employer and to society.

I state it upon the basis of my extensive experience as an employer that it is comparatively simple, where cash is handled to the amount of millions in a day, to safeguard the interest of the employer and stimulate the morals of the employees, by a system which in appearance amounts only to clerical checking, instituted solely to avoid errors and essential to the expeditious disposal of large sums, where the element of time is important and where three men are less likely than one man to make a mistake.

The same principle follows through all the ramifications of a great business or a national administration, but there is more scope for individual initiative and ability in a business than under any department of a bureaucracy.

The more each man in a great business can be made to feel that the success of the entire undertaking depends upon him, the greater will be its success. There is in every humble man a sentiment of personal dignity and pride which never fails to respond to an intelligent and sympathetic appeal. Such a man can be humiliated by nothing so much as a feeling of personal failure. The progress and good name of the great impersonal institution which employs him becomes a matter of personal concern to the most humble man and those in the poorest situations can be made to feel that their part in the great work is not only useful, but of real importance. The deep meaning of this policy was impressed upon me in a thousand ways in my own organization. On one of my daily tours of inspection over the works, this most beautiful of all sentiments of personal dignity was reflected in the attitude of a man occupying an unimportant and quite ordinary post when he approached me to announce that he was returning to his work in the country. He said he would probably not see me again but he hoped everything would go along all right with the business. He was only number two thousand and something on the pay-roll. It was considered that any ordinary man could do his work and there were, alas, probably a hundred applicants for his humble job! But I passed on with the feeling that the obscure man who was leaving had done his work in a beautiful way and that others might not easily take his place. He had ennobled his obscurity and deserved a better fate.

Alas, the blind waste of so much that is beautiful and which if used, as it is ever longing to be used, could in one generation make a paradise of our disordered world!

The old institutions in which the employees felt a personal interest and in which every man was in direct contact with his chief have passed and in their stead are the great anonymously controlled companies, depriving men of individuality and taking from them all sense of their personal importance, responsibility and dignity. These are together the most vital sentiments controlling all human action and they are never lost without a great and irreparable injury to man and to all society.

The wheels of time will not turn backward and the old feeling of individuality and dignity can be restored only through the system set out in my books, and through which the toilers would feel that they were interested in attaining the greatest efficiency because they would be working for themselves and for society as distinguished from the existing basis, upon which all production above the barest necessity of the toilers, goes to those who do not toil or spin but who pass laws and issue watered stocks.

The present industrial system tends to suppress all that is best and most social in men, and it quite unrationally removes the incentive for nearly all toilers to make the best use of their time. It consequently exercises a most injurious influence over the morals as well as over the economic activities of men, who cannot attain political liberty in any effective sense, except after or concurrently with the attainment of their economic independence.

I would write with all reserve concerning the institutions of a country in which I have spent less than two years, but in no other place except the prairie states of western America have I encountered a people with so much personal dignity and individual independence as in Switzerland. Nowhere else have I observed that personal liberty is so general and effectively safeguarded at so small a cost and inconvenience to the masses.

The masses in Switzerland are the most free politically because they are economically more independent than any other people. Their political and social institutions could never have been created in a nation of industrial wage-slaves, and if unhappily for them, modern industrialism should destroy the economic independence of the people, they would speedily lose their political liberty. Democracy would then mean no more to the Swiss toilers than it now means to the industrial toilers of France, England and the United States. It is because the actual rulers of Switzerland are not bonds and shares, but small farmers and shop-keepers, that there is more political, economic and personal liberty here than elsewhere. The isolation resulting from its mountains and language and the security and independence arising from the general ownership of property, are largely responsible for the special and favoured position of the majority of its people. It is due to the restraint which these classes exercise over industrial development and to the comparative absence of high finance and over-concentration of labourers and to the relatively small number engaged in the modern forms of industry, that Switzerland has suffered the least of any nation from the fatal tendencies of modern evolution.

In some other countries where the per capita production of wealth is less than in Switzerland, the absence of a dominant peasant proprietorship, the concentration of wealth in comparatively few hands, and the mendacious system of wage-slavery applied to the majority of the population, create a condition which would be unthinkable in Switzerland and against which this country will be protected so long as its peasants and small merchants maintain their direct interest in all political measures, which might even remotely tend to a curtailment of their existing powers. The chief dangers to the Swiss democracy are on the one hand, the temptation which is natural to a people so completely democratic and independent to lose interest in self-government and in the principles and policy which have made them free, or that the industrial workers may be so ill-advised as to lay aside the great and secure constitutional means which they should sacredly guard, and seek to take a short road to economic independence. It is only through the exercise of their constitutional rights, without violence of any sort, that the industrial toilers of Switzerland may hope to make secure progress and bequeath to their descendants those institutions of true democracy which have been so dearly bought and which must at all costs be maintained.

The point of comparison most important to observe as between the masses in Switzerland, France, England and the United States is, that in the former country we see genuine democracy and liberty in their most tangible sense, resting upon the economic independence of the masses. The more one observes the people the clearer it becomes that they could not have founded their social system at any time anterior to their economic independence, which is always an essential preliminary to political freedom.

I have observed by long residence in the agricultural as well as the industrial parts of America and also in Europe, that the economic independence of the small land-owner, as compared to the wage-dependence of his own class engaged in industry, renders the former a great and important factor in maintaining stability and at the same time opposing all aggression upon his political rights. In these two tendencies, essential to a genuine democracy, the industrial wage-earners concentrated in great centres may constitute either a dangerous element which can be too readily moved to drastic and unreasonable decisions, or who set aside the principles of democracy either through inattention to political matters, or because they feel bound to vote as they know their employer wishes them to vote. Also because they have learned that their ballots are of so little use. The secret ballot will be a decisive power in the hands of the masses only when men and women toilers formulate a definite program of their demands and unite solidly in the political and economic defense of their proper interests.

I was recently impressed with the practical value of a secret ballot and of the condition of economic independence which would permit men of ordinary sense and courage to give effect to their most important civic power. In a quaint old village near Lucerne, I witnessed this year the "Landsgemeinde." It is a romantic, beautiful and historical sight. Sunday afternoon in a down-pour of April rain several thousand people, some in quaint and gaily-colored costumes from the middle ages, gathered in the open on the mountain side to hear the report of their cantonal authorities for the fiscal year, to discuss the price of salt, the difficulties created by the war, and to pass upon the question of taxation. After some hours of speeches to which all listened with attention and which were probably interesting to those who understood German and who were to be taxed, with the crowds standing unsheltered in the rain, the votes were taken by raising of hands.

From appearances the negative votes were in the majority but the affirmative votes were declared to have won. There were many vigorous protests but no disorder.

Among people of economic equality when no one had a mortgage on his neighbours' farm, where no pressure could be exercised by one man over another, it was no doubt a just and effective method of expressing the popular will, especially when the numbers were small and could be readily and exactly counted, but I left the scene with the feeling that this is one more of the historic customs rendered almost sacred through hundreds of years upon the same spot, which changing conditions will one day replace by the ballot, to be secretly cast and exactly counted. Sometimes the most beautiful and historic things outlive their practical utility, or might be wisely abandoned for something more in keeping with a changed environment.

In the other so-called democracies there is no genuine democracy and no liberty in its most important sense, because the economic independence of the masses has not been achieved. In the great industrial nations they are homeless slaves, not because they are employed in industries, but because the basis of their employment has prevented them from rising economically above the level of an ordinary product. It is upon this shameful basis that their lives are bought and sold, and it is their necessity and not the value of their lives which determines the selling price.

It is because they are employed by machines and become a part of the machinery and because these machines are organized to attain definite economic ends, while the toilers are not similarly organized to attain social ends, that the machines are the masters and the men are slaves. The men have endeavoured to realize without organization, a freedom which can never come to them until they are organized and able to act in union nationally and internationally.

The toilers are struggling to unwind an endless chain. They are at work on the dome of their noble temple without having laid its foundations. They are seeking to make free men politically out of material which industrialism has already reduced to slavery. They are striving to obtain control of governments in order that through governmental powers they may dominate industry, but as society is now constituted it is industry which controls the governments and the toilers of nations.

This order cannot peacefully be reversed except through organization for industrial and political action, and even when the control of governments is so obtained, its stability will depend upon the ordered life of the industrial world. I believe this can be universally established and maintained through the system set out in my books and which is not only practically workable but scientifically, socially and ethically sound.

CHAPTER IV.

MAN'S ABUSE OF SOCIAL LIBERTY.

By nature and practice most men are polygamists at one or another time of life, although they do not generally acknowledge it until they have reached an age at which it is evident that their polygamy is at an end, or when they are in company with people who are truthful.

As society is now organized man's polygamy carries no social obligations which are legally binding upon him and which would tend to abolish a system inflicting great injustice upon millions of women and levying a terrible tribute upon humanity.

Men sail their ships of affection over many seas without incurring the slightest risk if they scuttle every ship. This is a condition which in honour and morals should be abolished, to the incalculable advantage and elevation of women and to the great and permanent benefit of the race.

In considering the social status of men and women in its economic and moral aspects, so far as morals may have relation to conduct, I would emphasize that in marriage the ideal happiness is to be found in the relation of one man and one woman. Whenever this is in fact realized it brings to men and women their most noble joy. In these pages there are no suggestions which seek in any way to interfere with such associations, so far as they now exist or may hereafter be formed. There is no wish to advocate any measures which, if adopted, would disturb the happiness enjoyed by the fortunate ones of earth, but on the contrary it is desired only to suggest measures which, so far as may be possible with humanity, would tend to afford protection, honour and true freedom to millions to whom these are now uselessly or wrongfully denied.

Through the pressure of a mendacious industrial system and the destruction of men by the shameful war waged in the exclusive interest of imperialism and high finance, the position of women is no longer tolerable under existing institutions. The tragedy of their situation has not yet dawned upon the world and will not adequately be appreciated even by the women most vitally concerned, until two or three years after the murder of men has ceased.

The purpose of these pages is to show why and how this problem must be fairly and honourably faced and to suggest the general lines along which society is destined to move in the great days when economic slavery, oratorical nonsense as to democracy, religious intolerance and our savage social system are all buried in a common grave, never to rise again so long as men love liberty, respect virtue and honour truth.

There are many stern indications that when the war is ended there will be a great demonstration of public indignation at the international murder of men and it may well be that it will result in wide-spread civil strife.

I indicate in these pages the definite and peaceful measures which the toilers may take in order to attain control of and not destroy the vast industrial mechanism created by their patient toil. They are sure to make a great and determined effort to rule or to wreck industrialism. Nothing but general ruin will follow violence and from such a catastrophe no class could hope to escape, least of all the toilers.

The millions of women whose lovers and natural protectors have been murdered have created a unique problem and their tragic misfortune will be regarded by posterity with pity, indignation and shame. If they are forced through economic pressure into a general industrial competition, there will be a steady trend of society towards universal depression and violence.

The classes which desire to perpetuate the old evils would not be materially affected in their habitual conduct through any alteration of the social system, while the measures suggested in these pages would abolish industrial slavery. The ruling castes have all the advantages and none of the responsibilities which should be inseparable from their mode of life and they find the present arrangements admirable and highly honourable. Our social order is neither more nor less honourable than our economic institutions. They are children of a common father whose shame is written in the exploitation and enslavement of men, the ruin and degradation of women and in the murder of children.

As matters now stand man's promiscuous relations do not impose upon him any definitive or binding responsibility, whereas they involve for women the most important social and moral consequences. Many men, who are what the world regards as model husbands, would not wish closely to contemplate the position of one or more women with whom they were once upon familiar terms, when they were either unmarried or were not quite such model husbands. And yet these women were entitled to the protection which the men should have been legally, as they were morally, bound to give. These women belong to the great and ever increasing class whose misfortune is the most pathetic tragedy of life. They are only a part of the great river of human misery which flows from a fountain of civilization, polluted at its source by a pretentious hypocrisy imposed upon mankind by aristocrats and priests.

It would be without purpose to seek either to justify or to condemn what is nothing more than the expression of man's nature as it has always been and is likely to remain, undominated by a high ethic or by true social conceptions or a spiritual religion. It is however essential that all men and women should be compelled to respond to the actual, eventual and even potential consequences of their conduct.

The attitude of society toward this all-important problem is such that men, who are in other respects the most generous and honourable, do not accept what ought to be the minimum responsibility towards the women with whom their relations have been the most familiar. These relations are begun and ended in circumstances in which women should never be placed and often under illusions on the part of the woman which amount in her eyes to an ideal of happiness, protection or security, while for the man they have no more than a temporary and often an inconsequential interest.

This great difference in the point of view under which women and men enter upon the most familiar relations may not arise from any intentional deception on part of the man. It is inherent in the nature of humanity that man will always be unable fully to share the attitude of woman regarding sex, because it has for woman a meaning, a natural purpose and a significance which it never can have for a man.

In considering the principles of liberty as they should apply to man's relation to the general body of society, and also to the more personal relation of individuals towards one another, there is a fundamental misconception to which may be traced some of the most far-reaching injuries to society. This is the contention that man is not accountable to society for acts which do not concern others and that those acts which may vitally affect others cannot properly be restrained for the protection of the ones who assent. It is difficult to over-estimate the evil consequences of this reasoning in its effect upon the conduct of men towards women. It is not sufficiently recognized that no assent on the part of a woman in a matter of such importance can be regarded as a free, voluntary and moral act, so long as it is influenced in the slightest degree by necessity, expediency or illusions. It will always be so influenced until women are in their natural place, where home and motherhood are accepted as the only social and ethical basis for their intimate association with men.

It would be too great a digression from the subject under review to enquire into the various evils which cannot be eradicated so long as personal liberty is allowed to conflict with the social interest. Considered in its application to the relation of men and women, the principle now followed is that important acts may be performed without consequence to others and even when such conduct may be followed by the most lasting and injurious effects upon others it cannot be restrained by society on behalf of those who were voluntary parties to it.

The results which follow certain acts of the most private nature, shared by the voluntary assent of two people, are so indefinable and may be so remote that they cannot be anticipated. It is therefore not only the right but the duty of society to surround such acts with safeguards against their logical and perhaps inevitable consequences. This leads to the necessity of establishing the relations of men and women upon such a basis that in exercising personal liberty they are bound to accept the natural and moral responsibilities which may arise, and so far as possible they must also anticipate and provide for such responsibilities.

The reasons for an association between a man and a woman are no proper concern of society and the causes for which such an association is terminated are even less its concern. This is only strictly applicable to those who are personally qualified to have healthy children and able to so protect their offspring that they do not become a charge upon society.

The greater part of the so-called evils may be traced directly to the general misconception of the rights of society to regulate personal conduct. It is not only the right but the solemn obligation of society to protect itself against the consequences of the most personal conduct of men and women but, as is usual with all man's regulations, they begin at the wrong end of the problem and deal with effects rather than causes. They seek to remedy what they have the power to prevent and something which they have no power to remedy, because some of the evils which befall men and women are past all remedy, as soon as they are felt at all. This is particularly true as regards the numerous and sometimes far-reaching results which follow man's conduct towards woman.

It is partly because men are now permitted to marry without making provision for the women and children that society has sought to render divorce difficult. Considered solely as an economic measure, seeking to prevent the individual from transferring his obligations to the mass, this is a legitimate and justifiable attitude. There is however a far larger aspect from which the problem must be regarded and this phase of the present system is examined more closely in the last chapter of this book.

Lesgislation restricting the grounds of divorce is enacted under the pretense and fiction of upholding so-called public morals, rather than sustaining bigotry and guarding the public purse.

The economic condition of the masses renders it impossible for most men to set aside in advance any fund for a woman's protection and it is therefore necessary to rely upon the toil of the man, rather than upon capital, for the support of the woman and children.

The toilers bear testimony through their patient labour and honourable devotion as to how faithfully this obligation is discharged.

It would be in the highest interest of these toilers if women were withdrawn from competition with men and given homes by the ones who should be their natural protectors and whose toil not only now supplies all the material needs of humanity but in addition bears all its follies, its extravagance, its waste and its outrageous destruction.

Neither women nor children should work in competition with men. It is as wrong as it is unnecessary. The place of women is the home and children should remain in school, if they desire to do so, until they are twenty-five.

In considering the relations of men to women, outside marriage, it is essential to examine to what extent the assent of women may be moral and to what degree it may arise from their ignorance and economic necessities. In most countries the age at which a woman's assent may be given is established at eighteen. I think it should be twenty-four, except in case of marriages contracted with the assent of parents. Under the system set out in these pages such an assent without marriage, would be rendered as impossible as it should be unnecessary—at any age.

When girls who have had no experience with men assent to intimate relations outside marriage, the decisions of the large majority are greatly influenced or altogether determined by their economic situation or by an affection for some man whose obligations or economic status would render marriage impossible or postpone it for an indefinite time. The number of married men with whom this relation is established by unmarried girls is greater than is generally believed and in an overwhelming majority of cases the result is disastrous for the girls in all that most vitally concerns their future, whereas it involves no consequences of importance which can be brought to bear upon men. The measures I suggest would put an end to this monstrous wrong. I state as my settled conviction that if men were by law in a position which enabled them to contract a legal marriage with every woman whom they were qualified to support and who wished to accept such a relation, and if the sexual association made this support in every instance binding upon the man, the evils I have outlined would be reduced to the point of extinction. If such a possibility were open to women they would not enter the relation except upon the basis of marriage and the effective assurance of protection and support. The fact that men could not enter upon such relationship without becoming responsible for the permanent maintainance of the woman and their children, would deter most men who do not now hesitate to form one or several alliances through which they incur no obligations, hardships or legal or social penalties.

Only the men who were able and willing to support one or more women and their children should be permitted to establish relations with women and this is the only class of men to whom such relations should be allowed. Instead of this system tending to increase polygamy on the part of men now married, or among unmarried men, its result would be quite the contrary.

Under the present system many married men, and a majority of those who are unmarried, have relations with more than one woman without incurring any financial or other responsibilities which either the women or society have the power to enforce. This is a direct encouragement of such relations. Under the system outlined in chapter eleven which places direct, inevitable and probably permanent obligations upon a man in respect to any and every woman with whom he has sexual relations, the result would be to decrease the practice of polygamy among irresponsible and dishonourable men and limit it to those who were able and willing to respond to their conduct.

Through industrial exploitation and wars there has come to be a great surplus of women over men. The mills of capitalism grind out the lives of men for the profits of plutocracy and constantly augment the surplus of women. This is only one of the ominous tendencies of industrialism which must be regarded with profound misgiving.

If the great problems which will press for solution at the close of the mendacious war were now to be set forth in their full significance they would be regarded as the fantastic creations of a confirmed pessimist, but one of the greatest and most difficult of these problems is the altered status of women and the part they must now play in the elevation of the human race, or on the other hand in completing the subjugation and enslavement of all toilers. I entertain no doubt as to the great and beneficent work to which they should in future dedicate their lives, while expressing the most genuine concern lest they be misled by senseless appeals to tradition, by the devices of the clergy and the pressure of plutocracy, to continue in their present course which will be disastrous to them and to the race, for reasons which I clearly show.

The clergy, composed of men who differ from other men chiefly in the arrogance they assume towards a question concerning which all men are profoundly ignorant, will contend that marriages are made in heaven and that heaven is opposed to any change in the present system. As the spokesmen of heaven they must feel some chagrin in the fact that the most important functions in making the marriage contract and all tribunals which are permitted to cancel or in any way amend it, are reserved to public servants appointed by men. Marriages are made by clerks and dissolved by judges and the majority of both are polygamists by nature and practice, but they and the priests would be afraid to profess what they are not afraid to practice.

It is not without significance that from the most remote antiquity the clergy has been on the wrong side of every great project designed for the liberation of men, the cultivation and development of the human intellect and the obliteration of any form of oppression, superstition and tyranny, notwithstanding it is upon the ruins of one form of bigotry after another that all religions have been established—including that of Christianity.

It was only a little while ago the church of England decreed that marriages regularly contracted were an invalid and illegitimate union unless the parties pretended to believe in its creed and were members of that church. If such an attitude were now assumed by any clergyman in the church of England he would be under the necessity of seeking useful employment in another sphere and his pretentions would be regarded as an impertinence. And yet if the church ever had such a right it could not possibly have lost it.

When we witness the misery of the toilers who create all wealth, and the arrogance of those who absorb it and when we regard the pretentions of the parasites who render no useful service to mankind, we marvel at the patience and stupidity of the masses and are forced to wonder if they will ever be able to create and maintain a social commonwealth.

For thousands of years it was taught that people were not to choose their own occupations and that a superior wisdom vested in some authority had the right to order the lives of the masses. This all tended to maintain obedience to authority and prevent the intellectual and social rise of the people. It also prevented the rise of individuals except under the favour of some persons whose sole right to exercise power was that they were sufficiently arrogant and strong to do so, without regard as to whether the power was wisely or badly used.

When we consider the great obstacles which the weak and helpless have overcome it is not surprising that progress has been so painfully slow. It must be remembered that nothing is more difficult to combat than the wrongs which are accepted as either unavoidable or natural and which are so well entrenched in the institutions of mankind, that they are not even recognized as wrongs. The monstrous pretensions of ruling castes are accepted as a matter of course and appeared for centuries to rest upon a right so absolute that it was not subjected to doubt or question and was not discussed.

There is something inherent in humanity causing it to

accept what it is taught should be accepted and to reject what it is taught to reject. It is upon this feeling that the church and civil authorities rely to perpetuate their particular superstitions in the one case and injustice and tyranny in the other. They know that people as a rule will be slow to doubt or question the authority and value of institutions which they have been taught to regard with reverence and whose decrees they feel bound to obey. It is only the most exceptional and the bravest men who will not only question and doubt but who will do what is in their power to induce others to doubt. The risk of disapproval for saying what is contrary to established beliefs is sufficient to deter most people from doing anything to improve the position of the masses as regards governments, religions and social customs.

If there is nothing to be feared from the direct violence of a tyranny there is much to be feared from the indirect pressure of public opinion, which is for the average man more terrible than any other tyranny. The old tyranny which put a man in the stocks and beheaded him, might make him a martyr, whereas the tyranny of public opinion makes him merely an outcast. This is a position which only a few men are courageous enough voluntarily to accept, but it is to such men, who are sufficiently farsighted to see in what ways humanity must be led that the masses may finally look for true guidance in the realization of an ideal social state.

It is time the masks are laid aside and that we scrutinize the pretentious institutions resting upon an exploited world of toilers and sustained by injustice, violence and murder. Our boasted civilization is a house of cards built of temporary expedients and standing on the shifting sands with an appearance of solidity. Nothing is what it appears to be. Laws enacted ostensibly to promote or protect public morals — whatever the pious ones may mean by the term — are only the devices of the exploiting classes to exercise through the schools, the church and the press, a tyranny over the minds, the sentiments and the conscience of mankind, and through governments, stock exchanges, banks and watered stocks, a like tyranny over the lives and toil of the masses.

In all this shameless affair the ones who control and use the masses are exempt from the tyrannies they impose. They escape the free schools by establishing an expensive private system of instruction. The masters of the world are not influenced by churches, because they do not believe in them, do not frequent them and pay no attention to religious teachings. They care less than nothing for the newspapers and purchase them only to be in touch with current events, to see which stocks to avoid, to observe the results of racing and other sports and to kill time, whereas the patient masses support the press and read it as they would the bible, believing all the clumsy lies they read.

The ones who establish the tyranny as to marriage and divorce are not actually its victims. They live according to their several tastes without incurring any responsibilities corresponding to their mode of life.

The whole of this wonderful creation representing the high intelligence, altruism, religion and morals of the ruling castes is not a high tribute to the intelligence of mankind. It is a monument which has within itself all the essentials of its own dissolution and it is rapidly being dissolved into its own elements. It is crumbling into ruins, never to be raised again by the hand of man.

It is still the practice in some countries to worship a bronze crab. Perhaps this arises partly from the fact that crabs only travel backwards, while the hope of humanity may be found in the few original and free minds which are able to form an accurate and impersonal conception of their own age and indicate the measures by which genuine and solid advancement is to be realized in the ages that are buried in the mystery of time.

CHAPTER V.

THE PSYCHOLOGICAL IMPORTANCE OF PREJUDICE AND TRADITIONS.

If it be accepted as a settled principle concerning which the greatest scientists have long since ceased to have any doubts, that a natural process of selection if left to itself, works solely for the good of each species and tends gradually towards perfection, it will be conceded that all interference with this principle, such as arises from industrial exploitation, social prejudices and an unsound marriage system are obstacles in the way of the natural and only steps by which the highest perfection of the human species may be realized.

The temporary happiness of the individual, or what may appear to be his immediate good, is generally in conflict with those measures through which alone an ideal commonwealth might be steadily approached.

We see nature constantly sacrificing the present to the future while man almost invariably sacrifices the future for the present. It should be the policy of society to harmonize these greatly divergent principles now manifested in the operation of the laws of Nature and in the laws of man.

The whole of man's social and economic system sacrifices the future to the present, without achieving the objects sought in the present and in violation of the manifest designs of Nature as to the future. We ignore the large and permanent interests of the race for advantages so intangible as to be of no real importance, even as satisfying our temporary purposes and we seek constantly to avoid by temporary expedients the consequences which must inevitably follow the pursuit of a discordant, compromising and short-sighted policy of conduct. It is due to the fact that the individual has no high goal at which he wishes the race to arrive, that his measures are only temporary and strictly personal, whereas they should be general and permanent. It comes to this that the individual and society seek their own ends, and that these ends are transitory and appear to require the adoption of means which can never realize great and lasting aims.

We perform our most consequential acts under the pressure of narrow limits of time and are entirely oblivious of the larger issues which are to arise in the remote future. We are almost unconcerned as to the effects which our actions must necessarily have upon ourselves, and others of our own and succeeding generations. When this sentiment is narrowed down to the ruling motives of average conduct it rarely takes into account the effect of its policy beyond its own generation and, as between the weak and the strong, it does not take into account even the present generation, except in so far as man's exploitation and savagery are reserved for strangers and their children, rather than expressed towards his near relations, which incidentally illustrates his conception and application of the golden rule.

If this is followed still more closely into individual conduct its concern does not extend beyond the individual and his immediate family. This is clearly a principle of action from which no progress or good of a great and general character can ever be realized.

If humanity is to move forward towards its greatest

destiny it is essential to proceed upon a principle which shall not constantly do violence to man's nature and which may respond to the needs and possibilities of his being, and through which his large and permanent interests are not constantly sacrificed to temporary expedients, involving the most unsocial disregard of the most numerous classes whose progress must in future be the standard by which we shall measure the success and judge the value of all civilization.

One of the most discouraging misconceptions is humanity's failure to realize that the useful and solid progress of man towards ends that are ever higher and more social must be judged by the material, intellectual and moral progress of the masses.

The vast accumulations of wealth in a few hands while the millions who toil are homeless and poor is not progress. The senseless luxury of the few, accompanied by the wretched poverty and misery of the many is not progress. The development of science and machinery, which are used to make machines of men and to devastate an earth which they could have converted into a paradise, is not progress. The comparative enlightenment of a few men who have risen above superstition, religious fear and tyranny while the masses remain in ignorance and superstition, is progress but so slow as to deprive the most sanguine mind of hope for the general elevation and ultimate liberation of man until there is an end to his exploitation and degradation, and until our actual monstrous economic and unsocial systems are replaced by one through which the most numerous and useful portion of humanity may take the definite and sure steps essential to an ordered progress towards education, morals and freedom.

It will long be a great misfortune that those who are

able to conceive the largest projects for humanity, have neither the positions, the executive talent nor the practical sense required to realize their ideals. Those who are most able to translate thought into action are the organizers of industrialism, who have rare powers which they know how to employ to their personal advantage, but which they seldom use in the disinterested service of mankind. This is a general and natural attitude of humanity and will remain until it is replaced by an impersonal social ideal of service and duty.

We have not advanced beyond the most primitive instincts in the motives controlling the use of either great or meagre powers. A few men are considered to possess special virtues when they give something they do not need, to the ones whose distress is the shame of the world. When compared to those who give nothing they are in fact exceptional men, but in the unethical struggle for existence the standard of comparison is not high. The basis of nearly all philanthropy is vanity and after men have acquired great fortunes and have earned only the curses of their fellow-men, they wish to do something to endeavour to receive the praise of men. If the motives underlying charity were as benevolent as they appear, there would be no need for charity of any sort, because this is only a means of advertising, or a method employed to soothe the conscience of those whose unmoral social acts have rendered charity indispensable in the modern scheme of life. Therefore their charity is as insulting as their exploitation—which is both the father and the mother of poverty, war and other crimes.

It would be looking towards an ideal and therefore an unattainable civilization, to hope for one in which the acts of men would not be greatly influenced by the praise or blame of others. Even the most aloof minds are not insensible to public opinion and it is due partly to this that the most grievous injustice and odious defects of all societies are so difficult to remedy.

Customs and institutions acquire a sacred authority through prolonged acceptance. Sometimes these are only the ugly relics of the ignorance and savagery of man. The whole organization and scheme of society comes under this condemnation. Instead of regarding it as a solemn duty to expose the whole of this shameful system, it is considered impertinent and revolutionary to suggest that the present state of existence is not the ideal of which humanity is capable. It is not man's nature but his institutions which can and should be altered. No one except a special type of shop-keeper, policeman, or priest will look upon the actual state of society with feelings other than indignation and yet this wonderful structure is regarded with awe by the vulgar, and defended without shame by the so-called elect of the world!

Those who are the most willing to expose the evils are generally the ones who know the least about them. They behold the ruin of the common man and charge it immediately to the wrong cause. They would divide the wealth of the few among the many, without realizing that such a division would not serve any useful purpose, that it is in any event impossible and that as matters now stand, if all existing institutions were destroyed to-morrow, mankind would the next day begin their reconstruction in substantially the same form. Society has been constructed upon the unsound and anti-social basis that the interests of the individual may be served without reference to the general welfare. This erroneous sentiment has led to all forms of injustice and exploitation. It can be eradicated only through the most emphatic teaching that man's largest personal ends are to be realized only through the general good. This teaching must be accompanied by such economic and social amelioration as will indicate to the masses that the general good is in fact attainable in our actual world.

The considerations of first importance are that the masses should have an open mind with reference to all criticism directed against anything which has come from the hand of man. We are constantly setting up images which for a short time we worship as sacred and then destroy as outrageous. This is one of the impressive lessons of history but it is ignored by nearly all men.

On all hands we witness the operation of laws and customs which are an insult to the good sense and honour of mankind and we do not doubt that some day these must pass away. The only means by which this may ever be realized is that the institutions, customs and prejudices shall be fearlessly scrutinized with the object solely of steady advancement upon solid ground. It is a curious and regrettable phase of human misunderstanding that those who see the most clearly are the most condemned as fanatics, even by the ones who stand in the greatest need of their teaching.

As one observes the attitude of the masses moving towards a common end whether it is recreation, work or war, one is profoundly impressed by the attitude of thoughtless people who feel the security of numbers and who do not realize that their greatest dangers arise solely from the greatness of their numbers.

The failure of the masses to realize that there is no permanence in the power of unorganized numbers is one of the reasons why they are so easily controlled by the organized power of the few. A man walking toward a precipice in the dark may have a sense of fear, the origin of which he does not understand, but when a thousand men are marching together toward the same precipice they have no fear, especially if they march to music.

The governing classes have not understood the psychology of mass sentiment or of their own prejudices, but they have had the practical sense to capitalize this psychology into political and social institutions which make effective use of it. The masses think they are supreme but it is a fictitious paper supremacy, because they never take the steps necessary to so organize that they may express their will either through the ballot, or in any other form.

The blindness with which men accept and follow the opinions of others is truly pathetic to witness. This is especially true respecting the attitude of the rabble towards war. If to-morrow the press, clergy and ministers of belligerent nations were to tell the masses that the only way to prevent a collision of the earth and the new star was to set up a row on earth, it would be accepted by humanity as the undoubted truth and anyone who questioned it would be under suspicion. He might even be a pacifist. That would be a new and sufficient reason for war.

When the priests told the masses that the inquisition was a divine invention to behead men, in order to save them from protestantism, the masses wondered how they got on so long without so beneficent an instrument of torture. They did not seriously doubt its divine origin until they had their tongues cut out for enquiring if it was in fact true that the earth was flat. Those who claimed to speak in the name of the Creator assured them that the earth was flat. Thanks to the genius of men who did not assume to know the divine mind, we have learned that the whole conception was false, that the earth is not flat, that the inquisition was an instrument invented by cunning devils, called priests and that it is not a capital crime to study, to wonder and sometimes to doubt. But the curious psychology of the masses—who follow like sheep in the wake of everything that assumes to speak by the authority of gods or governments,—did not permit them to see what was hidden in this leadership, nor can they now understand what is involved in the present similar and equally wrong guidance which they are following with a madness not heretofore equalled since the world began.

The inquisition destroyed only a few hundred thousand whereas the exploitation, the false teaching as to nationalism, the conscription, the tyranny imposed in the name of freedom, the spies and the lies are destroying millions. And he who dares to doubt the justice and morality of this sacred business is regarded as an enemy of his fellowmen! I entertain no doubt as to the verdict of posterity regarding this shameful war and the men who are directing it.

For reasons not understood and utterly devoid of any sense the masses give their noisy support and slavish praise to one or another man for a little while and suddenly become quite indifferent. Hundreds of such incidents have passed under my observation. Perhaps the most impressive was that of America's attitude towards Admiral Dewey who sank the Spanish fleet at Manila.

We sat in carriages along the line of march for six hours waiting for him to pass among millions of a cheering crowd and the night was ablaze with lights and hideous with noise, as the welcome of New York to a popular idol. A few weeks afterwards I saw him walking along Fifth Avenue in complete obscurity and exciting no more than ordinary notice when pointed out to strangers.

Some brainless freak in Paris appears in a hideous gown donated to her by a designer to be worn at races in the hope of attracting the attention of men and exciting the envy of women. Soon millions of women are aping this monstrosity for no better reasons than they would otherwise be out of fashion, which is taken to mean that they are too poor or too slow to invest in the latest fads. Women whose gray hair might be beautiful, make themselves frowsy sights by becoming blondes.

It is for similar reasons that people attend silly plays, read stupid books, and give deadly dinners to people who dont want to come and who are only glad when they get away! Like a bankrupt who groups his bankers and bakers together in order to finish an unpleasant job as soon as possible, so those who feel obliged to entertain for their business, their professions, or their almost unmarriageable daughters, bring together all the tedious people they know, and entertain them together. It makes more display and is the cheapest way to get through a disagreeable job. They know that things done wholesale work out at a smaller per unit cost in money, time and trouble. This is supposed to make people happy. I never found anyone who was made happy by it. The only moment of happiness is when the affair is ended and one may go quietly away through the soft night air and meditate upon the vanity of man. Happiness is at best evasive and not in the keeping of crowds or served at banquets. There is no happiness between people who wear masks, except on those delightful occasions when masks are supposed to be worn. To refuse to take part in all this common humbug is regarded as eccentric or stingy. Once more the psychology of following the crowd is the rule which only a few care to break.

It is a universal principle in nature that all extravagance on one side causes poverty on the other. We must always pay in quantity and kind for what we waste and finally what is useless must disappear. It is because our economic and social structure has been built up in violation of sound principles that it cannot stand. It is scientifically unsound and morally unbalanced and must therefore disappear.

It may be contended that there are no morals in the operations of nature and no evidence of an ethical purpose, but it cannot be said that there is no justice, while in our economic and social insitutions there are neither morals nor justice.

It may also be that man's life is too brief and restricted and his point of observation too low, to see in the operations of nature those high ends towards which it may cause all life to progress. Whether in distant ages this may or may not be known, it is sufficient and essential for man's ordered progress towards his highest destiny, that he pursues the principles which nature has disclosed and under which everything renders according to its kind. Neither in his economics, social relations or religions has man put himself in this secure way in which alone he may hope ever to attain the fulfillment of his own possibilities in the universal scheme, or establish relations of peace and justice in his actual world.

Man may deny to the operation of general and impersonal forces any ethical tendency because he is unable to find such tendency, but his failure must not be taken as establishing that such tendency does not exist. No one can safely attempt to set any limit to the exalted state at which the individual and even humanity may some time arrive. We know that the story of life is written through ages which embrace millions of years whereas the life of the individual passes as a shadow. For an instant man observes some isolated fact and tries to find its relation to other facts, only to realize that they are buried in a vast ocean whose mysterious depths no one can ever know. And it is only recently that man began to record the little he observed.

As man regards the world from an ethical point of view, he is impressed that the means adopted by nature to attain what appears to be its end are so contrary to what the highest type of man would regard as an elevated conception of sentiment and duty, that he is compelled to believe it is his restricted point of view rather than the unmorality of nature to which this may be traced.

I do not have any respect for the dogmatism of churches but I have a reverent appreciation of the philosophy of the great and exalted Nazarene. I am not prepared to say that he foresaw the entire significance of some of the great truths which he bequeathed as precious jewels to mankind, but I am persuaded that both ethically and scientifically he was completely right when he said that "the meek shall inherit the earth." Among the animals it is the meek which now inherit the earth and among men this inheritance is passing to the meek. In the light of what has transpired through the ages it is clear that there has been a steady progress towards the realization of this seemingly impossible phenomenon in the natural world and in the evolution of man this has been the constant tendency. The circle of influence of the most humble men has ever enlarged and if the events of the last few years mean anything in human evolution it is that they indicate a tendency to establish this as a universal principle among men.

More and more the meek are inheriting the earth in a material as well as a moral sense. More and more those who have been the weak and oppressed of earth are coming into their own as the true inheritors of their earth. The circle is ever extending. It may well be therefore, that what appears as a disorganized struggle of unethical forces are in reality the sure steps by which man is to establish a high ethic and thereby realize his place in the ordered march of a universal nature which arrives at a spiritual goal. It is quite clear we cannot estimate the importance of the whole by any restricted evidence to be obtained from a part, and that we must consider universal tendencies, rather than isolated incidents.

Upon this basis of valuation, it may be that everything moves towards a goal which is entirely spiritual and man may one day understand that it is only his blindness, rather than a nature devoid of ethics, which has caused him so long to ascribe to its operations the absence of an ethical aim.

These considerations are put forward, not with the idea of endeavouring to show that such an aim exists, but rather for the purpose of suggesting that we do not have a sufficient grasp of the vast designs of nature to generalize from the fragmentary phenomena which we have been able to observe and which we have tried to estimate and value.

The whole idea of brute force as the arbiter of the fate of men has been destroyed and it is recognized that the ideal may create its own force, which rises above all material power.

It is by this principle that the present world tendencies are to be measured and it is in the light of this experience as a general human tendency that the great epochs in the life on earth are to be regarded. It may therefore one day be established that what was announced as the dreams of individual men, was in fact only a true forecast of the trend of events, which man will be able to follow to ends now regarded as fantastic, but which in reality are the high goal of an apparently unethical nature.

As man rises above savagery and enlarges the scope and elevates the nature of his sentiments towards others, he acquires qualities which are exclusively personal and which tend to indicate that no definite limitation can be set for the universality of man. It would be difficult to over-estimate the significance of this divine endowment. Man can rise to great heights only from a foundation of justice in its legal and moral sense, and he must abolish all injustice in his own acts before he can act ethically and with moral significance attaching to his acts. When man follows unfailingly the principles of impersonal justice, he may find an earthly paradise in which he will be able to express the benign altruism which might lead to a true conception of the highest attributes of that Supreme Nature, towards which all that is most beautiful on earth appears to move.

Man would then in all serenity say: "O World, all things are suitable to me which are suitable to thee. Nothing is too early or too late for me, which is seasonable for thee. All is fruit to me which thy seasons bring forth. From thee are all things; in thee are all things; for thee are all things. One man says, O beloved city of Cecrops. Wilt thou not say, O beloved city of God?"

We are at a loss to account for an absolute justice devoid of any great and universal ethic and yet we see in nature everywhere the evidence of the former, apparently not accompanied by the latter. In man's ethical attitude towards society he is inclined to regard our humanity as a great family in which those who are related to him are not only father, mother, wife or child, but everyone who touches his sorrows, his aspirations and his joys, or who has encountered grief on the way of life. Also that his brothers and sisters are all men and women who stand in need of his courage or his strength.

Against this attitude, which man feels to represent his highest attainment in his relations towards others, there is that natural, and in most cases dominant instinct, which not only tends to exclude from these noble and ethical sentiments all the vast world to which he is not directly related, either by the ties of family or the intimate associations of life, but also to implant in each breast a sentiment which more highly regards the interest of the child than it does that of the parent.

At each step in this strange contrast between sentiments, which seem to be dictated by a nature working towards unknown ends, and an ethic which looks to moral ends, there appears to be a more direct and personal interest in what is obviously most useful to the continuation of the creative program than that which is felt for those whose part in direct creation has already been played. If this is viewed in its human and sentimental aspects it would appear that there should be more attention paid to the weak and aged parents of a man than to his children —but the reverse is true in the natural world.

A man will neglect his father and mother when he would not neglect his child, notwithstanding he is in greater debt to his parents than to his children. In ethics this is undoubtedly the position, but nature, to arrive at more distant ends, implants in men strangely contrasted sentiments, which do not give first place to a sense of duty based upon compensation and gratitude. This is one of the mysteries to be solved in the sentiment and philosophy of man before he can realize why his impulses run counter to his ethics and how he may so harmonize both that they will become in his own mind, as they are no doubt in the Universal mind, one and the same thing.

There is a general tendency to consider that what has been long sanctioned must be right, that it must rest upon something which, if it cannot be understood, must be worshipped and that so long as it is not generally repudiated it deserves to be defended and justified. Unfortunately this attitude is not confined to the ignorant and vulgar. It may be the general sentiment in a given age and supported by men renowned for their greatness and wisdom. Plato and Aristotle, whose philosophy has justly entitled them to the veneration of mankind, both endeavoured to justify the Greek custom of throwing infants to the wild beasts or murdering them in other ways, when they became too numerous or their support too difficult. This would now be regarded with horror even by savages.

One of the lessons to be drawn from this is that no minds are ever sufficiently great or detatched to be completely above the reach of the prejudices of their own age and able to reject everything which is foreign to their sentiments. If this is true as regards the most exalted minds it is not suprising that the masses follow with unthinking regard what their predecessors followed in the same way.

As a boy on the Indian reservations in the Dakotas I observed among the Sioux that no amount of personal suffering was ever regarded as a justification for the least display of pain and that sudden news of the most distressing or pleasant nature was always received without the slightest emotion of any sort. No amount of contact with more impressionable races seemed to alter this stoic indifference. As I hunted with these Indians I became convinced that such traits of character could be accounted for by the necessity for personal bravery which is essential to their mode of life.

They expected no quarter either from nature or man and each one was taught by example that only those who suffered without a trace of emotion and met death without fear, were worthy of another life in the happy hunting ground or were entitled to be ranked as men. To act otherwise would be to incur the contempt of those around them and this is as potent a force among savages as among so-called civilized men. When they followed the buffalo across the plains, if an old man or woman became too ill to travel, they were left behind to die, because the caravan could not wait and its instinct of self-preservation forbade it to divide. All must go forward together for purposes of offence and defence. If one or more should be left to die alone it did not impress them as anything unusual, nor could they be induced to see that it was other than natural and just. Any academic discussion was always met by the response that they acted under the pressure of necessity and this was quite true. They were following their game and the game did not wait. This is still as true in cities as on the plains—especially among our rich industrial savages.

The Indians, who individually were as indifferent to pain and pleasure as stone images, were also able to display the most intense suffering and joy, but never separately. This is an impressive evidence of the strange and allpowerful influence of action in the mass, as distinguished from individual action. Without artificial stimulants of any sort these people in their Sun Dance, Messiah Dance, War Dance and in their Dance to Death, displayed emotions of hope, joy, terror, fortitude, hatred and revenge, in degrees quite unimaginable among white men. What was regarded with disdain if shown by an individual, was considered as natural and attended by great traditions if done by a tribe. In no collective action did they ever display fear as regards dangers of any sort. They had strange traditions and were true to them in season and out of season. They too disbelieved in any change!

There is only one true attitude which man can adopt towards the great tendencies of his own age, no matter what that age may be. He should reserve an open mind as to everything which tends towards the greatest good for the greatest numbers and evolve his institutions in accordance with nature, which does not appear to make any hopeless attempts at projects of equality, but which renders unto every man according as he sows. These are the last objects now sought by the institutions of man and that is one of the reasons why his institutions cannot endure.

It would be a dismal picture if we were unable to see anything ethical in man's attitude towards others, but his general attitude and policy are unethical. Great importance is attached by some to the increase of charitable institutions as showing that man has ethically progressed and that considerations of general moral interest are increasingly expressed. The increase in the number and scope of these institutions has resulted from the multiplied productive power of men, working with machines and creating a surplus beyond their essential needs. The few give what they do not need, to minister to the misfortunes of others who are for the most part the victims upon whose ruin rests the favoured position of the few. This is not due to a general advancement in the sense of moral responsibility but arises from increased and concentrated wealth.

If we seek to find evidence in our laws to prove that man is a moral being we will completely fail. In so far as man's laws are at all just, they arise from a sense of sympathy with those who suffer and a desire to reward those who would protect the weak. Even such laws may be traced to the necessity of establishing rules of protection and self-defense. They do not result from ethical considerations. Men seek to punish most severely those acts of personal violence which may be expressed to the most direct and personal detriment of the individual—hence the stringent laws regarding murder where one life is lost through violence, because we do not wish to be murdered individually, but there are no laws to punish the indirect and terrible murder committed against millions through industrialism and wars.

The grievous wrongs which afflict our age cannot be cured by the ethical conduct of a few men and women and majorities may never be guided solely by ethical considerations. The ones whose positions and powers give to their acts the greatest significance are precisely those who are not generally dominated by an ethical sentiment. It is because this will remain a permanent tendency of conduct that we must not look to persuasion or to morals, for the solution of the general problem which lies at the root of human misery. It must nevertheless be solved as a preliminary to a durable civilization, from which exploitation and war would disappear.

The despair of all who seek even a remote approach to an ideal commonwealth is that morals governing conduct exercise a controlling influence in the lives of only a strictly limited and small minority. The dominant elements in society will never be guided by a noble ideal of action based upon ethical consideration for others. This permanent and natural tendency of mankind must be brought under a restraint. The solution is not to be found in any system which relies for its success solely upon an instinct of moral justice, because there is no indication that in hundreds of years this will be found either in the most numerous or the most powerful members of the human race.

We record to the lasting honour of human nature that great and impersonal principles of morality and altruism are the governing force in the lives of many men and women. This is not new in human experience. If it is now expressed more generally than in the past it does not arise from any higher source than the increased independence of greater numbers of men and women and the increased pressure put upon those who are rich through the organizations of those who are poor.

There are two classes of people who have always illustrated altruism and morals by their conduct. These are the philosophers and dreamers, whose personal position in society was to them a matter of complete indifference. Whether they happened to be poor or rich they saw humanity through the eyes of ethical beings and their attitude toward society has set before mankind its only standard of true morals.

The other and more numerous class has been so situated by its economic independence that it could and did adopt towards charitable institutions a course which on the surface had the appearance of ethical conduct, while in fact it could never have any moral significance because it was generally devoid of real altruism and made no sacrifices for the common good.

It is most remote from my philosophy to suggest that the highest good, or in fact any permanent good at all, may come from giving. I would only point out that in its general tendencies of exploiting and destroying the common man, society has never been so immoral as at present and that the great increase in so-called altruistic institutions does not indicate any advance in ethics or a higher sense of responsibility among men. Our apparent generosity in giving something we do not need is without any moral importance or value. It merely expresses the vanity and arrogance of exploiters, whose virtues are advertised by a puffing press, at so many shillings per line, depending upon the number of readers and the cleverness displayed in disguising the fact that what they are reading bas been paid for!

CHAPTER VI.

THE PRINCIPLES OF EDUCATION AND POLITICAL RIGHTS.

In the first chapter some of the defects of home discipline and education are considered, but it will be useful to pursue the enquiry as regards the principles of education and their application to social and political institutions.

The defects in the character and application of what is taught do not arise from the stupidity of the ruling castes but rather from the fact that they devise the system which is most likely to realize the objects they have in view. In so far as the clergy can influence education it would close the doors to all enquiry, speculation and doubt in order more easily to impose upon the superstition, the credulity and the fear of mankind.

As regards autocrats their influence is always directed to inculcate a slavish respect and reverence for the institutions most calculated to prevent men from obtaining political independence and true liberty, while the plutocrats uphold both the clergy and the autocrats in order that they may maintain the economic slavery of the masses. As plutocracy is interested in upholding a despotism of its own choosing, it sometimes joins in deposing autocrats who have obtained their positions either by inheritance or force, but plutocracy has no interest in seeing the establishment of institutions which will tend to the religious, political and economic independence of the people. These are some of the reasons why the masses are not educated in any liberal and useful sense. There are additional causes for the deficiency and failure of education and these are that we have continued to hold to traditions which are out of harmony with the spirit of our age; we have paid too much attention to theology and classics and too little attention to the microscope and the telescope and to the economic and social problems which lie unsolved at the root of all our institutions and which polute all the streams of life at their source.

In most countries there are laws imposing what is dignified as "compulsory education" without the essential requisites existing to give effect to such laws or make them of any practical value. The first requisite is economic independence for the masses for whose ostensible benefit the laws were passed and the second is the creation of an intelligent system of primary, technical, scientific and literary instruction which at present does not exist in any nation to an adequate extent.

So long as the children of underpaid toilers must at an early age enter the ranks of toil in order to enable their parents to maintain their miserable surroundings, any general and useful education of these children is economically impossible.

So far as children of either the poor or rich are educated at all it is generally of little value because it is conceived in a spirit so narrow and defective as to make it almost as useless as no education. It is in the hands of insufficiently trained, small minded and underpaid public servants who have had no useful education and its result cannot be well-balanced men and women. The poor are not prepared for anything except to be inefficient cogs in the great industrial machine, and the rich are taught a quantity of rubbish which they learn as parrots and which is without the slightest use in the great and serious affairs of a practical or truly cultivated world.

Plutocracy for its exclusive benefit arrives at a conquest of world markets for machines by making mere machines of men and women. It builds foreign and domestic trade and industry upon the degradation of an underpaid and overworked world of toilers. The poor to whom health is an essential, are taught nothing important as to the laws of health and although their lives are to be spent among machines they know nothing of the laws of mechanics or of the laws of nature which all must obey because nature is not paternal. If it were it would give man several chances before it struck and often it would never strike, whereas on the contrary it always strikes directly and without warning of any sort.

All education like all employment is too restricted and mechanical. Pupils learn a few unimportant things by rote and forget them in less time than it took to learn them. They are taught that certain things are so, without the slightest notion as to why they are so. They are not instructed as to the principles underlying the subjects taught. They know only a little about certain effects without the slightest understanding of the causes to which all effects must be traced, in order that the knowledge may in future be used in finding the principles from which all material and moral facts have inevitably arisen.

A fact is soon forgotten but if the principle in which this fact has its origin is once profoundly understood, it will never be forgotten and will serve as an explanation of countless facts which are constantly met in the ordinary experience and study of life.

The teaching of history is also typical of the senseless

methods employed in the so-called instruction of mankind. It consists for the most part in memorizing dates and forgetting them, in describing battles and glorifying the murderers on one side or the other, according to prejudices arising from nationality, politics and religion. In the United States an important part of domestic history consisted in learning to hate England, and this will now be changed to instructing the youth to hate Germany, notwithstanding all are Christians and it is written that "ye shall love one another." This because hatred only injures those who hate and to forgive your enemy is much more important to you than it is to your enemy.

The defect involved with respect to the teaching of colonial history in America consisted chiefly in its lack of discrimination as to those who were responsible for England's colonial policy, in that Britons as a nation were made responsible for the short-sighted, vindictive and arrogant policy of a crazy German who happened to be king of England at the time.

Historians of the future should make a clear distinction between those who mislead and misrule the masses and the patient masses themselves who are so misled. This principle must be once more applied in weighing the responsibility of the few autocrats and the many plutocrats with respect to the present war, in order that posterity may make a clear distinction between the few who in all lands waged war as a business and the millions who were duped and destroyed by the few.

History, as generally taught, deals with isolated and sometimes unimportant events rather than with the tendencies in the life of men and nations and ignores the fundamental causes underlying the great social, economic and religious movements through which races and nations evolve, decline and disappear. It notes the signposts along the path of time without attempting to explain or even to read what is written on these signs. The greater part of all so-called history is quite useless and the more serious studies under this heading are of importance chiefly because they furnish the material which may some day be used by a great and original mind as the basis of raising history to a science, which will illuminate the principles, the tendencies and the epochs recorded in the life of mankind.

In a branch of education which has such important possibilities as reading, there is no suitable instruction as to what one should read and as to why some reading is worse than useless. The teaching in this respect is so deficient that it rarely implants any genuine taste for literature or establishes the foundation for the great and refined enjoyment to be derived from the extensive reading of good books. It makes the study of classical literature so stale and unprofitable that the average college man never looks at a classical book after his days of punishment at the college have ended, and too often he has neglected the great literature of his own language and has little or no inclination to pursue it amidst the interruptions of an active life.

One also constantly observes that nearly everyone has read to little useful purpose. If he has not read enough, his opinions are formed upon a basis which does not take into consideration the experience of man and the experiments which have been tried and found wanting and the lessons which they should convey to his own age; neither is he able to form any personal conclusions as to why some of man's most laudable enterprises have failed. If he has read a great deal of the harmful rubbish which passes as history and philosophy, he has no power of original judgment and ceases to be himself. He becomes somebody else or nobody. In all castes nearly everybody talks a common nonsense, professes the same opinions and feels the same limitations, because either they have not read enough and have learned little or nothing by experience, or they are under a common limitation imposed upon them by books and by ignorant teachers and priests.

The defects in nearly all other branches are as great. As regards writing, it is badly and loosely taught and the result is that only a small percentage of so-called educated men and women can write correctly about anything. The majority cannot convey in written words what they may have to say upon any subject and not one in a hundred thousand can write with ease, simplicity and elegance.

In the higher as well as the lower grades of schools, there is taught a slavish respect for the validity of long accepted notions as to authority, religion and government, without the slightest attempt to enquire profoundly as to the correctness of existing views or as to the evolution and science of the important subjects involved. There is also no encouragement offered to students to make independent enquiry which might result in conclusions of the highest value to mankind, even if they might also destroy some of its long cherished beliefs.

To those who may be interested in pursuing this subject at greater length I commend *"The World Allies"* in which I have set out not only new principles as to liberty and political economy, but have also conclusively shown that the principles upon which both are founded as enunciated by those whose authority is universally accepted—cannot longer stand and that they were never properly applicable to society and that they could not be, for reasons inherent in nature and in man.

If for the purposes of the present enquiry the special defects in the education of women are considered, it is evident that quite apart from the error of omitting instruction of the highest importance, the whole system is wrong because it is founded upon principles which in their results only emphasize and aggravate some of woman's greatest defects without giving to her the high advantage of a natural and useful counterpoise.

Girls are more emotional than boys and while emotion, as applied to art and to imagination has great and important uses, its cultivation to the extent now reached is detrimental to women and consequently to the race. The greater part of a girl's education tends to accentuate her emotions and this is not accompanied by a counterbalancing influence to be derived from the study of science, mathematics, history and politics, and by needlework and physical labour. In many schools the subjects mentioned are taught, but they are not profoundly taught or seriously considered, whereas the studies which appeal to and magnify the emotions, receive the greatest attention, and even aside from this teaching several hours are devoted daily to music and to reveling in sentimental poetry and this can have no other effect than to increase a tendency which should on the contrary have been restrained.

The girls who receive a training best calculated to result in their normal and useful developments are those belonging to the lower and middle class, and the daughters of artisans, in whose homes some degree of family life exists, consequently receive a useful training at home which is supplemented by an education in free schools, devoted to more practical and less sentimental instruction. The difference in the education of daughters of the poor and rich arises not so much through any rational conception as to what the education of women should be, but rather because of the feeling of insecurity which pervades the lower classes, there is a tendency to instruct their daughters along the same lines as their sons, since the trend of modern industrialism is toward the ever-increasing employment of women in competition with men. The women of the poorer classes rarely ever feel that they are securely placed beyond the possible reach of this competition and it is therefore natural they should endeavour to prepare for eventualities which are likely to arise. This class as well as the rich does not devise a system of education calculated to develop the most normal and perfected types of women but rather as regards the poor the most useful type, and as regards the rich, the most decorative.

The latter hope to adorn a world in which they will not be called upon to take any part in the competitive struggle for existence, while the poor fear that this competitive struggle will fall to their lot in the natural course of events, and they seek to do what lies in their power to prepare for this emergency. The point upon which special emphasis must be laid is, that the training of the poor is incomplete, because the girls are not fitted for a serious and equal competition with the boys and this is essential if they are to be forced to become parts of the industrial machine, otherwise their natural handicap is only augmented and they must toil longer hours for less pay. On the other hand, they are not sufficiently trained to the care of a home and children if they are spared the necessity of industrial competition with men. They are therefore not properly educated for anything. In *"The World Allies"* and in these pages I show how this competition may be avoided and give the reasons why any other course will be disastrous for mankind.

In the education of all classes a great defect is that they are taught a little about many things, and are never sufficiently instructed as to anything. They never master any subject. The result of this mistaken policy among the classes financially independent is that the women are over-emotional, superficial, indolent and uneducated. They are not serious-minded, restrained and reasonable and they lack the great and important qualities which they could and would acquire under sound, thorough and rational training from which emotional and sentimental nonsense should be eliminated.

The results of these mistakes are far-reaching and may be seen in the ever increasing and general strife between men and women. This is a tendency which can be witnessed only with feelings of misgiving and sorrow by all who would promote the welfare of mankind. Step by step women are being led and driven farther and always farther from their natural and highest spheres of usefulness and are unconsciously preparing the way for their own enslavement, along with that of the men, although they are being given the ballot and are actually persuaded that all this tends toward a larger and truer freedom.

From the commencement of modern democracies the suffrage has been determined upon a wrong basis. All men are not competent to vote and some women are and have always been competent to do so. The demand made by women for the ballot has increased in proportion to the rise of industrialism and is most general in countries where women are most in competition with men, each working for their own independent ends.

It is not because women labour with men that they have made increasing demands for political rights, but rather because they have laboured without being in their natural relation towards men, without having the protection of man and deprived of the most important natural associations which should exist between women and men.

It may be due in part to other causes which lie too far below the surface to be discovered in the limited study I have been able to make in Switzerland, but I entertain no doubt that the absence of any general or particular demand for the ballot by the women of Switzerland may be traced to the economic independence of its people, to the more natural relations which exist between its men and women as compared with England and America, and to the fact that they labour together rather than in conflict with one another. The small farmers and shop-keepers who constitute the majority of this remarkable democracy dwell beneath their own roof, cultivate their own spot of earth, manage their small business and share as men and women a family life which is calculated to remove all conflict of interest between them. The women live in co-operative relations with their men, where conditions have been most favourable for the establishment of a sound and genuine democracy and where the terrible evils of industrial concentration and high finance are unknown. They are content to leave politics to the men because they are in their natural relation towards men. There can be no greater error than to suppose that men and women who are essentially different in nearly everything, should be similarly employed.

Women are more tender but less generous than men. This is constantly illustrated by their acts, as they may be studied in biography and it is also one of the outstanding impressions formed by the observations and experience of actual life. Women who may be capable of the most genuine heroism and self-sacrifice, are often quite unable to express a generous attitude toward great or small defects, which in the more abstract judgment of men are regarded with magnanimity. Women as a rule look at matters as they are likely to affect themselves and they are therefore the great conservative element in society, while man is its speculative, constructive and creative element. The woman's instinct is to provide against the future by saving what she has, while the more courageous instinct of man is to scatter what he has in projects where the harvests may be great, even if they are long deferred, in the same sense that the farmer scatters his seeds abroad in spring-time on the chance and in the hope that they will return to him a multiplied abundance in the sunshine of autumn.

It is because of the special functions which nature has entrusted to woman that she will permanently express tendencies entirely unlike those shown in the conduct of man.

Quite apart from any questions of ethics or education, men and women are by nature endowed with the qualities best calculated to serve the distinct and special interest confided to each by nature in pursuit of its own ends. What these ends may be neither men nor women will ever be able to divine.

It is because nature has equipped men and women with different tools suitable to widely divergent tasks, that it is a violation of their natural rights and against the interests of humanity to bring these two interdependent beings into relations of competition. In proportion as this competition exists, the designs of nature are defeated and all true progress is retarded.

The industrial exploitation of women is not in any sense in their interest and tends only to defeat and destroy the natural objects of womanhood. It is of the highest importance to humanity that women should be spared the fate which is now being prepared for them by plutocracy and unless they are saved from this calamity they and all industrial toilers will be enslaved. They will not be in chains because chains interfere with work, but they will be bound by stern necessity and poverty to the wheels of industrialism where their lives will be slowly taken for a few pennies a day. This can be avoided only if the toilers take the steps I have outlined in "*The World Allies*" and through which they could rise to economic independence and have the resources necessary to protect the women of their class from industrial exploitation and degradation.

It may be taken as a general principle so long as the present basis of exploitation continues, that anything which increases the supply of competitive wage-earners is in the interests of the plutocratic employers of labour and directly against the interest of all toilers. The interests of plutocracy for the future would suffer through the shameless destruction of millions of toilers unless their place in the industrial machine can be filled from a new source of labour supply. In the view of plutocracy there is only one possible substitute for the millions of men who are dead as the victims of the greatest crime of plutocracy and this substitute is the labour of women. Through the destruction of these poor and patient men, plutocracy has gathered a harvest of milliards of paper fortunes and if women can now be forced into industrial slavery, the future operations of plutocracy will not suffer from the havoc and destruction it has wrought. The larger the percentage of the masses who can be forced to toil, the greater will be the value of their production and the percentage which goes to each one who toils will be correspondingly reduced—while all the surplus will go, as in the past, to plutocracy.

If on the other hand, through the measures outlined in my books, the toilers take the steps necessary to establish industrialism upon the basis of payment for production, rather than upon the present barbarous basis, they will not only be able to rise above economic slavery but will keep for themselves a free industrial field and make it unnecessary for women to continue a course which can only end in the complete enslavement of both. Unless men are economically able to support women and permitted to accord such support, the great industrial army of men and women will be reduced to hopeless economic bondage.

This is a prospect so completely against the natural rights of both men and women and so contrary to their sentiment and interest that it must not be permitted to become a reality. The decisive issues rest with the toilers and the women of their class and as soon as the war is ended it will be the opportunity and the solemn duty of these men and women to make a decisive strike for their economic and social freedom.

It is only five years ago that women were being imprisoned in London for the violent methods employed in their struggle for the ballot. Those days are buried in a past which now seems remote, and the ballot is being granted to millions of women. They and their men believe that this constitutes an effective weapon in the hands of the masses, but they will learn, when they have taken their cup of bitterness to the last drop, that the ballot in the hands of women will result in nothing more than passing a few laws of little importance and then repealing them and in doubling the numbers of votes cast for candidates nominated by political machines.

Nothing of large or permanent value can ever result

in multiplying the already too numerous votes cast under a political and economic system in which numbers do not usefully count.

Even under the most ample and democratic system outlined in chapter seven, the remedy for the problems which weigh most heavily upon the masses must be found outside parliamentary action and it can exist solely upon the basis set out in these pages and in *"The World Allies."*

If the right to vote, for what it may be worth, is regarded in its philosophical aspect, it is evident that considerations higher and more important than those of sex should be the basis of all civil and political rights and obligations.

There is no more justification for establishing the right to vote upon the basis of sex than there would be to determine it by the colour of a man's hair. To give the ballot to stupid, depraved and indolent men, merely because they are men and to withhold it from intelligent, cultivated and honourable women for the sole reason that they are women, is as unsound and illogical as it is unwise and unjust.

There is no relation in life concerning which it is more important that men and women should be instructed, than in what constitutes their highest usefulness and duty to society and yet there is little or no place in modern education for this instruction, even as applied to men and none at all as regards women.

The majority of men who vote in all industrial nations have no accurate notions as to the origin, evolution and scope of the political institutions controlled in theory by their ballot and are generally ignorant as to the history and tendencies of civilization. They have been given a theoretical power which they are in no way intelligent enough properly to use or to convert into a real and effective instrument for the political control of democracy. This cannot be attained by a mere extension of the franchise to women, but rather by the establishment of suffrage upon an intellectual and property basis, to include both sexes upon equal terms. These terms should be more exacting but wholly different from those now generally applicable to the franchise of men.

As the masses remain disinherited by plutocracy it would be an unfair discrimination against them to lay stress upon the ownership of property. The millions of industrial slaves have no resources except the potential value of their ability to toil. In so far as this is applied to produce an income it should entitle them to the same position as a similar income would create if it resulted from the ownership of property, which would mean that a man or woman who earned 5000 francs a year would have the same position as one who might own 100,000 francs of property. No man should have more than one vote and no one should be qualified to vote unless he can read and write and has sufficient understanding of the political institutions of his country to pass an examination as to its history and the principles upon which its government is founded.

In the leading industrial nations not one voter in ten thousand has more than the most vague notions as to the tendencies of society even in the last century or as to the origin and history of the offices and institutions which it holds in reverence or regards with slavish respect.

They would consider in England that the office of Prime Minister was as ancient as Fleet Street, although it was not officially recognized until this century and probably would never have been thought of except for the fact that George I. being a German and unable to speak English, was bored by attending meetings of his cabinet. This has no greater importance than attaches to the fact that George V. following the custom of the Germans on the London Stock Exchange, drops his own name and takes an assumed one, because in war time Windsor is popular and Guelph is unpopular. In a little time this will rank among the other traditions.

Among all classes there is a general tendency to accept what exists as something which has the right to exist and has perhaps always been and therefore must always be. We find this attitude displayed on every hand towards everything. It arises from an insufficient knowledge of history and from the restricted views natural to men who cannot disassociate themselves from their surroundings or make any comparison of the present with the past. Also from the general sense of dependence felt by most men who prefer the ills they know to others which they cannot know. The margin between most men and want is so slight and the institutions to which this great evil may be traced are represented in a manner so impressive to the average mind that there is a general tendency to accept, rather than to seek to cure the monstrous wrongs which are regarded merely as the will of a divine power and consequently beyond all remedy.

It is due to the moral and material pressure which the few exert over the many, and to the wasted energies of exceptional men who seek to remedy existing social wrongs by measures which are not adapted to society and which cannot therefore in practice be applied, that the progress of humanity as a whole is so depressingly slow.

Those who have the power to establish a new era of prosperity and freedom for the masses have no material interest to do so, and as ethics are the exception rather than the rule in human conduct, there is nothing to hope from any plans which rely for success upon men in general, acting ethically rather than selfishly. One of the most melancholy misfortunes of the masses is their inability to discern the connection between their exploiters and the institutions which dominate their sentiments and they fail to realize that the things which they regard with unthinking awe and slavish reverence are in reality the most potent instruments by means of which they are exploited and oppressed.

To know the origin and evolution of political institutions is beyond the education and capacity of the toilers, but to be able to understand that every man who toils is the economic and social brother of every other toiler is so simple and self-evident, that it may be understood by all men.

It is upon that basis and in that realm rather than politically that these men must unite and act throughout the world.

They may be joined in this great movement by the women who are now engaged in the economic war, struggling against their sisters and who are taking a course which offers nothing but profits to plutocrats and disaster to the masses.

Those who are accustomed to the control of men and women know how important and even decisive is the part played by sentiment in the most trivial and also in the most momentous decisions of the masses. This will long remain the dominant force in all action in the mass and will only gradually disappear through centuries of sound education and a more general economic independence. If women happen to be more sentimental than men it remains to be seen whether they will also be more stupid in following this sentiment to the ballot box where they may throw away their votes.

While I do not attach great importance to the ballot either for men or women so long as they are wage-slaves and guided by plutocrats and priests, I would impress upon women that the ballot will have an importance for them only in proportion as they may be able to lay aside sentiment, cast off old prejudices and all unsocial aims and nationalism and cease to fight an industrial war in competition with men.

The men who control the credit and industry in all great nations and who play upon and exploit mass sentiments, are themselves uninfluenced by sentiment. They know the path of their self-interest and follow it. They name their apparently competing candidates for all political positions and the masses acting like sheep, accept the blind leadership of the blind and follow the banners and bells into the pits dug for them by men who do not dream or indulge in sentiment but who organize, and coldly and deliberately follow their unsocial interests. The extension of the franchise has in the past meant little more than increasing the number of votes cast for one or another straw man made by political machines, and as the ones who control these machines expect that the ballot for women will result in nothing more important than doubling the number of votes to be cast in the old way, they consider they are in no danger from the votes of women. Probably they are right since neither men nor women in the mass ever understand their own or the social interest and always act without judgment, reason or good sense. THE GREATER THE NUMBER OF WOMEN WHO CAN BE MADE TO BELIEVE THAT THEY SHOULD HAVE THE SAME CAREER AND FOLLOW THE SAME VOCATIONS AS MEN, THE GREATER WILL

BE THE PROFITS OF THE EXPLOITERS AND THE MORE COMPLETELY WILL MEN AND WOMEN BE INDUSTRIALLY ENSLAVED.

Great hopes might have been entertained from giving the ballot to women if it were not that some centuries of experience have shown that whatever may be the theory of government, the practice is that democracy is an illusion, that the masses whose numbers might make them supreme have no effective voice in the management of nations and no assured veto over the most important and destructive designs of the ruling castes, who have created and maintained the machinery of despotism under the cloak of democracy in every belligerent land.

These conditions will not be altered even if the ballot were to be given to every man and woman and it is one of the most discouraging signs of our times that this is so little understood by the masses to whom it is of such special and vital importance.

If the right to vote has been given some emphasis in these pages, it is because of a desire to deal with the matter in its philosophical aspects rather than because of any importance which I attach to it as an effective means by which the masses might now obtain either economic or political freedom. It is discussed not with regard to its economic importance to the masses, but rather abstractly as to who should in fact be qualified to vote. Even if this were the most fairly and generally determined it would never put into the hands of the toilers the means by which a proper commonwealth could be established, so long as men retain their unsocial instincts.

It is one of the special grievances of plutocracy that while some men own or control property to the value of millions and employ thousands of men, they have only one vote along with the most humble man they employ. The toilers cannot attach great importance to this theoretic equality, because the employers exercise in fact a political power quite in proportion to their economic position. It is by their orders or manipulation that candidates for all offices in the preponderating political parties are named and the masses have no alternative except to vote for the nominees of plutocracy. If the minority parties, such as the socialist and labour groups, nominate third and fourth candidates for office, their natural followers are so short-sighted and unorganized that they vote against themselves in favour of plutocracy, instead of voting in their own interest.

In so-called democracies such as the United States, the industrial masters exercise impudent and coercive power in many direct and open ways and through almost countless hidden sources.

To such an extent had the industrial toilers in the United States been mastered in 1896 that they were directly menaced with unemployment unless they voted for William McKinley the Republican nominee for president.

In that campaign I was the owner of Republican newspapers and knew McKinley personally and yet I could not refrain from expressing my resentment that millions of men, in a so-called free country, could be forced by threats to support the candidate of the money trust through fear of losing their position if they voted against him. It is mere humbug and cant to refer to the sacredness of popular suffrage and the right of every man to vote as he desires, when at the same time on the Saturday preceding the election of McKinley, millions of men received a printed notice in their pay envelopes to the effect that if he were elected they might resume work Wednesday, otherwise the factory would remain closed. At that stage in American history the toilers should have voted as one man against the system which had the impudence to destroy the most important and precious of all rights supposed to belong to the masses. The money trust had no intention of closing their factories against which the fictitious paper fortunes of American plutocracy had been issued, but so dependent were the so-called free men of America upon their industrial masters that they did not dare to face the issue raised by plutocracy. They voted as they were ordered to vote, and returned to their wage-slavery with somewhat of their manhood gone, because they had submitted like sheep to an insult against their personal independence and against the integrity of their political institutions.

A president and congress elected by such measures of coercion could in no sense be considered as the free choice of an independent democracy. They were, on the contrary, the instruments by which plutocracy was to impose its will upon the American people and it must be said that they carried out the designs of their creators.

If, as should be the case in all countries, there had been the initiative and referendum, and if congress had no power except to enact measures which would not become laws until they were ratified by a majority of all votes cast, the methods employed by plutocracy to elect its candidates would be used to secure the vote required to give sanction to its laws.

It is because the tendencies of democracies are toward an absolutism effectively imposed by plutocracy, that the interests of the toilers cannot be protected through political institutions. These interests must be consolidated by an economic, as well as a social organization of the toilers upon a world scale, upon the basis and to obtain the objects set out at length in my books.

At a time not so distant as most people imagine these vital issues will be pressed by the masses and it is the solemn duty of all who would serve mankind to warn the toilers against all leadership which seeks to take a short and violent road to freedom through civil war and the confiscation of property. There has been too much violence and destruction under orders of the plutocrats and if international murder is followed by civil murder it will result in complete disaster for humanity. There are many indications that this calamity will follow the war, since the rulers of the world are blind and will drive the masses to despair.

Let no hands of violence be laid upon the property which stands as the monuments of toil and no violent measures be adopted to dethrone the existing rule of plutocracy. For reasons clearly indicated a disorderly and violent mass always degenerates into an enslaved rabble, whereas by general organization and immediate but peaceful pressure the toilers may become masters of the world.

In considering property I do not regard the mountains of paper debts (which represent nothing but the crimes of exploitation through war) to be property in any rightful or legitimate sense and it should be one of the first results of a genuine rule by the people to take effective steps to prevent anyone who has made a penny out of the war from retaining that profit in any form whatsoever.

The milliards of bonds issued by belligerent nations and now safely locked in the strong boxes of the plutocrats who have exploited the misery of mankind, murdered millions of toilers and mortgaged a thousand years of posterity to the bandits of high finance, should be dealt

with upon the basis set out in chapter five of "*The World
Allies*" and respected in so far as they represent wealth
as therein defined, and which was not acquired directly
or indirectly through the war.

The armament makers in these nations, whose influence is one of the most subtle springs from which flow
the torrents of ministerial eloquence as to the reasons
why the war must be waged until there are no more men
either old enough or young enough to be killed, should not
be allowed to rob this and succeeding generations of
poor toilers whose brothers they are now murdering by
millions. Every penny which they have made from this
shameful affair and which is represented by bonds should
be cancelled as so much waste paper, which no government should have had the power to issue for such destructive and disgraceful ends, and the toilers should
never again allow the manufacture of arms. It is clearly
shown in my books how the whole of this atrocious system
may be abolished and peace, security and economic
justice may be realized by mankind.

Through thousands of years the patient masses have
struggled for peace and the right to life and to the enjoyment of what they create, but this has not been
attained in any nation. These objects represent only the
minimum rights of the toilers and yet they now appear
forever unattainable. I believe they will never be attained
except upon the basis and through the measures I have
indicated. The hope of humanity lies in the fact that the
system I urge is based upon natural and peaceful measures
which the toilers have full and exclusive power to put into
general effect, if they are inaugurated without delay.

In the violence of their despair and rage the masses
have time and again through centuries destroyed property
and beheaded kings, only to find that the property they

destroyed must be replaced under the dictates of other masters who were usually worse than the kings. The masses can never realize economic independence or political liberty through violence. They must follow the example of plutocracy and organize—not to destroy what is useful in society and never to destroy property—but in order that they may exercise an effective restraint over the industrial masters of the world enabling the toilers and intellectuals to establish an economic system based upon the principle that *the ones who sow may reap and that plutocracy shall no longer reap where it does not sow, and that all steps to be taken must lead to the complete socialization of all property which collects rent and employs toil.*

It is worthy of special notice that men who are able to acquire and exercise great powers outside of politics almost invariably have no desire to exercise political power. They are endowed with large capacity for organization and with the executive ability to give effect to their principles and policy. They look upon governments merely as instruments to be used in carrying out the economic policy of capital which dictates the course of governments and consequently controls mankind through what appear to be democratic institutions.

The result is the impersonal autocracy of unknown masters who execute their designs through the nominal representatives of the people. It is natural under existing conditions that those best qualified to conceive and execute great projects do not take part in what amounts to the clerical administration of governments. They are too preoccupied, too arrogant and egoistic to seek the doubtful honour of acting directly in the name of the people, since it is more effective and less annoying to have this work done by vain politicians, who are usually lawyers, nominated by machines and elected and paid by the masses.

If the real masters of the world were to take into their own hands the direct outward control and active conduct of governments, the people would be able to see the class by which they are ruled and the small men now employed by plutocracy to run governments would be left without any occupation and would incite the masses to unrest and violence. It is due chiefly to the fact that the outward show of power is confided to talking politicians that plutocrats are secure in the possession of final control over the masses. I recall in this connection a conversation I once had with the great ruler of Mexico, Porfirio Diaz, when I complained that I could not obtain protection for some of my property in a remote part of the Republic without paying tribute to a lawyer who was senator from the State in question. After arranging for the necessary protection through President Diaz, I asked him why he kept such rascals in Mexico City and in the Senate. He replied: "So long as he is in Mexico City and able to make a few thousand pesos a year I can watch him and he is therefore comparatively harmless, whereas if I sent him back to his state without an occupation he would create trouble in three months." It is because politicians live from the crumbs which fall from the tables of plutocracy that the rule of the plutocrats is possible.

I have known bankers and masters of industry whose autocratic sentiments completely incapacitated them as candidates for parliaments, but they exercised a silent control over the financial and industrial life of nations which enabled them to dictate all important legislation affecting domestic and foreign policy. They are the despots who rule democracies.

The successful politician usually talks his way into prominence and power. He addresses the multitude in terms they can understand and tells them what they wish to hear. Above all he assures them in the most impressive manner they are free and the press echoes this solemn assurance. But for the eloquence of oratory and editorials the masses would never suspect that they are free.

The politicians who constitute parliaments are only slightly less ignorant than the masses as to the problems which most vitally concern mankind. They are continuously passing futile legislation for the ostensible control of trusts and the regulation of capital, without having the slightest conception of the issues involved and, without the least understanding as to the measures which might be adopted in the interests of the masses. It may also be asserted in all confidence that as parliaments are now constituted, no adequate measures could be passed in any great nation, even if they were intelligently conceived and seriously put forward.

Most men do not desire to hear the truth unless it happens to be in accord with the notions they have formed as to their position and powers in the state. The masses wish to remain under the illusion that they constitute the final sovereignty. There are in all nations numbers of small men seeking political power who are willing to perpetuate this illusion. There are also in these nations a small number of men who hold no political positions, but whose sanction is indispensable in all measures of national and world importance. These silent masters of the world achieve through nominal democracies the great and substantial objects which attend industrial exploitation and conquests at home and abroad. Their tools in parliament who must answer to the so-called democracies always have a ready answer.

The effect of all this shameful business is that the

ones who constitute the majority in industrial nations and create the wealth of the world are without any useful powers which they can exercise through the creation and peaceful use of an organized force to apply direct pressure upon the economic life of the world.

CHAPTER VII.

A SOUND BASIS FOR POLITICAL POWER AND THE SCOPE OF A LEAGUE OF NATIONS.

There is a general misconception as to what men term the "right to power." So far as this refers to political power it may be strongly contended that no man has what could be termed an inherent right to power. In its practical, rather than its philosophical aspects, and in its application not only to peoples but to individuals, this question has been brought into great prominence through the war. Until the world had witnessed the destruction of millions of men and the establishment of tyranny in all the great nations of earth in the name of liberty, it would not have been considered of more than academic importance closely to scrutinize the questions as to what constitutes the right to power, whether any man has such right and if so in what manner it arose, to what extent it should be exercised and how it may be most reasonably and effectively controlled.

It will, however, now be generally conceded among intelligent men and women that these are not only large and important questions but also that the basis upon which they are resolved is of the most vital concern to mankind.

Governments which have the power arbitrarily to destroy millions of men and thousands of milliards of property without the necessity to consult the ones whose lives and property are to be destroyed until it is too late to consult them, could never render to an intelligent people any reasons sufficient remotely to justify the use which they make of such vast, terrible and arbitrary authority.

The belligerent governments have shown that such powers are vested in and used by a few men, that these men are not the greatest or even the ablest in their respective countries, that they are in most instances not only untrained but unqualified for the discharge of the duties which they have assumed the right to perform and that in effect they are the means through which a few armament-makers, shipowners, meatpackers, bankers and other exploiters make fabulous paper fortunes, while the entry on the other side of the ledger is a record of debts, destruction and death charged to the patient toilers and to be paid by them in instalments. The present instalment is being paid with their lives, and future ones will be extracted from the descendants of these unfortunate men. That any men should ever have the power to inflict such horrors upon a patient and suffering world of toilers, would be monstrous enough, but that it can now be inflicted upon such a ghastly scale, for reasons so ambiguous, so frivolous and so unreal and by the mediocrities who rule and ruin the world after centuries of struggle for liberty, is an indictment which men will find words insufficient adequately to frame in the distant future, when reasonable and thoughtful minds are able calmly to survey and accurately to judge the immense crime which is now being committed against the property, liberty and life of mankind—and to place the responsibility where it must be placed.

In my book I venture to anticipate the verdict and to there assign the responsibility where I am confident it will ultimately rest.[1]

It may be taken that the object of power should be to establish government and that the chief functions of

---
[1] *"The World Allies."*

governments should be to maintain order and to compel men to settle their disputes by arbitration rather than by force. Also to insure, so far as possible, an equality of opportunity and responsibility among men and to promote the welfare and happiness of the governed. It follows as a necessity that such an institution can only be realized in practice through the exercise of power by a limited number in any state. How this number shall be selected, what powers should be confided to them and under what circumstances their mandate must cease, are questions which have always been of first importance but which have now become vital through the trend of modern civilization.

Until the latter half of the last century it was considered in so enlightened a country as England that the Jew could not be allowed to hold any political office or take part in legislating for so-called Christians. The objections to the Jew were not taken upon the ground of his fitness to hold office or to legislate, but upon the basis solely that he was a Jew, that he was a member of an international clan, that he hoped to return to Palestine, and that there were too many irreconcilable religious differences between him and the Christians.

To withhold political power from a race upon these grounds was wrong, but to deny political power to any individual of whatever race on personal grounds is and will always be right. Those who seek political power evidently consider that an honour is being conferred upon them. Upon this theory society has the undoubted right to confer or withhold these honours at its discretion but only upon personal and never upon racial or ecclesiastical grounds.

It has been the general experience of mankind that wherever ecclesiastical and government powers were centered in a single office, there was a tyranny both as regards religion and government. There can be no true toleration and genuine religious and political liberty until the church and state are separated and until it is generally conceded that the beliefs of a people are no proper concern of any government and also that no church has the right to interfere with, or attempt to control the utmost liberty of private judgment, conviction and dissent. So little is this understood that in some of the most advanced nations men are now taxed to support an ecclesiastical system in which they do not believe and which is maintained as a part of the machinery of governments. Any religion which has a true and important meaning for those who profess it, does not require any official support or government subsidy and any religion which can only exist by such means is useless and does not deserve to exist. This is a contention with which most Protestants, Pagans and Jews will at once agree.

When religions are subsidized by the state the clergy is more independent of the feelings of the people because it does not directly depend upon them for support. It is therefore bigoted and reactionary and in a country like England the result is that the members of the established church, in proportion as they advance in knowledge, are not influenced by its teachings and take their religion and their tea as matters of routine without troubling to enquire more closely into the origin of the one than of the other.

In countries where the people are more benighted the power of the clergy is in proportion to the general ignorance, superstition and poverty. The idolatry which is inseparable from the religion of an ignorant people only changes its form as the masses slowly emerge from darkness. Instead of worshipping idols they now worship saints and the pagan Cybele, who was mother of the Gods and whose special day was 25th March, is now replaced by the

Virgin and the day called Lady-day without so much as changing the date. These mummeries and idolatries have obscured the sublime and simple beauty of the original teaching in which justice was founded upon sympathy and was truly poetic, such as all justice should be, and which looks to no higher reason for a man having happiness in the next world than because he has had undeserved misery in this one.

Whatever may be the religious sentiment of any man it is certain that in so far as governments attempt to influence or control the freedom of worship, as a right which is inherent and sacred to all men, the tendency is to reaction and tyranny. It therefore follows that any attempt to exclude men from office on religious grounds amounts in itself to tyranny and is the more objectionable because it could only be practically effective when exercised by substantial majorities. The danger of religious tyranny can only entirely disappear when people do not longer pretend to be religious or when true liberty of thought can arise through general instruction in natural science. The tyranny which is established upon a basis that makes it acceptable to the majority, who do not in fact recognize its nature and extent, is the most effective and will the longest endure, as has been so generally shown in the history of various nations.

The Jews and Christians cannot have greater religious differences than exist among Christians, neither do they desire to return to Palestine. The Jews are a people who thrive only when they mingle with other races which are productive through agriculture or industry, since they are no longer an agricultural people and have never been industrial toilers. They are traders and money changers whose prosperity is founded upon their association with those who create rather than hoard wealth and who are also in general less intelligent than the Jews. These reasons taken in connection with the religious bigotry of the Scotch account for the scarcity of Jews in Scotland.

The Jews have obtained the legal right to political power in England and the greatest British prime minister in the last hundred years was Disraeli, but in practice they are still under the disability which results from religious prejudice and bigotry. The ablest men in England, France, the United States and Germany are Jews and through their financial ramifications and racial clannishness they constitute an international power which, if fully and generally understood, would command the wonder of mankind and would also be deemed the proper object of serious concern. As matters now stand the national budgets are framed or dictated by the Jews and only in so far as this is in practice effective can the great national budgets be said to represent any financial intelligence whatever. It must not be considered that I am ascribing to this extraordinary race any abilities beyond those which it possesses, as the time has long passed when their wonderful economic talent and civic virtues can be regarded without respect except by those who, in earlier stages of society, would have been persecutors and who are now bigots. There are individual Jews in London whose signature is worth more than the signatures of five kings and whose word stands higher in the discount markets of the world than the paper of any Republic. Yet at all points where the lives of these men are in contact with unthinking Christians they are still subject to unreasonable prejudice in the minds of the vulgar majority, who do not realize that property and credit create the highest form of effective power and that the ones who rule the banks and the stock exchanges are in fact the rulers of the world.

There is no doubt that this power may also account

for some of the aversion shown the Jews, since humanity has not made sufficient moral progress to be able to admire a class with which it is unable successfully to cope. Also as we must reap what we sow we are now getting from the modern Jew the natural harvest of the injustice so long suffered by his race and which implanted in him those qualities of evasion and deviousness which might qualify him to be a modern diplomat, but which do not tend to inspire sympathy and arouse affection.

The Jews are in the modern financial life of nations what the Moors were in the life of Spain when they were expelled at the dictates of a bigoted and fanatical clergy. They exercise a power over the activities of great industrial nations which is out of all proportion to their numbers or their political position and which is in fact exercised outside all discernible connection with governments. It may be that their idealism and fanaticism are to enter upon a new phase of world importance in social and religious realms, through the lines of influence that will be projected from the new Zion which, for political reasons will be set up in Palestine, under a British protectorate. Once again there will come from Syria a dynamic power which will have a profound significance for humanity and which will interpret the true meaning of Zionism in the world.

I have mentioned the instance of the Jews because it is typical of other prejudices equally unfounded and still all but generally held. In most nations the Jews are not under legal disabilities but they are and will remain under other disadvantages so long as people profess to believe in existing religions.

The lines upon which democracies evolve are such that the effective control of the masses falls to the lot of a few men whose interests are not identical with those of the most numerous classes. It is beside the question to say that the majority have the ballot, that the votes count by their numerical importance, that the toilers are the most numerous portion of nations and that if they do not control governments it is their own fault. The fact is that the ballots of the masses are cast for a choice between two men nominated by intangible political machines and these machines are created and controlled by small groups whose interests are not those of the masses. The superior intelligence and more effective organization of the few as compared to the many, place it beyond the power of the majority to control the institutions which have been set up in their name and for the ostensible purpose of achieving general independence and freedom. As governing bodies are now selected the masses have no power which they are sufficiently organized to use in order to remedy this evil. Even if they were not disorganized at the polls they could not create the political machinery necessary to obtain the power which should correspond to their numbers. It not infrequently happens that the qualities which enable a man to obtain power with popular approval, are those which least qualify him and in fact disqualify him for the exercise of the power obtained. In their most consequential acts the masses are controlled by sentiment and this is a dangerous guide in matters which should be decided solely upon the basis of reason and self-interest. This basis of decision should be more strictly applied to politics than to any other of the concerns of life.

There is a great difference between the legal and moral rights to power. It is one of the most inherent and inevitable defects in the hereditary system that large powers may pass from one who was legally and morally entitled to them, into the hands of one who is totally unqualified for the exercise of power in any form. The right to such power arose from a theory of government which should never have been imposed upon mankind and its further maintenance should be repugnant to the sentiments of justice and freedom among all intelligent men. It rests upon usurpation and violence and will never be of service to the masses. It follows upon a principle of conduct and policy which can be maintained only through the continuance of the injustice and exploitation upon which it was founded.

The recipient of the most important inherited political powers is not called upon to submit to any of the tests which are applied in the elective selection of men who are to discharge the most humble duties. The holders of hereditary powers in governments are not subject to any of the reasonable restrictions which the masses should have the right to impose as conditions precedent to the exercise of any political authority. They represent the class interest of castes which have done more to retard the progress of liberty than all other agencies combined and they stand for privileges which have never been generally or fairly shared by those to whose moderation, patience and toil the world is indebted for its security and prosperity, upon which rests all enlightened progress.

It is not the least evil of such a system that it is sometimes able to bring over to its support the most illustrious philosophers and men of conspicuous ability and genius, either through patronage or the conferring of titles which carry some so-called honour or political power to be passed on to their descendants in the hereditary scheme of society. It is inevitable that the new aristocracy of wealth, arising through modern industrialism, should seek to associate itself with the more ancient aristocracy created by wars. The two fields of conflict engaged men of radically different types and it has thus come to pass that the Duke of Burgundy may sit at the right of the Duke of Mulberry whose claim to such distinction arose from his successful manufacture and sale of jam and to the gratitude of hungry politicians for an open purse.

It happens also as a further alloy in this pure gold of aristocracy that my Lord Snooks whose ancestor fought with King John, sits by the side of my noble Lord Snobs who has no ancestor and whose sole merit is that he knew how to make Yorkshire hams in Chicago.

The only hopeful sign to be found at this bargain-counter of nobility is that what becomes cheap and ridiculous is less likely to endure than those institutions which maintain their ancient traditions, to which men attach distinction or which they associate with glory.

If all hereditary titles were abolished and honours were to be conferred only upon men who are benefactors of their race there might be something justifiable in the custom and attach to it a true and enduring value, but so long as titles are bestowed by politicians they will be given only to those who contribute money to parties or to popular charities, or who have the appearance of winning a certain amount of fame in pursuit of those transient and unimportant things which now engage and will for ages occupy the attention of mankind. If titles were bestowed upon those who deserve the homage of mankind they would belong to the great scientists, dreamers and philosophers whose genius is always an honour to their age; instead of being sold as corn in the market-place to small, vain and pompous men and then solemnly conferred upon them under the pretence that they are in recognition of some worthy service to their fellow men. No doubt these transient and empty "dignities" would not be in the least valued by men of genius or great merit who would never attach the slightest importance to any so-called honour so long as it can be borne by people who have done nothing worthy of consideration of any sort.

It would be interesting to see the opinion which philosophers of the future will pass upon the psychology of our age and the grotesque institutions which now command the slavish respect and even the veneration of thoughtless millions in the most enlightened nations, where a few men are sowing hatred and murder among the masses and a harvest is being gathered which can be measured in terms of fabulous riches for exploiters and financial bandits and in untold misery, ruin and death for the most numerous, useful and deserving classes. At the same time under the plea of future self-defence there is a general intention among the exploiters and plutocrats in all belligerent nations to continue the fatal game of armament and unless this is completely rejected by the toilers and rendered impossible through their economic union, it is a matter of mathematical certainty that greater and more terrible wars are in store for the human race.

The time has long passed when this had merely an academic interest for a few reformers because it is part of a system which keeps the masses in ignorance, the wage-earners in senseless competition, reduces all toilers to a mere industrial commodity and designs to increase armies and navies which are fatal to the liberty and peace of the world. How this should be now dealt with is a matter of the highest concern to mankind. There must be a readjustment of the creation and exercise of political power even in the most representative states and an alteration in the theory and practice of elective selection. Such measures would completely abolish all hereditary political power and the trumpery of so-called "majesties" with their trains of flunkeys called princes, dukes, counts and lords, also the small decorative frippery such as barons, knights, etc. Future generations will consign the whole of this political rubbish to the oblivion under which mankind has buried the fragments of some of the most horrid images which once it worshipped with the idolatry of slaves.

The right to exercise power should be earned by each man for himself and (without ostentation of any sort) should be confided for only a brief and definite time. There should be no "majesty" among men except that which arises from knowledge, wisdom and character. These can never be inherited. The recognition of any other claim to "majesty" tends only to make pretentious autocrats of a few men and snobs of all the rest.

The slavish respect for inferior men who bear "honours" they have done nothing to deserve, presents one of the most discouraging aspects of human nature, when considered in the relation which it bears towards the sentiments most essential to achieve the economic and political independence of mankind. There can be no proper commonwealth so long as the thoughtless masses are content to bestow homage upon eminent nobodies whose show of superiority is possible only in a society where pretentious men are used to decorate the sordid actual tyranny of bonds and shares which dictate the policy of governments in all industrial nations.

If the so-called dignities are traced to their origin it is observed they had no higher claims to "majesty" than their ability to make use of the loyalty and toil of the unthinking masses and build palaces through the slavery of the common man. Their method during generations has undergone changes only in form, while the old policy of exploitation and violence remains, and through the use of science and machinery is effecting the conquest of nature and consolidating the subjugation of man. So long as there are nominal and actual kings there will be palaces and slums. The palaces are the grotesque relics of autocracy and the slums, which arose from primitive exploitation and injustice, have been extended and their misery has been intensified through modern industrialism. These two monstrous extremes of life have no place in the ordered affairs of an intelligent humanity.

The undemocratic character of so-called democratic governments in industrial nations is the logical result of the natural inequality among men and arises as one effect of the theory that great and arbitrary powers, centralized in a small group, or in one man, are not dangerous to popular liberty because they are confided for brief and definite periods of time. The fact is however that the powers so conferred are permanently exercised by castes representing only a small minority of mankind. The machinery of government is under the permanent control of a strictly limited number, whose names only are changed through elections, but whose interests are and will continue directly opposed to true democracy, to industrial independence and to all important measures which might bring about the liberty and well-being of the common men. In my books I have shown how the tendency of all governments may be traced to motives which are general and in their nature permanent and also how a peaceful and effective limitation and counterpoise may be established by the industrial toilers, in order to restrain all abuse of political power and put an end to their economic subjection.

It will be at once apparent that those who control the activities of mankind will most strongly resist any system which would arrest the present tendency of civilization and turn the great currents of independence and wealth into wider channels. As any consolidation of the present means of exploitation must favour the class now dominant, so all measures to promote more general intellectual, moral and economic independence must result in a corresponding suppression of the power, exploitation and arrogance displayed by plutocracy.

It is essential to emphasize that in so far as political power is conferred by the ballot it does not fall to the lot of men most competent to exercise it, because the ablest men in every nation prefer to control governments through nominees who will do their bidding and who are placed in power by impersonal forces operating through political machines.

It is due to the ignorance and vanity of politicians that they make such a poor show in trying to carry out the wishes of their creators and that they accomplish the designs of their masters in the most clumsy and expensive ways and often in ways most disastrous to the masses. The types of men who seek and obtain power do not greatly change from one generation to another in the relation which they bear to their contemporaries. They are on the average only a little less ignorant than their constituents. They are rarely ever men of first intelligence and would but occasionally rise above mediocrity in the most important and difficult affairs of life outside politics.

These vain politicians are taken too seriously by a thoughtless public and are not subjected to the restraints which must accompany large and discretionary powers. The decisions even of wise men, when influenced only by the highest motives, may be the result of a defective judgment of particular circumstances, and it should not be within the power of any man, or even of any elective body of men, to inflict great and irreparable injury upon other men without their express and direct assent and it should never be possible for the lives of men to be put in jeopardy upon a great or even a limited scale without a like assent.

Decisions for war are made by an individual or by a

parliament under influences and pressure from which the masses in a general and secret ballot would be free. Men do not lightly vote away their lives and if there had been no secret diplomacy and no power by which any government could murder men without their consent, there would have been no war in 1914, or at any other time in modern history.

In chapter five I have considered the influence exercised over the masses through their feeling of security in numbers, which leads them to do or consent in the mass to what they would individually repudiate, but it may here be stated that in spite of this fact it is quite a different matter for people to support a war with enthusiasm after they become infected with the microbe of war and hate, which the press fans into a disease, than it would be for people deliberately to choose war. This arises partly because during the time which would elapse while their decisions were being taken, their passions aroused by the press might spend their force, or be allayed by intelligent and sober advice as to the horror they would encounter through violence. To get such advice before the public would now be the great problem in all countries, because the press is in principle interested in sensations which sell the paper or it is the direct or indirect tool of plutocracy. It is however one thing to create the microbes of war before the conflict begins and quite a different thing to propagate such microbes after they have been scattered over the world by a war actually being waged.

I have shown in *"The World Allies"* the extent to which democracies may in practice be democratic, the forces which effectively and generally control all important acts of governments and the reasons why the toilers must form, outside all governments, an effective world influence which may be succesfully and peacefully applied. Also it is there shown why the most explicit and closey drawn constitutional restrictions which can in practice be established as the bounds of executive and even parliamentary discretion, will not operate as effective safeguards against the destruction of life by executives and parliaments upon a basis which would never obtain the assent of the people. I further show why it is essential that the new counterpoise to be exercised by the toilers must be both national and international in character and how it is to use its control and ultimate veto without reference to politics.

In the same book I have given fundamental reasons why no treaties among nations can prevent future wars. Before the idea of a League of Nations was suggested I pointed out that decisions of international tribunals can only be enforced through wars so long as there are armies and navies as now, at the bidding of plutocracy and so long as the world organization of the toilers upon the basis and for the objects I have proposed remains unformed. Since that was written a number of eminent men have put forward, with more plausibility than sound logic, the idea of a League of Nations as a safeguard against the pedatory methods of plutocracy and the general muddle of governments.

Even though the present war was officially inaugurated by governments, it must not be regarded as an accident to be attributed to secret diplomacy, but rather as the necessary and only possible result of a long sequence of events arising from a mendacious system of society which will not be obliterated by the actual havoc. Its origin lies deep in the foundations and policy of international imperialism and exploitation and in the senseless and wicked national and international competition of toilers. Its cause lies at the root of human society and no proper commonwealth can ever be established until this cause is definitely and completely eradicated.

No such patch-work as government ownership and the

employment of women, or a League of Nations can solve the national problems of economics or the international problem of war. The former will tend to the complete enslavement of both men and women and to the establishment of political tyranny through a centralized and national bureaucracy and the latter will result in a new grouping of nations, vast armament, an unpardonable waste of human energy and a repetition of the ghastly horrors of war.

It is well understood by all who are acquainted with world tendencies and who have eyes to read the signs of the time, that we are moving towards internationalism, that humanity is national in nothing except name and prejudice, that a great international understanding is inevitable and cannot be long deferred. It is therefore the hope and determination of plutocracy to use this great world tendency in such a manner as will be best suited to its own designs, in order that a higher, more effective and more noble use of it shall be forestalled or altogether prevented. The design of the ruling castes is that the world understanding shall be signed by governments rather than arrived at by peoples, because the governments are and will continue to be controlled by plutocracy. Their contention is that the people can only be represented by their governments, whereas the facts are that in no industrial nation is the government in the least representative of the people. A world League of such governments will only mean the formal world compact of plutocracy to uphold and perpetuate the existing exploitation of toilers upon an organized and well-defined world basis.

The classes which now control governments are those which have everything to gain and nothing to lose through national exploitation and international wars, whereas those who must form the only international League which can serve effectively the interests of humanity, have everything to lose and nothing to gain by exploitation or war. The basis of a world understanding which will bring security and peace to mankind and upon which a proper commonwealth may be established, must rest in the solid union of all international toilers and not upon any phantom such as a League of Nations, which in fact means a world league of exploiters, expressing its powers in a new, a more subtle and a more imposing form and through which it will make steady preparations for the next and inevitable wars.

Against all these shameful designs the toilers alone have the power to erect a solid barrier. It must be constructed by the labouring men and Socialists in one international economic union which can peacefully impose its will over world-industrialism and thereby over all the activities of men—including governments.

It is the solemn duty of these men to now reach an international basis of accord and a definite plan of action in order that they may put an immediate end to the shameless murder which disgraces humanity and is ruining the world.

They represent the only force which can bring order out of the chaotic horror into which mankind has been plunged by the ambitions, greed and tyranny of international high finance and they owe it to themselves and to posterity to take immediate steps to this high and noble end. They have borne too long and patiently the abuse of power by a few men who have assumed dictatorship throughout the world and who are now engaged in carrying out a policy of international hatred and murder on a scale which threatens to bring irretrievable ruin to all belligerent peoples and which will be followed to this ghastly end unless the iron hands of the common men can be united for international action without delay. It is necessary now to force the hands of the ones who are destroying humanity and to bring the unforgivable outrage to an immediate end.

The avidity with which the whole world appears to cling to all the phantoms created to perpetuate the rule of plutocracy is an indication of how desperately mankind stands in need of real leadership and how little likely it is to follow anything which may be practically effective in the attainment of true liberty and enduring peace. If all these tendencies were not so melancholy in their display of the almost unbelievable blindness of humanity, they might be regarded with less misgiving by those who have no illusions as to the actual social order or as to the steps which must now be taken for the genuine service of mankind.

The blunt truth is that the masses have no notion what they are fighting for. If they knew what the issues were, there would have been no war. The politicians in belligerent nations have exhausted all their resources of oratory and pretence as to the reasons why there is war, also as to the responsibilities of their enemies and as to the aims of each nation and incidentally how war may in future be abolished. Like drowning men who grab at straws, these vain and superficial politicians now enthroned in places of arbitrary power, will grab at and exploit any suggestions which afford them the slightest opportunity to talk plausible nonsense to a long-suffering public, who seem to forget that these men have for four years put forward one reason after another as to why there is war and that these reasons have constantly changed in the different countries to suit the changing conditions, with a rapidity which does not flatter the memory of the masses. It is perhaps fortunate for the politicians that only editors and philosophers keep files of newspapers. As the editors have a constant forum which the public is willing to pay for the privilege of attending and as the same public will

not read the message of a philosopher even if they are
paid to do so, the editor has his temporary hearing and
is soon forgotten, but the philosopher who once obtains
a hearing is never forgotten.

Political power is never exercised directly by philosophers or by the men who can look to the distant future,
because such men would not be deceived as to the designs
of the invisible masters who control governments, neither
would they sacrifice to the whims of the masses any part
of their intellectual or moral independence. It is in the
highest interest of mankind that this should be maintained, because the masses are habitually unable to trace
effects back to their causes, or to forecast with any accuracy what must be the inevitable consequence of world
movements, which only a few ever understand and a still
smaller number are able accurately to define.

It is less difficult to measure the savagery of man
than it is to comprehend or imagine his colossal stupidity.
If anyone had attempted to describe this stupidity in
adequate terms before the war he would have been accounted
raving mad and yet no man is sufficiently gifted or mad
to picture the length to which this dullness and folly
have gone. Man's stupidity passes all bounds of human
understanding and is beyond the reach of every human
sentiment, except that of pity or sorrow. There are dark
days ahead for those who seek to play upon this stupidity
as a facile instrument in hands which now use it as a
means of international hatred and murder.

It will also be a dark day for humanity as a whole if
it should witness any great or general movement which
is not inspired by a high ethic and which attempts to repay
injustice and violence in its own coin, since nothing of
permanent and real value can ever be accomplished by
such means. This is written upon all the sign-posts of

history but it appears to be lost upon a blind humanity. If the masses had eyes and used them, they would realize that once more this same inscription is now being written in language of blood and fire and its end will be what it has always been—and that is disaster. There are no indications that any belligerent government intends to adopt wise and general measures to avoid the rise of a tide of hatred and revenge which nothing can resist if once it sets in, against those now abusing the patience, credulity and heroism of the men and women who carry the world on their backs.

Fear of governmental tyranny has made millions of men and women hypocrites during this war, but underneath this hypocrisy there is a smouldering rage which beholds justice as a mockery, liberty of conscience violated by punishments in prisons and all the sacred rights of freedom, home and life destroyed and buried in a common grave. It will be well for those who now tyrannize in the name of liberty to look to that day when the iron hand of their own creation turns against its creators.

Those who have erected in all belligerent nations the vast machinery of destruction and murder fail to take into account that the vital part of this wonderful creation, which has been put to such monstrous use was made up of millions of poor and patient men who had nothing to gain and all to lose and who have lost all. They have been lured by extravagant promises of a new world, by offers of a new standard of human freedom, by the hope of personal and collective benefit which no government has the slightest intention or the least power of bestowing upon its people. They have been misled and betrayed. They have left behind them enough anguish to drown the world in tears. Their blind and heroic sacrifices cry aloud to heaven for a redress which is beyond the gift either of earth or heaven.

These millions of broken and murdered men, born of the indescribable agony of women, cared for by them with a tenderness and solicitude which is beyond all praise and cherished with a hope for their career which should have touched the depths of human sympathy—alas how unutterably pathetic is their lot! What a use to make of all this noble power and high courage! And what a contrast between the masses with their desire for home and peace, their lowly toil, their love, their sacrifices, their simple following of what to them is a vague ideal and on the other hand their exploiters who have no ideal and whose religion is ambition, money, power, titles and cheap but transient fame!

One of these noxious human pests who is a French armament maker said to me in Paris in April 1914 that the best solution of impending labour troubles was to set the toilers to cutting one another's throats. I must say that this armament maker was a moth-eaten, fox-faced devil, with eyes and hands of a dead man and with a heart of stone and he prowled through his factory with a cat-like stealth, but lacking all the noble dignity of a cat. He has not been at the front but has hoarded his vile profits made in a gloomy dungeon which he calls an office and extracted from the suffering, the heroism and the murder of his fellow-men. He is one of those eminent villains who insist that the holy cause shall be vindicated, that the stream of paper wealth shall continue to flow to the exploiters and that if a few million more men are murdered they can be replaced by women and thus the ideal of plutocracy, which is equal slavery for men and women will be realized and the principles of liberty, equality and fraternity will stand as tributes to the benevolence of his class.

Those who are acquainted with the most eminent politicians and who know the influences which control the metropolitan press in all belligerent nations will not be surprised that the scheme embodying a League of Nations as a protection against future wars, appears to be seriously regarded by everybody who speaks or writes upon the subject. It should however be examined with the view of weighing its reasonable claims to meet the objects it is professed to serve. In one form after another various nations have made leagues of offense and defense and have as often broken them by wars. In the days when men and money were not world commodities, and when the world was not dominated by stocks and bonds, such a League might have had even greater prospects of success than it can now possibly claim. Neither in the past, present nor future could any such League afford effective and peaceful restraint over those elements which control the policy of nations and whose interests are well served by war.

The whole scheme of a League of Nations is a fantastic illusion in so far as it is regarded as the means by which wars will or could be abolished. No doubt the League will be formed but that is not even a step in the direction of abolishing war. The conditions which create war are inherent in the very fabric of the civilization of each country now at war and of nearly all countries not at war. It is only when these conditions are remedied or when the power of the toilers outside all governments is able to counterbalance and defeat the designs of plutocratic power, that the occasion for wars will disappear and it is only when the *common men* make war impossible that it will cease.[1]

In my books are set out the measures which must be

---

(1) As a great part of the press and public, in their amazing ignorance, have considered that the idea of a League of Nations originated with the politicians now in conference in Paris, there is published as an appendix to this volume a short history of the origin and evolution of the idea, which completely exonerates the actual rulers of the world, from the charge of having originated anything in the least degree new! This bibliography was prepared for me by my friend Dr. Nicholas Roubakine, author of the great work "*Parmis mes livres*" etc. etc.

taken to establish industrialism upon a basis in which there would be no place for exploitation or war. As these objects can be attained only by peaceful means and with the passing of time, the toilers must now act if they would not be permanently enslaved. I have indicated the principles which must immediately be followed to avoid a future war. Neither the League of Nations nor any other suggestion which has been offered has the most remote possibility of achieving this object.

A League of Nations will arise from the war, chiefly because it will furnish plutocracy the most plausible excuse for maintaining great armies and navies and it is an idea which causes the masses to hope for better conditions, for which they think they are now fighting and which plutocracy would wish to hold permanently beyond their reach, in order to keep up the eternal struggle, founded upon an illusive but eternal hope.

Any League of Nations will be followed by an industrial grouping of interests within the League and the conflicts and ambitions of plutocrats and imperialists will raise questions which will be dignified as vital to the national interests or honour, when in fact they will represent nothing more than the vulgar grabbing of international finance for property, markets and power, which have been usurped by a nominal rival. In all this game the toiler has not even so much of an interest as a miserable room he can call his own. These international quarrels of vulgar plutocrats will be submitted to the court created by the League of Nations, because they will be represented as national and not as caste questions. Whatever might be the decision of the League upon any matter affecting a powerful member or group within the League, such decision could only be imposed by force. If this should take the form of economic pressure directed against one or more members, the nations so boycotted would resort to arms as soon as they were sufficiently grouped to do so.

It is never difficult to so interpret the issues created by international finance that they appear to involve questions which are dignified by the name of national honour and sovereignty and when so clothed they are not regarded as properly subject to outside interference. So long as men are blind enough to remain under the prejudice of nationality and to wave and worship national flags, these so-called questions of national dignity will hold their present exaggerated importance. It will be a long time before these harmful prejudices, created by the ambition of kings and priests, are effectually overcome and it is therefore necessary that the generations which will pass on their way to this rational and high goal shall be protected from the fatal consequences of sentiments which have been so long cherished and are so difficult to alter. If men will for ages continue to be unable to recognize that their lives flow from a common source and that their nation is the whole world, they should at least be able to now recognize that to whatever class they may belong they have a common world interest which as it affects their economic independence and political liberty can be protected only by world measures, designed to secure justice, not as between nations but as between castes, because humanity is not divisible into nations but into castes, which are international. The great and arbitrary powers now vested in the hands of plutocracy have only been rendered possible because this caste has recognized its international status and interest. The absence of such power which is expressed in the lamentable slavery and poverty of the toilers is only possible because they have failed to recognize their international caste and interest. Until these distinctions are grasped by the great industrial caste its millions of members will remain disinherited and continue to be the victims of those who appropriate the vast product created by the toil, the patience and the misery of mankind.

The head of one of the belligerent governments in Europe, in a recent speech said that the rulers of his country were appalled at the shocking state in which the toilers of that nation had lived. It is one of the strange ironies which this war has rendered possible that the sole deduction made by this politician from the shameful abuse of the toilers of his country was, that it had been shown by medical commissions that through this outrage there were a million men between 18 and 41 who were unfit for military service and who if they had been properly fed and housed might have been sent to the front to be killed[1]. If the statement of this outrage and the reason why it was deplored were not in the highest sense a tragedy one would be able to understand why this disgraceful revelation was greeted with passive indifference. When regarded in its gloomy aspect, as reflecting to what extent the abuse and subjugation of the common man has been carried, its recital to thousands of toilers seems as incongruous as the insipid jokes which some parson, sitting as a magistrate, has the audacity to perpetrate in a Court where the liberty or the life of some unfortunate victim of society is at stake.

It should not be difficult to see that, quite apart from

---

[1] The actual language used was: "The results of our examination are startling and I do not mind using the word appalling. I hardly dare tell you the results. The number of grade II and grade III men throughout the country is prodigious. So much so that we half suspected the doctors, but there were re-examinations which did not make very much difference. What does it mean? It means that we have used our human *material* in this country prodigally, foolishly, cruelly. I asked the Minister of National Service how many more men we could have put into the fighting ranks if the health of the country had been properly looked after. I was staggered at the reply. It was a considered reply, and it was: 'At least one million.'" Extract from a speech by Lloyd-George, Prime Minister of England.

the questions which man's national prejudices will not now admit to be subject to any arbitration whatsoever and which would constitute a formidable obstacle to the effective value of any League of Nations, those questions upon which the League might render its decisions would in the end involve the world in war, as society is now constituted and as it will remain after the present war.

The decisions of any tribunal, in order to have the least importance, must be so sustained that they can be effectively enforced. The value of local and national tribunals consists in their ability to render just and final decisions and in their power to enforce such decisions. When local questions are involved this power is exercised through the police and upon larger lines by national armies. If courts were without the power to enforce their decisions their reason for existence and their value would be at an end and men would revert to the settlement of their differences by private force.

This general and settled rule is equally applicable to international tribunals and no decisions of any international court will be binding unless they can be surely and invariably enforced. To what extent the wish of an international court might voluntarily be respected by any nation would obviously depend upon a variety of circumstances which do not admit of generalization. This is the more difficult accurately to define because there can be no precise boundary set upon interests which are not national and which are constantly assuming ever widening world aspects. It would therefore follow that any general pressure put upon a powerful nation would affect other nations allied to it geographically or by finance and trade. This would result in a definite divison of the "League" upon the first occasion when its decisions were to be thus enforced.

The menace of a boycott may profoundly influence or

altogether control the policy of small and undeveloped nations, whose well-being depends upon foreign markets for their products or upon foreign finance for their development, but both groups of nations now at war have long passed beyond that stage. There is no great belligerent whose vital interests are inseparably linked to any international markets, either of products or finance, which any group or League of Nations would be able permanently to close. There is in consequence no peaceful means at the disposal of any such League by which its decisions could be effectively enforced as against any of the great belligerents and it is only in respect precisely to such nations that the purposes of the League are of any great or general importance.

It is perhaps natural that the people of Switzerland, more than any other, will attach importance to the idea of a League of Nations, because they feel that they have themselves successfully applied the principle in their own history and that their Federation is a miniature League of Nations. They point to the fact that although the people of their cantons, with identical interests and similar languages were once at war under the leadership of aristocrats and priests, they have now secured permanent amity through a Federation and that if this experience is successful as applied to Switzerland it offers a strong presumption that it can be extended to include all states. If this is closely examined it will be seen that the peaceful relations existing among the Swiss people are not the result of any Federal organization. Peace among small states, such as the Swiss cantons, or among great states such as those now at war, has never been and can never be secured through any form of agreements among governments. The people of Switzerland did not secure peace until they had rendered powerless the ones who were able to declare wars and whose interests were served by such wars. So long as Switzerland was under the rule of aristocrats and priests, whose feuds of families or property could embroil the people, there was no end to war. Peace and feudalism cannot exist concurrently either in Switzerland or elsewhere. It is because Switzerland is in fact ruled by small farmers and merchants, nearly all of whom own their farms and small places of business, that the basis for peace exists. It is one of the logical results accruing to the only true democracy which is now in existence and it rests, not upon any Federal constitution, but upon the sole foundation upon which peace can ever securely and permanently rest and that is upon the effective rule of the people as distinguished from the rule of a few aristocrats or numerous plutocrats.

The great and dominant powers once held by the feudal aristocrats in Switzerland have passed into the hands of the masses and are effectively exercised by them; whereas similar powers formerly held under feudalism in Germany, France, England and in Europe generally, have passed from a few aristocrats to many plutocrats and the feudalism of modern industry — which is directly responsible for all modern wars — is a class feudalism, strongly intrenched in all great industrial nations and is an effective barrier to peace among those nations. Its powers will not be reduced or in any manner curtailed by any international League which the governments under plutocratic control may create, or by any contracts which they may sign. It is the hourly experience of individuals and corporations that contracts are constantly broken or that the parties refuse to agree as to how contracts shall be interpreted and this occasions the steady interference of tribunals with their elaborate system of officials and police to enforce the decisions rendered.

The extent to which nations, governed by industrial

feudalism as at present, can be relied upon to act according either to the spirit or letter of their agreements, will depend solely upon the shifting interests of international industrialism and trade, as it affects the plutocrats, rather than as it may concern the toiling masses.

The most remote and the most recent history demonstrates that compacts are only enduring so long as they are in accord with the interests of their signers and the only compacts which can have an inherent certainty of permanence are those which rest upon the indivisible world-interest of the toilers. Such compacts cannot be made among governments controlled by industrial feudal chiefs and imperialists whose interests are founded upon the exploitation of labour, the subjection of weaker races, the grabbing of territory for the exclusive profit of the industrial rulers who grab it and who will do all in their power to maintain the armies, navies, colonies and industrial slavery which are a disgrace to our boasted civilization and the inevitable occasion of future wars.

The powers which were once exercised by the feudal tyrants in Europe and which enabled them to wage local wars against neighbouring communities, such as were formerly waged under similar orders in Switzerland, slowly passed from many hands into the hands of an autocrat in each nation. Through civil wars in all the leading nations the powers of the autocrats have passed through the hands of unorganized rabbles, calling themselves democracies, into the hands of plutocracy and such powers are now vested in bonds and shares, although they are outwardly expressed through lawyers, parliaments and priests.

The new industrial tyranny of joint stock companies is only less autocratic because it is more impersonal than the old tyrannies. The rulers of the world are not personal autocrats with souls which might be touched by human suffering, or with bodies which might be seen and therefore kicked.

If the people of the United States have been happily free from the old form of European feudalism they have unfortunately not been able to escape the new industrial feudalism in its greatest and most powerful form. The strength of that nation rests upon the wide diffusion of property, upon wages which are uniformly high and upon a prosperity which in normal times is general. If the slums of its cities display the most sordid and gloomy degradation and suffering these are not due to the permanent misery of the millions of foreigners who constitute the slums, but rather to the steady stream of pauper immigration which continues to bring from Europe other millions into the slums, as their predecessors rise to better conditions.

Concurrently with the rise of the masses in the United States there have been created the most fabulous fortunes and the most odious and tyrannical plutocracy which exist on earth.

In no other nation are the industrial tyrants so organized, so mendacious, so powerful and so well in command of the avenues of production, transportation and manufacture in all great industries and so completely able to dominate money and credit. They are exploiting a great continent possessing vast riches. When the national resources shall have been so dissipated as to place American production upon a competitive footing in all respects with Europe, the exploitation by the industrial masters in America will be transferred from the land to the toilers and they will then become only an international commodity, with an international value, instead of a national commodity as at present with its slightly higher value.

Individuals and parties may come and go but the industrial plutocrats go on forever. Their names pass as sombre shadows along with those of the nominal rulers, but property remains on the one hand with its feudal powers and the masses on the other hand with their struggles for life and with hellebore in the bottom of their cups.

The conditions of economic independence and therefore of effective power, must be created in all belligerent nations before elements will exist upon which may be founded an enduring world compact. When the great industrial power which now dominates the life of nations and determines all international relations is under the effective counterpoise of a general international organization of toilers, there will be no need for a League of Nations, created by debating societies called parliaments. Until such time any League that may be formed will only tend to perpetuate existing conditions and will be without the slighest value as a means either to abolish armament or to protect humanity against the horrors of war.

The net result is that a League of Nations to enforce peace must be a League equipped for war and so long as nations are equipped for war there will be war. There is only one sure course open to humanity in order that this may in fact be the last war and that is through an international organization of the Trade Unionists and Socialists into such a union as I have defined in *"The World Allies."* Concurrently with this measure there must be general disarmament and an end of all standing armies and of military service of every sort. There must be an end of legislation against trade and of all restrictions upon the movement of world products. The peoples who are now held as colonies of all nations must be raised to positions of self-government and in the meantime they should be controlled by an international board and their markets freely opened to the commerce and finance of the world upon equal terms. There must now be an end of all imperialism, no matter under what form it is established, since it has been and will always be the most potent occasion for wars. There must be an end of all navies and in their stead should exist only a small international fleet controlled by an international board, and strictly limited to a patrol of the seas against pirates.

There should be an end of international hatred and revenge. If one does not esteem his neighbour, the best revenge is not to become like him. Hatred harms only those who cherish it and generous sentiments are important chiefly to those who entertain them. There are noble qualities to be found in all our common humanity, but only by those who themselves possess such qualities.

The laws of compensation and values which are general in this world and therefore probably universal, cannot be set aside and no man can place himself beyond their operation. In this world, and undoubtedly in all worlds everything renders according to its kind and in its own season. This is as true in the spiritual realm as in the material and its lessons have been so often and so painfully learned by some men in generation after generation that it would seem unnecessary to now learn them afresh; but such is the blindness of men that they do not look beyond things to principles and do not realize that the machines they set up to destroy others will turn against their makers. They do not know that there is a oneness in the world which cannot be violated in any manner, that there can be no proper, real or permanent divisibility of human interests, that all the sciences merge into one science— that we are our neighbours' keeper whether we will or not and even if we fail to know or understand it. There is a common and universal law over the seed-time and the harvest and in the end only what is fitting can endure.

There is final and absolute truth only in nature and this may be the common heritage of all.

The world will pay in blood and tears a terrible tribute to the hatred which is now being fostered among men to serve temporary and base ends and which is constantly arousing, upon an ever increasing scale, those sentiments of violence and revenge which are the most harmful to the ones who harbour them the most and which, when aroused to such a degree and over so vast a range as at present, cannot fail to be fraught with the most disastrous consequences to all the peoples involved. We are sinning against posterity in a manner and to a degree as shameful as the crimes now being committed against our own age.

It will be to the permanent credit of all men who have been sufficiently wise, courageous and free to take their stand solidly against the whole of this mendacious and horrible business.

Anyone who will now take the trouble to read the speeches made in the British House of Commons during the early stages of the French Revolution will find that the hatred and revenge then so freely poured out against the French, who were there called ruffians and savages, and the assumed right to dictate to that great and spirited people what form of government it should adopt, were the seeds whose harvest was a European war lasting twenty years and costing the lives of millions of men. This sinister sign-post of history holds a warning against the suggestions which are now being so recklessly made as to the dismemberment of existing states, the crushing of great and powerful peoples, and in the blind policy now pursued towards that immense and wonderful Russia which is struggling to find its way from one despotism through another, to that high destiny which awaits a people, remarkable for their virtues and quite capable of attaining a position of first importance in the world. They, more than any other people, have the natural resources and personal qualities which enable them to become the true evangel of a vast and new social movement in which will rest the highest hope of mankind. When their revolution shall have run its course, in which the experience of our common humanity through the ages will be repeated and when they establish their local and international policy upon a high ethic, when they do not enthrone a new injustice in place of old ones, there will arise a new and greater Russia whose course through generations will command the gratitude, the wonder and admiration of mankind.(1) The ones who are able to unite the ethical, intellectual and practical genius of this people upon a sound economic and political platform from which all exploitation, confiscation, oppression and violence are removed, will lay the foundations of what can become the greatest future commonwealth and will leave to the most remote posterity the heritage of imperishable names.

Viewed in its world aspects and also as it more closely concerns the Russian people, it is pathetic to see that the international hatred and murder now so general over the earth, and the ambitions of imperialists in the east and west, render it all but impossible for Russia to save herself and to avoid those temporary alliances which may prove so difficult and dangerous to sever and which may impair her greatness and long retard the rise and liberties of her people.

The toilers should be most solemnly warned that international armies have always been and will always be the most useful and potent instruments in the hands

---
(1) Writing a few days after the fall of the Czar I predicted in *"The World Allies"* the principal events which have since transpired in Russia.

of plutocrats and autocrats for the suppression of the liberties of mankind. An international army is, unfortunately, not a new invention but rather one of those grim horrors from which men suffered for thousands of years and which has left its trail of death and destruction over the whole earth. Let there be no illusions as to the dangers involved in equipping an international League with an international army, numbering millions of men and it is only through such an arrangement, or through general armament by all principal nations constituting the League, that its decisions could be enforced unless there is complete disarmament, and only a small international fleet under the control of a League of Peoples and conducted by men who must answer to free parliaments. It is upon these grounds that the idea of a League of Nations is an illusion, in so far as it is put forward as a preventative of wars.

If such a League is formed it cannot do more than bring to bear upon all questions submitted to it those judicial considerations which may be taken to represent the conscience of mankind, in so far as this can ever be represented by proxy. Its deliberations would not be unlike those of the Hague tribunal and its scope could never be properly extended or safely sustained to a point enabling it to impose its decisions by force of arms. It could not resolve the international quarrels of plutocracy and it would not be permitted to deal with the vital domestic questions which now threaten the stability and progress of every European belligerent, neither would it be able peacefully to intervene in those issues of race and prejudice which the ruling castes have raised and fostered to serve their own ends. Even its most fair and impartial judgments could be ignored by its most powerful members.

Under whatever theory or upon whatever pretext the League may be formed, the interests of its members will continue to evolve on lines which are well defined and which can be projected into the future with almost as much certainty as they can be traced backward into the most remote past. These lines mark the national and world ambitions of the exploiting classes and indicate a movement which will be permanent and which will change only in its appearances, unless it is brought under the power of the toilers who in future may so organize as in fact to create a new world.

Any compacts signed by governments mean a perpetuation of nationalism which is the most harmful of all sentiments and most contrary to the interests of the common men and women of the whole world. Instead of bringing understanding, prosperity and peace to the masses, all attempted national isolation and local prejudice, dignified by the name of patriotism, and every institution which follows in the wake of such mistaken sentiments, tends to keep mankind divided into hostile camps and perpetuate the ignorance, poverty and economic slavery of the masses.[1]

As humanity has a common interest and moves towards a common goal, it must at all costs avoid every form of conflict which involves the destruction of the toilers, whose interests are identical and can only be served through peace.

International war must be rendered impossible and this can be accomplished; not through a League of Nations, whose decisions could only be enforced by war, but through complete disarmament and a world organization of toilers who have nothing to gain by violence. International boycotts can only lead to hatred and war. The strongest instinct in every realm of life is self-preservation and that involves a

---

[1] Happily for humanity, the time will come when men will refuse to carry passports. These are suited only to animals and slaves.

corresponding repugnance to violence. The unchangeable natural determination to preserve the individual life and the resistless passion to reproduce such life are the most general and potent forces of action in all the sentient world and every form of destruction, no matter in what realm, is a violation of the sacred law of life which is universal and changeless.

My scepticism as to the value of a League of Nations does not arise from any disbelief in the importance and possibility of such a League but rather because the actual rulers of nations will not establish the only basis upon which it would be possible to create an effective *League of Peoples.*

The only foundation upon which a League could rest is *complete disarmament for all nations* and this essential requisite will not be imposed by those who unfortunately will sign the treaty of so-called peace.

Neither exploitation nor war can be abolished so long as nations maintain naval and military establishments.

Before an effective League of Nations can be created there must be general disarmament and a strict provision that no arms are to be made in future except in one international factory strictly controlled by the League and the arms so made must be at the exclusive disposal of the League, which would maintain only a small international fleet to police the seas.

Any League of Nations which can now be organized will be nothing more than a political compact among governments controlled by capitalism and this does not afford any proper basis for general reconciliation or peace.

The creation of a great number of small states among people not accustomed to self-government, is fraught with dangers which can only be reduced to a minimum if no nation has at its disposal any armament and if all nations are obliged to refer all controversies to the final decision of the League.

The only way by which the decisions of the League could be imposed without future wars is through complete disarmament of all nations and the exercise by the League of measures of economic, political and social isolation. Such measures could not be imposed upon nations independently armed—without future wars.

The idea of a League of Nations is an illusion, not because it is wrong in principle, but because the only basis upon which it could be securely established is one which the forthcoming congress of "peace" will not create.

The imperialists and financial brigands who control all belligerent governments are too short-sighted and selfish to take the great steps which alone could save humanity from the disaster which now threatens organized society.

In *"The World Allies,"* published in 1917, I warned the ruling castes of the impending danger and gave reasons why the international murder might be followed by civil wars which would engulf all nations.

The steps which could be taken to avoid this calamity will not be taken and underneath the present show of power and the arrogant and tyrannical measures of belligerent governments there smoulders a volcano which is soon to explode and which will shake the foundations of social order throughout the world.

The rulers of mankind fail to realize the consequences which must follow as the logical sequence of their teaching, that under certain conditions it becomes a sacred duty to destroy the lives and property of other men.

There has been inculcated throughout the world a disregard for the sacredness of life and millions of men have been taught to believe that murder may be committed as a right in the defence of principles.

Under the orders of plutocracy the common men of the earth have scattered the lives of men as ashes over the sea and they have been honoured and applauded by a senseless world in proportion to such destruction which also included the property created by the disinherited toilers of earth.

It is inevitable that the patient and deluded masses will turn the whole of this mendacious system against its creators.

When the disillusioned millions, who were heralded as heroes realise that they are expected to return to the old grind of wage-slavery, it is inevitable that they will turn their terrible powers from the destruction of their brothers at the front to a dethronement of their exploiters at home.

In the face of this menace, which threatens the foundations of social order, the blind rulers of humanity are doing nothing to avert the world calamity which they have brought upon mankind, and there is no indication that any steps will be taken in this direction.

The allied rulers refer with indignation to the treaties of Brest and Bucharest, but they will probably impose similar treaties upon the Central Empires, failing to realize that the treaties they impose may be annulled by revolutions in the nations which impose them.

Instead of seeking an honourable reconciliation among peoples, there is every reason to believe that when the so-called statesmen of the Allies meet to settle their so-called peace they will do nothing more useful than to inflame the passions of men and turn against themselves a spirit of hatred and revenge which may lead to general violence as destructive as the unforgivable war. It may also lead to the creation of a second so-called League of Nations, composed of Russia, democratic Germany and Austria — with the Balkans, China and nearly all neutral states as members. That would be the final act but one in the forthcoming tragedy. It is to be hoped that such a course will be rendered impossible through the veto of Labour and Socialism.

Unless this is in fact done, humanity must not look to a League of Nations as an effective means of preventing wars, but rather to the measures I have prescribed and which alone can make it materially impossible for nations to engage in wars.

The value of a League of Nations rests solely in its ability to bring moral pressure upon one or another nation when there is involved a breach of good faith or justice, but when the issues are wholly imperial and financial and regarded as highly important, the division of interest will be so definitely marked that the judgment of mankind, in so far as the League might properly speak in the name of humanity, could only be given practical effect by a calamity from which mankind must be permanently rescued.

There are no questions having any legitimate claim to the consideration of men which cannot be settled by peaceful means and no issues could ever arise which can be justifiably settled by force. There is no proper division of interest among the millions in various nations and it is the solemn duty of the oppressed and exploited classes to make it forever impossible for the private designs of plutocracy to precipitate the general murder of men through war.

Nations are only gradually evolved. Their forms of government come slowly into being and are altered through the shifting of the balance of power from one class to another, or to several classes, but resting at all times in the hands of those whose interests are so organized as to give them the opportunity to make laws and the authority to enforce them. This obviously places in relatively few hands the great powers which may long be employed to defeat all popular aspirations and in some nations postpone almost indefinitely the measures desired by the masses who are unorganized and not effectively represented.

To change these conditions from within, when the people are not pressed to do so from without, is at best a slow and difficult undertaking. When however there is an outside attempt to dictate in the domestic affairs of a powerful people, it is likely to be used by their rulers as a means for the further consolidation of their powers through those appeals which never fail to find a response in the senseless pride and vanity of men, who will be told that their nation's independence is endangered by an outside menace and that they must show their national spirit and honour by ignoring all attempted outside interference in their local affairs[1]. That this will be the result of the present agitation admits of little doubt unless the masses resort to force and that is a course which they should at all hazards avoid.

This leads me in complete fairness and free from any conscious prejudice, to note an important difference which is strongly emphasized in the evolution of the people of the United States and Germany and because

---

[1] This tendency is only deviated from when national ruling castes are no longer able to resist outside military pressure and if they capitulate, under such circumstances, the power passes from autocrats to plutocrats but not to the people, because the masses do not rise to genuine self-government except by slow degrees. A democracy cannot be established by decrees or proclamations but only upon the foundations of general economic independence, personal self-government and a universal and popular initiative.

of which there is inevitably a wide divergence of view among the masses in these two nations respecting all questions as to the proper scope of governments. Also as to the importance of individual initiative and personal independence so strongly expressed in the United States, as distinguished from the German sentiment which attaches an exaggerated value to the power of the mass and to a discipline through which individualism is effaced.

There is in Germany some remnant of feudalism from which France and England so long suffered but from which America has happily always been free. The prerogatives which aristocrats take unto themselves, tend in Germany to aggravate caste distinctions more than in England, because they are exercised in Germany by those whose chief desire is to hold a military post, whereas in England the chief desire of the aristocracy is to do nothing whatever. The arrogance therefore of a high official in the German army arises in the line of first importance because of his caste in German society and through which he would in any event disdain ordinary people. When this is coupled to the pretensions of the military caste it results in a special type of man not to be found in France or America. This is due to the fact that in these latter countries there is a total repudiation of hereditary aristocracy, except among the vain and the rich who still desire to associate titles which mean nothing, to money which buys nearly everything. In England where they flunkey to the old titles and sell the new ones, those who belong to the real and therefore the ancient aristocracy do nothing unless they are quite poor and the new crops of industrial aristocrats are so occupied with money-making that they know nothing about anything else. When the titles which once stood for some great distinction in England are held by poor but deserving aristocrats, so long as the holders can keep out of the bankruptcy courts, they are useful as decorations on the boards of joint stock companies or their possessors live in modest obscurity and are unknown except to those who diligently study the Blue Book or Whitaker's Almanack.

Until the whole of the pretensions now assumed by aristocrats, plutocrats and priests are set aside through the international union and rise of the toilers there will be no proper commonwealth, no freedom from arrogance, no general economic security, intellectual independence or international peace.

If the castes which are responsible for the present ghastly position of the masses are not entirely blind to their own interests they will see that these interests are for the future inseparably linked to the common interest of all men. The ruling classes will be well advised if they do not seek to place any obstacles in the way of the patient masses who may yet be induced to pursue their ends without violence, but who may also easily be led into the folly of a destruction which will be more disastrous than the shameless war. As these lines are being written in February 1918, the fuse is laid and reaches around the world. The common man is at bay and when he has ceased to murder his brothers at the front it will require more than the shallow speeches of ministers and the vague promises of governments to prevent him murdering his only actual enemies who have not been at the front, but who in his own land, have made fabulous paper fortunes upon the ruin of those who create all wealth. If the proposals I have put forward[1] in which I have shown why the toilers must not resort to violence, are not followed, there will be no escape from a general social revolution

---

[1] *"The World Allies."*

which will be more extended and terrible than any of the mighty tragedies enacted since the world began.

In the United States the common soldier who passes his time in idleness in the barracks is regarded as a worthless fellow who is either good for nothing or who has failed at everything. His position is lower than that of the most ordinary labourer, whereas the officials who are trained at West Point represent a reliable but not a brilliant type of young Americans, but it is almost impossible for young men to enter such a career without the aid of influence at Washington. It must however in fairness be said that the most intelligent and promising men do not find any attractions in a military career which are at all comparable to the great inducements offered in business and the law. It is for these reasons that the ablest men in the United States do not aspire to a military career.

Usually these men are either quite poor or have only modest incomes and therefore are free from those temptations to arrogance which always surround the children of aristocrats and plutocrats. The general aversion of the people of the United States towards a standing army, the restricted career which it affords even to officers and the feeling so strongly held by the people of that country that one man is as good as another, that the great man is the one who does things on the biggest scale and that the only men who are worthless and to be despised are those who do nothing, all tend to prevent the display of any arrogance on the part of military officers towards civilians.

In England when the son of a gentleman or of a prosperous shopkeeper has no talent or ability, every effort is made to provide him a place either in the army or the church, since neither the one nor the other offers the least inducement to men of the first order of capacity and intelligence. The effect is that as intellectual and practical pursuits are everywhere multiplying and their scope, variety and importance are constantly extended, they engage an ever increasing proportion of the best men, with the inevitable result that the intellectual and executive capacity of those who follow the professions of war and religion is constantly declining and will continue to decline. It is a movement which has been in progress for centuries, not only in England but throughout Europe, and while it may appear to offer occasional exceptions, the great and steady trend of this important aspect of civilization has in fact been uninterrupted. It points to a definite end which, if it may be remote, is none the less inevitable and that is the complete loss of authority, honour or respect for both of these professions. This desirable result will be brought about by internationalism, which will abolish war, and through the progress of science and general intellectual culture which will put an end to intolerance, existing creeds and priestcraft.

The importance which this movement has for humanity is beyond the power of imagination now to forecast except in its broad outlines, but it is one of the most inspiring consolations to be gained by patient study that this tendency is shown upon all the pages of history and that it has been accompanied by the corresponding rise in the intellectual life and in the liberties of all peoples. This must be taken in the sense that all true progress depends upon the elevation of the masses. Only those movements which have the power to influence and raise the people, as distinguished from a selected caste among a people, can be classed as of first importance to mankind. The ideal commonwealth of the future towards which man slowly moves, will be one in which the only good will be the good of all, and the only greatness will be the collective freedom, independence, intelligence and dignity of the whole. How remote this is from our generation it would be idle to forecast, but the steps by which it may be hastened and attained are indicated in my books. They are steps which must be taken and which humanity will take, be it soon or late, because they must follow in the sequence of events which have carried our civilization to the brink of ruin and from which it can be rescued only by measures adapted to its present and its future needs and conceived in the interests of humanity as a whole.

In America the spirit and practice of the people is to do what they are forbidden to do, whereas the contrary is the spirit and practice of the masses in Germany.

The paternal interference of the government from which England is so free—and which so long stood in the path of the French and from which they still suffer greatly—is more pronounced in Germany than elsewhere among the leading Western nations. It is the most serious obstacle to be overcome by any people in their rise to the right and power of self-government.

Government regulation of private actions and its interference in the occupations or habits of the people takes a form in America which is less harmful than in Germany because with one exception, which I shall presently note, the interference of government in a paternal sense in America is confined almost exclusively to tariff legislation. Fortunately for the people of that country the protective spirit, usually so pronounced among Puritans, has not been a guiding principle of control in the most important realms of human endeavour. It has created vast monopolies which involve problems of the highest concern in the minds of those who wish the ordered progress and the general welfare of that great country. It has made vast fortunes for a few men but it has not prevented the opening of a rich and beautiful continent as a place of refuge for scores of millions of the oppressed and wretched ones, who fled from conditions which they were unable longer to combat in Europe. The ships of hope, upon which have sailed millions whose only asset was despair, were anchored on the shores of what has been in fact a promised land.

The fusion of these races into a mighty nation, devoted to ordered progress, records the most outstanding and remarkable example of the capacity of men and women of all races to rise under tolerable surroundings and to live in amity and peace.

The exception above noted in which the governmental authority in the United States has sought directly to interfere in the personal liberty of the people upon a great scale is in its legislation respecting alcoholic drinks. It may be laid down as a principle, which is illustrated by all human experience, that crime results, not so much from the inherent viciousness of the offender as from the surroundings in which he is placed. It is upon this theory that those who are responsible for prohibition in America contend that the government is justified in direct and paternal interference in the most personal liberty of the people. In principle the homes and the countries which are best governed are those in which there are the fewest prohibitions and in which the people are therefore the most capable of self-government.

If the right to enact legislation prohibiting the sale of alcoholic drinks is admitted—not as a sound principle of government but as a protective measure against what may be a disease—it follows that it is both the manufacture and importation of alcoholic drinks which should be prohibited, rather than the sale and that in order to be effective in America this prohibition must be upon a national scale. As long as such drinks are made or obtainable in any part of America they will be consumed in prohibited territory and the consumers will be demoralized more by the hypocrisy involved than by the drink consumed.

It may be said for prohibition in America that its saloons are a horror, only approached by the public houses in England and that they greatly aggravate the drink evil. Also that where prohibition is the most general and effective it is enacted by substantial majorities who were in practice teetotallers without reference to prohibition and who regard the drinking of alcohol in any form as a disease from which the minority must now be protected, even against its will and from which future generations must be freed. Considering the present state of society and the tendency of mankind to imitate the vices of others in preference to their virtues, there is much to be said in favour of prohibition if it is general and effective wherever it is sought to be applied. Those for whom prohibition is not necessary, because of their moderation, may tolerate this interference in their liberty and this departure from the sound principles of government on the condition that it is not extended to the general and other concerns of life.

It may be said that a great part of the paternal interference in personal affairs in Germany is by the wish and with the moral assent of majorities. In so far as this is in fact true it only the more clearly illustrates my contention, which is that in proportion as a people are willing to admit the right of others to regulate matters which are not the concern of others, they continue in a state of moral and political infancy which is well suited to the purposes of aristocracy and priests, but not suitable as the solid basis of personal independence and consequently of collective self-government.

When people offend against themselves through a violation of natural laws, they learn in time that there is over them a nature which strikes the offender as often as he offends and he thus learns a self-control which does not violate his nature. When he offends against propriety and good taste the sole restraint should be that he forfeits the consideration of others and this will ultimately act as the most effective deterrent which can operate among free men. When however, it is sought, by prohibitions and government regulations to prevent either of these classes of offence, the effect upon the people is to delay their attainment of personal self-government and suppress those great and noble sentiments of personal dignity and independence. Force is suitable only for slaves, but self-respect is the highest attribute of free men.

It is precisely in this line of legislation or in executive policy that the German system of government enters into the ordinary affairs of the daily life of the people in ways which have naturally tended to retard self-government, because there are too many things which are either prohibited or paternally controlled.

The German masses are sentimental and unaffectedly simple and as they also believe in specialization it is natural they should regard politics and war as highly complicated professions which must be left to experts. The use which has been made of the confidence, the patience and the docility of the millions of toilers is a shameful outrage against the most sacred rights of man. One of its unfortunate effects will be to long interfere with the diffusion, in other nations, of some of the most important riches of the human intellect.[1]

---

[1] It may not be amiss here to note that I am an American, whose

This great people who before the Reformation looked to the clergy for guidance in all things, naturally fell into an error almost equally fatal of allowing the government to assume the places from which the priests had been cast down. There inevitably followed a form of temporal paternalism which can only be gradually suspended, but which must be generally eradicated as a preliminary to political and personal freedom. It will require a long time before the German people will cease to look to the government for anything and will have a government which must in all things look to the people. The only way by which the route to this goal may be shortened is through the combination of the labour unions and Socialists in such an organization as I have urged, but the measures essential to secure a government which will be liberal and at the same time stable, must not comprehend violence in any form. They must not seek to substitute a new injustice for an old one. They must seek a more fair and general distribution of the vast material and intellectual wealth which has been created. I would lay special emphasis upon the latter because of the almost impassable gulf which separates the intellectual aristocracy of that country from the masses. In science, philosophy, literature and music, Germany has long occupied the highest place in the world and to her belongs the honour as the birthplace of the originator of that great and far-reaching movement which resulted in the liberation of the human intellect from some of its most dismal superstitions and

---

family has resided continuously in that country since 1641 and whose paternal ancestor was the first treasurer of the Dutch Colony in America. Also as these lines are written, my son aged 19, is a volunteer private soldier in the American army and is now serving in an air squadron in France. He is another of those young men whom the press, the priests and the politicians induced to leave school in England and offer his life under the illusion that this shameless war is a crusade for liberty, when in fact it is nothing but an international murder of innocent men for imperialism and high finance.

fears. The credit for these high achievements does not attach to the government of that country, since governments do not lead but always follow human progress. It attaches to those immortal men whose genius often conducted them to prisons, but rarely admitted them to palaces. The philosophers of Germany have reached intellectual heights and a comprehensiveness which are not approached by the men of any other nation, but the great light of these intellects has remained the property of a strictly limited number, forming an intellectual aristocracy to which alone the most bold and profound speculations have been addressed, while the masses of the German people have remained superstitious and almost uninfluenced by the great freedom of thought and genius of their most illustrious countrymen.

As a direct contrast to this condition we observe in the United States that the gulf between the greatest minds and the masses is so narrow as to admit of being crossed by millions. This may be accounted for by the fact that the standard of philosophic attainment is not high in America and that the small contributions which that country has made to speculative thought are widely read and understood. They are read because they were written in a language which the masses could read and understand rather than in an involved, complicated and discursive language such as the great German philosophers employed and which only a philosopher can read and comprehend.

Important as is the effect of government policy upon the masses there is a still more powerful agency which operates in the life of all peoples and to which may be traced not only their personal and collective evolution and freedom, but also the form of government which is alone applicable to their various stages of development. This agency must be measured by the height of intellectual culture, speculative philosophy and ideals of political independence attained by a few men and the thoroughness with which these ideals are spread among the people and generally understood.

If the great philosophers of the latter half of the seventeenth century in England and of the eighteenth century in France had written only to their own class and in Greek, the vast movements which raised the people in these two countries and set in motion the great aspirations for personal independence and the rights of man would not have been recorded. The philosophers in those countries might have attained greater heights, but they would not have so profoundly influenced the people.

German philosophers ignored the masses and while they thus rose above the restrictions imposed upon a man who seeks to address the public, they likewise remain uncomprehended by the public. The masses were therefore deprived of those teachings which they might have followed to the attainment of personal and collective liberty and to the realization of a mode of individual and national life which would not need to be governed by prohibitions and in which the term "Verboten" and all that it implies, would not become the most general and conspicuous evidence of authority. It logically follows that the attitude of a people who must on all hands pay heed to prohibitions will be more influenced and impressed by force than a people such as the Americans, among whom "Thou shalt not" is almost a negligible quantity and who would not play the flunkey to someone whom fortune has placed above them, or kick those whom misfortune places below them.

The self-control voluntarily and continuously imposed by an individual over his own acts is the most important safeguard for himself and for any society which seeks to establish the institutions of justice and liberty by the assent and under the sovereignty of the people.

So long as men are governed by constant prohibitions they cannot attain the independence and reliability of character upon which alone the institutions of genuine freedom may be founded. All such policy on part of the church and state is wrong and constitutes one of the principal obstacles on the path of human progress.

America has produced only one intellect in any way comparable to the illustrious philosophers of Germany and his speculations are directed to such different ends that there is no ground for comparison, except to say that in future generations, to be measured by centuries, the great Emerson will be read with an ever increasing sense of veneration for his genius and of profound gratitude for the lofty and noble sentiments which he bequeathed to mankind. These cannot now be read without a feeling that much which he might have said remains unwritten through his amiable deference to prejudices which he did not attempt directly to oppose. As might be expected he did not stoop in any manner to gain popular favour and held aloof, as befits all who would serve mankind, from any flattery of the public. He belongs to remote posterity because of his greatness and his contempt for those transient honours constantly bestowed by an unthinking public upon men whose intellectual frippery is touted as wares in the marketplace soon to be buried in oblivion. The wind passes over them and they are gone, while the great contributions to human speculation directed to a higher and a freer age remain the permanent heritage of man.

How slowly great and essential reforms must be brought about is still to be learned through many generations. How little this is realized or at all grasped is shown in almost countless ways; some of which are strangely touching and would be truly admirable, were it not for the dangers which lie hidden under these sentiments, through the use made of them by an impersonal plutocracy, which has no sentiment.

I received the other day a letter in which one who occupies a great position with men at the front is quoted as follows: "All the troops are talking about, is the beautiful new world that will follow this war. Soldiers say it is the only thing worth going over the top for. An admiral has told me it was the same in the navy."

Alas! the new world to which these men will return! They will learn with indignation and sorrow that it is only they who have been changed by war. The men who sent them to the front have not changed and these men rule the world. The ones who have made sacrifices at the front belong to the same classes that have suffered at home, but the ones who dictate the policy of nations have not been near the front and have not suffered at home. They have, on the contrary, built palaces of paper wealth upon the general ruin of the common man. Out of his torrents of blood, have come rivers of wealth for plutocracy.

Upon a world which they have plundered, shattered and smothered with debts, these exploiters and imperialists will try to build a new structure of so-called civilization which will not be unlike the old, except in its more general and effective economic pressure and its more complete subjugation of the common men. The most shameful aspect of this monstrous policy is its design to snare millions of women and chain them by starvation wages to machines and they are reaching out after the children with the same grips which have held the men. The reception of the poor soldiers is being prepared in advance. If they were but able to understand what it all means they could now read it on every hand in the banking, shipping and industrial amalgamations, in the plans being made by armament makers for the continuation of their nefarious business, in the schemes being put forward for extension of government ownership and dominion in private affairs, also in the proposed impossible boycott of nations and in the ballot for women. Also in the employment and training of millions of these deluded women as competitors of men and in the campaign of sowing hatred among the common people of the various nations, in order to prevent them from coming to an international accord for the protection of their common interests and the honour of their class. At the same time these exploiters are making all preparations to resume their old international understandings and create new ones upon financial and industrial lines as soon as peace is signed. Capital will continue to be international, without country, race or religion, with its old creed of exploitation, profits and power and will always act upon the golden rule of plutocracy which is "Do unto others what others wish to do unto you—and do it first."

The ones who exercise great, although indirect political power through the possession of property are able to pass this power on to posterity for only a limited time. This should be the subject of further restrictions and the right of inheritance should be radically curtailed. No man should be able to accumulate the great fortunes now made possible through industrialism. Until they can be no longer accumulated, the right to dispose of them through bequest should be strictly controlled, allowing only a reasonable sum to be passed on—and then only to one generation. The whole of the remainder should not be employed upon armies and navies but in ways which would enable every man who toils to own his home and a spot of earth where his last years may be spent in security and peace.

Usually the men who make great fortunes are aware of the dangers involved for those who are to inherit what they did nothing to earn and which they generally do not know how to use. Such men have not seriously objected to the enactment of measures which would tend to prevent the indefinite bequest of their wealth, as applied to third and succeeding generations. This is partly due to the slight interest which most men have for distant posterity and partly to the feeling that property which they bequeath may be passed on to future generations through continuing bequests if only from one generation to the next. Were it not for the constant proof to the contrary which man has thrust upon him from all sides, he would not believe that one who has nothing to do but spend the income he has inherited, would be so short-sighted as also to squander the capital, because he is totally unqualified to make a fortune. If the money collected by governments through income taxes and death duties were wisely and judiciously spent by business men, under a sound system of control and the rigid application of business methods, instead of being thrown away by politicians in great part for harmful and destructive objects, the average rich man of business would find even a higher incentive to make and bequeath money than he now has. He now realizes that what he acquires by his toil and self-denial is likely to be thrown away by harmful governments or spent in idleness and indulgence, without the slightest service to society and to the permanent harm of his own offspring.

It will be considered that restrictions upon a man's

right to bequeath anything beyond a definite and specified sum may retard human progress through the removal of one of man's highest incentives to create and keep wealth; that if a man could not bequeath to his descendants what he creates, he would not make those great sacrifices which are indispensable to all important success in life and that this would be a distinct loss to mankind. This does not in fact have the importance which appears to attach to it, because those who work for salaries and wages have no alternative but steadily to toil for their current needs and by way of hoping to make provision against age; while those who succeed in establishing a moderate or great business are not able to abandon it for a variety of reasons. If they retire from business they usually die in a short time from inactivity, because the average man has no great intellectual or other interests to which he can turn when his business career is at an end and he is therefore reluctant to retire. Again those who create or dominate a business feel themselves indispensable to its continued success even after they have long ceased to be requisite, or it may be difficult for a man to discontinue his connection with a business because he is in fact indispensable to it. In all of these circumstances men continue to devote their lives to what may amount to money-making when in fact they have no need or desire to make money. The ones who come under this heading constitute a greater percentage of the total of successful men than will be realized except by those who have had the opportunities of associating upon equal terms with men of great material achievements and of being able to judge as to the motives which dominate their lives.

As all things are relative and as most men who enter business with the primary object of making money, continue for the reasons given, long after they have made even great fortunes, the basis of inheritance could be established at a definite maximum, not too high, and above which a man could only bequeath a small percentage of what he accumulated.

This is partly dealt with through the inheritance tax in some countries, but the percentage of inheritance tax is not sufficiently great and the uses to which the money is applied by the state are so wasteful, senseless and destructive, that either a wise or prudent man resents the feeling that what he has earned or saved will not be spent, either by his descendants or in ways that are of the slightest use to strangers and still these considerations do not deter men from struggling and accumulating all their lives. As restrictions upon the right to bequeath property at death become more rigid the bequests will be made during the life of the donor to give effect to his natural sentiments regardless of all laws which seek to repress or regulate human affections. The right to make bequests of what belongs to a man while he lives is so elemental that it should never be interfered with or in any way questioned and could only become of concern to society in so far as it was used for the obvious purpose of evading a just tax. As humanity will always have before it such experiences as those of old King Lear there will not be a general or reckless giving of fortunes during the life of their possessors.

It is confirmed by all experience that most men are disposed to abandon their most legitimate aims in proportion as these appear to be incapable of realization. If it were not for the perseverance and greatness of exceptional men there would be no political or intellectual progress and what now constitutes the whole of man's inspiring achievements would have been unrecorded.

It is because some men conceive designs for a better society and persist in the struggle for their attainment that society has made any progress through the ages. As parliaments always follow but never lead public opinion it is essential to institute means which will enable a small minority, to whom all progress is due, to force the issue upon all questions of importance. This can be accomplished on political grounds only through the establishment of the initiative, which would require that measures should be submitted to a general and secret ballot upon petition of two per cent of the electorate and when sanctioned by the majority of all votes cast, they should become law. This would remedy the almost hopeless inertia of parliaments which now have the power through evasion and inaction to delay for years the most important measures tending to benefit the masses. So difficult is it to induce legislators to take affirmative action upon large and general lines that in some instances more than a generation may pass in the agitation of most pressing reforms which, under the initiative could be forced to adoption in a few months.

In Federal governments, such as the United States and Switzerland, this initiative should apply to the local affairs of States and Cantons as well as to the Federation. Any self-governing body should have the right to use its most ample powers for any steps it might wish to take in advance of other parts of a Federation to which it belonged. No measures passed by local or federal assemblies should become law until they were submitted to a general referendum of the voters in the locality or nation.

As voters do not wish to be too often called upon to vote, unless it involves a holiday, such measures would tend to diminish the number of laws passed and this would be a great boon to humanity. It would be sufficient if one day in a year were set aside in which to vote upon projected laws. These should be printed in booklet form and placed in the hands of all voters six months previous to the balloting.

These powers would place in the hands of the masses a means by which they could compel the opportune adoption of measures deemed essential by the majority and prevent the enforcement of any legislation which might be contrary to the wishes of the people.

There should also be generally adopted a "nominating ballot" to apply to municipal, county, state and federal offices and which would transfer the selection of candidates for all offices from the dictates of political machines into the hands of the people. So far as I am aware this would be quite a new method of selecting candidates, as distinguished from voting for a choice between "a" and "b" in whose selection the voters have no effective voice.

The names of candidates should be written upon ballots by each voter and any man eligible to vote should be qualified to hold any office which the people might wish to bestow in their discretion—uncontrolled in any way by political machines. Any voter who refrained from using his franchise in nominating a candidate should be disqualified to vote at the election. Even under such extensions of the rights of franchise the political groups would continue to exercise through the press a far-reaching influence in the selection of candidates. The press has the power to create and use public opinion in ways so indirect and subtle as to be incomprehensible to the masses. Most people do not realize that they have no opinions of their own and that the press does for them what little thinking there is, respecting the merits of men and the importance, meaning and effect of given measures of public policy. This will long remain the experience of mankind.

Anyone who has attended local and national nominating conventions is aware of how little importance are the wishes of majorities. They are almost as unimportant as in time of war. In local primaries the most responsible voters rarely take any active participation because they know that the machines have decided upon their candidates and that their decisions will be effective.

In national conventions the hundreds of delegates are nothing but figure-heads to record what amounts to the nominal sanction of the millions whom they are supposed to represent. The political machines prepare a list of the various committees. The officers of the convention are agreed and the majority of delegates do nothing except to vote as they are told to vote, or as is generally the rule, they go to the conventions with instructions from their local machines as to how they must vote. In this latter case these self-important delegates are nothing but the messenger boys of the machines which created them and their vote might with equal effect and with much less noise, trouble and expense have been registered by post. It is however all a part of the decoration which adorns the so-called democracies and which, under a show of popular participation in government, tends to keep the public in a state of mental and political sleepiness so well suited to the designs of plutocrats and so enthusiastically admired by priests.

The candidates who emerge from the heroic labour of these imposing conventions are men most likely to appeal to the fancy of the rabble, which does not look beneath the surface, from men to principles and which does not therefore discern its own vital interest. The votes of democracies are divided between the two dominant parties and whichever wins, the toilers who constitute the majority of all voters, invariably lose. They lose because they do not know how to advance their economic interest through the one political means at their disposal and they do not effectively organize in order that they might use the economic power available to them through industrial union.

The ideal candidate for the political machines is a man whom the press has glorified because of his successful murder of men through war, and when such candidates are available they are invariably selected by nominating conventions. It never occurs to politicians to choose a great scientist, whose patient research may have saved the lives of millions and to whose discoveries man owes his most important conquests of nature, neither would they nominate a philosopher to whose principles future generations will pay tribute. Political machines choose either the popular hero of war or some apparently innocuous person, whom they believe will carry out their designs and from whom the people will not withhold their votes on account of some racial or religious prejudice. If a war hero is not available the ideal candidate for the machines is some outwardly respectable person whom nobody has ever heard of and whose activities have been so modest, so obscure or so inconsequential that he has incurred no powerful enmity. This enables the press to paint his portrait in the style dictated by the party machine in order that he may appear to respond to the divergent sentiments, whims and interests of the masses whose votes are sought. He must be all things to all men and must know how to play upon the cupidity, vanity and ignorance of mankind, which if done upon a national scale is no mean achievement for a man who seeks temporary fame.

It is interesting to note that no Roman Catholic has held the office of President of the United States and that no political party has risked the nomination of a Roman Catholic for that office or in general for the most important elective offices in the nation, although there are millions of Roman Catholics in the country and probably no candidate for the presidency could be elected against their united opposition. Such a division of voters is not likely to occur because men are controlled more by their interests than by their religion. They may profess to believe that it is essential to be a Catholic or a Protestant in order to be saved—whatever may be meant by the term—but in practice they postpone the intangible things of another world to the tangible affairs of the world in which they live, but it would be unthinkable to nominate a man who did not profess any religion or belong to any church!

That state in the emancipation of the human intellect will be attained only in the remote future. It holds those precious gems to be found only after the passing of ages and to be treasured only by greater, truer and freer generations who will follow the slow-moving hands of time. We may mourn over the delay but humanity takes the longest route to arrive at its surest ends and we must deal with humanity as it is. This does not justify any hopes that its freedom may be readily attained. The greatest achievements of man are still reserved for that superior race which will look back to our bigotry, superstition, ignorance and injustice with feelings of pity and scorn.

There is a long road to travel before mankind can arrive at anything approximating the ideal social state

and this can only be surely attained through an evolution
which will raise man above all that he now holds as the
most essential and even considers the most sacred of his
institutions. One of the chief obstacles to human progress
is the slavish regard for traditions which give authority
to some of the most reactionary and oppressive measures
established by the few to consolidate their control. If
these traditions are traced to their origin it is seen that
they could have arisen only in a world in which a few men
were masters and all the rest were slaves. This is not a
condition which the common man has the least interest to
perpetuate and yet he is in fact most reluctant of all
society to abandon what he should never have believed
and what he must reject before he can hope to be free.

This strange and most depressing tendency of the
masses would seem to be traceable to the fact that they
have never thought for themselves, that in principle
they are incapable of ordered reason and that they can
be easily led to see a danger to themselves in what
only threatens the special interests of their oppressors.
The excessive respect for caste is more strongly shown
among the dependent and ignorant than in other grades
of society and because of this feeling the masses are prone
to look outside their own ranks for intellectual guidance
and material leadership, without having the intelligence
to realize that those upon whom they rely have their
own interests to serve and that these are in conflict with
the interests of the masses whom the ruling castes
inwardly despise, whose elevation out of their lower ranks
is feared and into whose ranks those more highly placed
seldom have the desire or courage to descend. Because
of the dignity inherent in the breast of every man, the
most humble look for their possible rise to other castes
as more natural and less an occasion of remark or wonder

than a similar change would be regarded from a higher to a lower station.

In war and industry the tendency of men is to more readily obey an order which comes from a caste superior to their own, than from one of their own social or economic rank. It is therefore the policy of aristocracy and plutocracy not only to perpetuate but to augment this sentiment. There is only one remedy for such an attitude as applied to men in general and that is the sense of personal dignity arising through economic independence, which enables men to feel that it is by their own right and power, rather than through the favour of someone else, that they are entitled to their position among men.

The ones who control the means by which men live control their lives. The independence of the small peasant arises from the fact that his means of life are exclusively under his control, whereas the millions of industrial toilers are only a commodity controlled by world forces, and their constant and pressing necessities compel them to accept whatever they can get.

These poor and oppressed men cannot await the favoured opportunities of season, neither can they profit by the bounty of nature through laying in stores when they are comparatively cheap. Thus it is that human life, instead of being sacred, is everywhere for sale at all hours of the day and night and is purchased at a price and under conditions which should make the angels weep.

It is not possible or desirable to reduce the industrial importance of machinery in the great productive activities of man, but it is possible and essential to so raise the importance of man that he shall be the master and not the slave of his machine, that he shall have a capital value as well as the machine, that he shall be cared for and that when he and the machine are both worn out he shall no longer be consigned to the same scrap heap as a machine which has served its use. The steps which must be taken to attain this end and how little practical use the toilers can make of any political institution so long as they are unorganized are shown in "*The World Allies.*" Until these steps are taken there will be no economic justice, no proper commonwealth and no peace.

It is evident from the manner and bearing of certain men that they are by nature endowed with the capacity for power which implies the possession of a surplus of brute force, generally lacking in the most perfect types of men. Those whose philosophy and purposes are the most noble are generally deficient in the animal energy essential to constructive action and indispensable in the exercise of great but strictly temporary executive powers.

The men who are regarded in all justice as the most notable benefactors of the race were unable to do more than indicate the ideals of a new social order, while it remained for inferior men of action to take all the steps which have been taken towards the realization of the ideals. These men of action bear to the philosopher a relation similar to that of a carpenter or brick-layer towards the architect who designs a beautiful and noble temple. Each is indispensable to the other, each underrates the importance of the other and considers his own part as the only one which is essential. It is because of this difference in intellect and interest that great projects are designed and that they may be carried to completion. When man has risen to sufficient intelligence and the sentiments of humanity are enlarged beyond those narrow boundaries of local and national divisions of mankind, there will evolve a means by which the wisdom and greatness of exceptional men throughout the world may directly and usefully intervene in political matters with results of the highest importance and value for humanity. It may be reserved to a remote future, but the time will come, when the great scientists and philosophers will be called to legislate because men will have outgrown a policy of evasion, compromise and patch-work. Legislation must follow the ordered and unchanging principles, which are understood only by scientists and philosophers.

If the intellectual and moral elite of mankind could be directly represented by its own members chosen from its national or international class, they would profoundly influence parliamentary action even though they were not of sufficient numerical importance to control any parliament. At present the highest value of these classes is unused because they cannot bring their views to the attention of legislators in a form which would compel them to be seriously considered and openly debated before the public.

A large percentage of all legislation which retards human progress is enacted in ignorance of its significance because it is framed by ignorant men. Even when it is not influenced by personal or ulterior motives, it is at best only a succession of wretched piecework, without large conception or design, and quite inadequate as the sound basis of an ordered progress toward the highest ends well within the reach of mankind.

If men like Darwin, Pasteur, Kant, Hume, Locke, or Adam Smith could have a direct part in the drafting and parliamentary discussion of laws they would soon put an end to a great part of the senseless rubbish which is now dignified by the name of parliamentary debates. As parliaments are now constituted they never contain any of the most illustrious men, because such men will never sacrifice any part of their intellectual independence or descend to the level demanded by the rabble from men who are hunting for office and therefore begging for votes. Not until men of great distinction or highest attainments can enter parliaments as the representatives of their own class and answerable to no one for their opinions and placed above all ignorant popular prejudice, will such men ever have the slightest personal participation in political power. Even under the most favoured circumstances they would only consent to such an intrusion upon their time, if it were recognized that their presence conferred an honour upon any congress and that no honours within the disposal of any group of politicians were of the slightest importance.

No great business could be conducted to any end except ruin unless it had in all departments men who were experts in a given line and yet the great and important business of legislation, upon every conceivable subject, is carried on by men who are specialists in nothing but making shallow speeches; whereas it should be framed by those who are the most learned in political economy, natural sciences, social history and philosophy.

Such men would be wise enough to so legislate in accordance with great, enduring and general principles, that there would soon be an end to the legislative quackery and experimenting displayed by parliaments.

These debating societies spend this year in repealing laws which they solemnly spent last year in passing and they consider their labour of both years as an exhibition of the highest political wisdom.

CHAPTER VIII.

INDUSTRIALIZATION OF WOMEN AND NATIONALIZATION OF INDUSTRY.

If the position of women as toilers and their relations to men are regarded comprehensively, there is seen the constant and general tendency for women to depart from their natural sphere of labour in proportion to the difficulty encountered by men in providing the means of life, or in proportion as the products of toil are diverted from the productive to the non-productive classes. The effect of industrial exploitation is now seen in the rapidly altering status of women. This is one of the most sinister aspects of the great problems whose solution cannot be long deferred and which will be aggravated in proportion as the labour of women is exploited by capitalism along the great lines of industrial conflict.

In primitive stages among uncivilized tribes while the men hunted and fought, the women did all the other work. Among roving tribes there were no houses to care for and the woman's time was spent in preparing food, making coarse garments, caring casually for the children and arranging the camp.

In the tropics where a bountiful nature made easily possible an excess of production over consumption, there resulted an accumulation of wealth without which no class would enjoy sufficient leisure to enable any people to rise above savagery. In that state of society the masses were slaves and the few performed no labour of any sort.

In the gardual evolution of humanity the position of master and slave has been maintained, although the basis has constantly altered. Passing through feudalism to a more extended distribution of property, there was still a great concentration of land in a few hands and those who tilled the soil were wretchedly housed, poorly fed and passed their lives in drudgery and want. The evolution from this stage to that of tenants was only accomplished through wide-spread struggles and civil wars and the position of the average tenant remained much as it had previously been. The children of these tenant-farmers were generally forced to find employment as wage-earners.

This condition is still in an aggravated state in England. In France, Germany and the United States the small holders have gradually increased, but there are indications that a new form of concentration is evolving in most of these nations, either through the sale of small farms to larger landholders and the migration of the former owners to industrial centres, or through the extensive mortgaging of farms. To some extent these mortgages represent the rise of the tenants to the position of proprietor, but not to the extent that is desirable for the best results to agriculture or the genuine independence of this important class.

During the thirty years preceding the war the greatest changes took place in the United States; due in part to the development of vast areas not before under cultivation and to the abolition of the extensive cattle-ranges in the southern and western territories. Conditions in Europe altered more gradually and have been so influenced by local causes that any generalization upon the subject, amounting to the definition of a world tendency, is extremely difficult beyond the broad principle that small farms, in the hands of their owners, have been proved to be not only the most efficiently and economically worked but also that their increase in numbers, and in the percentage of the total farming areas, afford the most solid basis for the stability and well-being of all states, and that only in proportion as that movement is accompanied by the elevation of industrial toilers to the proprietorship of their homes, can the creation of a proper commonwealth be approached.

Farming, as distinguished from industry, does not prosper through the amalgamation of a great number of units into one enterprise. As farm machinery can be purchased by the small farmer and as science has brought the means of fertilization and rotation of crops within the easy reach of those who cultivate only small areas, there is more to be lost than gained by attempting generally to apply to farming the principles of industrial centralization.

It is safe to predict that the small farmer will remain a great and increasing factor in the life of the world. There is no independence enjoyed by any other form of labour which can be compared to that of the class which owns and cultivates its land. If one observes the attitude of men living in an industrial community where there is only one employer of thousands he will realise that this employer has more power over the lives and often over the sentiments of the people, than the distant parliament or king who may be their nominal ruler. When these toilers are compared to the small farmers on the prairies of America or in the mountains of Switzerland it is amazing to see the difference in their attitude of independence and liberty. The farmers are free men and women because they are economically independent, while the industrial toilers are wage-slaves, whose precarious economic status is a handicap to all political progress and a barrier against all sturdy independence.

In the ancient autocracies and under all forms of feudalism, the liberties of the people were in proportion to their economic independence of the ruler. This arises from a principle which will never change. It is as true in the present industrial feudalism as in any ancient time.

In localities where the land is held in small tracts by peasants or where conditions of soil or climate require the maximum of labour for an average or minimum production, the men, women and children share in the common lot of toil and this is not an ideal condition. By comparison, however, with the industrial wage-earners the whole of the material and moral advantages rests with those on the farm. They are working for themselves in decent surroundings and pure air and may reap what they sow, whereas industrial toilers work for an impersonal master who has reduced exploitation to a science. As improved machinery and more scientific cultivation increase production, the women will be able to withdraw from the fields and devote more time to the care of their homes and children. In countries where land is cheap and the most humble farmer may own a hundred acres and cultivate it with horses and machines, one rarely ever sees women working in the fields. One of the most striking experiences for an American on his first visit to Europe is the sight of women toiling on the farms.

With the concentration of toilers into great industrial centres and the ever increasing tendency to consolidate the ownership and management of great enterprises into trusts and to expand the scope and power of trusts through amalgamations and by crushing small industries, the toilers have been forced into an increasing competition amounting to the shameful barter of their lives for a few pennies an hour without regard to the values produced, and under social and moral surroundings which are a disgrace to the name of civilization.

This outrageous exploitation of the most useful and numerous class draws an ever increasing number of women and children into industrial pursuits and intensifies the congestion and competition of labour. To some extent this alarming tendency was checked by trade unions, but the measures adopted are wholly inadequate, and the balance has been completely destroyed by war.

I regard the basis of trade-unionism as unsound, not in its theory of combination, but in its principle of a uniformity of payment and a restriction of output. A uniform wage removes one of the greatest incentives to efficient work and the evils of all restriction of output falls upon the toilers, because they never have more than the residue of production after initiation, direction, rents, profits, reserves and watered capital have been provided for.

The position of the toilers and the principles upon which they would do well to organize are dealt with in "*The World Allies.*"

In addition to the outrageous evils against which the toilers were forced to contend before the war, there is added the industrial competition of millions of women. If this industrial employment of women becomes permanent the problem will be aggravated beyond peaceful solution, and violence will never solve any problems; not even those which arise directly through violence.

The industrial masters are doing everything in their

power to convince people that unless women now generally become industrial toilers there will be an insufficient production to meet the world's needs, and that the toil of women is the only way to offset the murder of millions of men.

If this proposition is closely examined it will be seen that as things stood before the war, the world's needs represented a payment to labour upon the minimum basis at which men and women could live and rear more industrial slaves. The whole of the vast surplus created by their toil was handed over to their exploiters by way of excessive profits, rents, interests and dividends upon fabulous sums of watered stock which represented neither the products of toil nor the gifts of nature, but which stood for natural monopolies, concessions and privileges which men should be unable to capitalize for their private account. It represented also in part the capitalization of surpluses created by the toil of millions and improperly withheld from its creators.

The solution of this problem must not be left to plutocrats. They must not be permitted to murder millions of men and send more millions of helpless cripples into a disorganized world and avoid the consequences of their shameful exploitation and murder by reducing women to slavery and grinding out their lives and those of their children in factories and mines. The remedy is to be found in quite another direction and if applied it will serve as a solemn warning to all succeeding generations that the common men cannot longer be crushed for the profit of plutocrats and still allow their destroyers to keep them in slavery and on future occasions send them to destruction.

The ones who have exploited and destroyed the toilers and created mountains of debts, hope that their fabulous paper fortunes may be given some tangible value through the absorption of the life-toil of a world of underpaid workers and that a new army of helpless and dependent women may join with the homeless men in rebuilding what plutocracy has destroyed.

The view of plutocracy is that the whole of the fictitious fortunes and usurped wealth, which are directly responsible for all poverty, for nearly all crime and for all war, must levy their permanent tribute upon mankind. After this tribute has been paid the remainder of the product of toil, such as it is and whatever it may be, would be doled out to labour. That is the intention of the ruling castes and the chief reason why they will use every possible means to force women to enter all spheres of labour on vast and permanent lines.

This greatest of all crimes against the masses cannot be effected unless millions of women take upon themselves the industrial slavery from which their men have been freed by being murdered on the fields of conflict at the behest of imperialism and high finance. Even the mere prospect of such a state should be sufficient to arouse the masses to a sense of their peril but it has already passed beyond a prospect. Through the tyranny of all belligerent governments, it is a reality, daily assuming more menacing aspects and which will bring unbelievable misery, suffering and destruction to the masses unless it is completely suppressed.

The solution does not consist in a further exploitation of the common men or in the enforced toil of women, but rather in such an alteration of the economic life of the world as will result in a fair distribution of all production. Also in stopping the manufacture of every kind of armament, abolishing all armies and navies (except a small international fleet to patrol the seas against piracy) at the same time doing away with all military service, which wastes years of the life of many millions of men. All this destruction and waste must cease and men be allowed freely to dedicate their time to useful toil, aided to a greater extent than ever by improved machinery, which may one day reach such variety and perfection as to abolish a greater part of the drudgery now performed by men and to free women altogether from drudgery. Thousands of useful inventions are unemployed because they conflict with some private interest although they would have an important social value. One of the activities of a League of Nations could be the creation of a World Commission to which all inventions might be sent and so far as they were useful, they should be given freely to mankind for its general use and the inventor should be paid by the League a permanent income in proportion to the social importance of his invention, thus completely abolishing the manifold evils of patent monopolies.

No source of strength or creative genius should remain unused in the great task which lies ahead of man in completing his subjugation of earth and abolishing all subjugation of men. In the great days when industrial and agricultural labour will be combined upon a vast scale, the day in the factory will not exceed four hours, and two shifts might be employed. But no man should be permitted to work in both shifts and boys and women should not be employed in factory work at all.

If women realized the dangers involved in their universal industrial employment, they would not take up the work of their dead, in the conviction that they are doing a courageous and beautiful thing. As matters stand they are only falling into the pit dug for them by their exploiters, whereas they should completely withdraw from industrial competition with men as one of the steps which will lead them to their natural career as wives and mothers.

The giving of votes to women is merely a war measure by way of a reward to obtain their silence, co-operation and labour in furthering the atrocious murder of men. It was important and essential that women, as well as men should be made to share in this ghastly business, otherwise it would have ended years ago, but plutocracy looks to the future, while the masses either do not look at all, or only at the present and past. Every step taken to put women upon an apparent equality with men and lead them into the folly of doing men's work— is a step towards the general and industrial employment of women. All the paths of this policy lead to the treasure-houses of plutocracy, which only accomplishes its designs in proportion as all men, women and children are forced to carry their riches to its mill and go away with empty hands, as drudges in a disinherited world.

While women are being flattered with the illusions of equality and greater liberty and independence and are thus being led or driven into the industrial nets, there is a further fictitious remedy being offered in the form of extending government ownership. As this is one of the most imminent misfortunes which might overtake the great industrial nations now at war, it should be exposed to a clear statement of precisely why it must at all costs be avoided.

The means of production and distribution must not be nationalized and directed by an incompetent bureaucracy, but socialized and directed by business men, experts and manual labourers.

There are permanent and fundamental reasons, resting in the nature and illustrated by the experience of man, why all extension of government ownership, under any form of government that men are now sufficiently advanced to establish, will increase the dangers of tyranny, discourage all initiative and progress and bring about lower wages.

The more favours a government has to bestow, the more lucrative positions it can offer to men of high intelligence and the more it increases its hold over the industrial and economic activities of a people through the ownership of enterprises, the less democratic and consequently the more despotic it becomes. This appears to be the opposite to what one would expect from a great and general extension of the active functions of government, because the larger the number under direct government employment the more readily it would appear possible to make the terms "the Government" and "the People" synonymous. But this is not in fact the result.

Every person who works for wages desires to obtain and keep the good opinion of his immediate superior. This begins at the bottom and extends to the top of every enterprise and establishes an autocracy in the hands of the man in whom rest the final powers of decision. No king, howsoever despotic, ever had a more tyrannical control over the lives of men than that possessed by the man who now rules a great business employing thousands. The respect which these men feel, or which they pretend to feel for their master and the awe with which he is regarded on his periodical inspection of the factory, are more profound and apparent than that entertained for any king, as society is now constituted. In order to understand the full significance of this, one must have been in the position I have described and must also have been so constituted by nature and affected by human sympathy as to be deeply touched and influenced by this attitude of his employees, expressed towards him, often quite unconsciously and arousing in him profound pity. I was always deeply moved by this feeling in my own business and impressed with the sense of my responsibility towards those whose lives had become parts of the vast mechanism of my industry.

So long as the state is not the employer, the men will feel they are free to oppose bad measures of government or unsuitable candidates for office and that they can do so without any risk of their positions. They would not attempt any measures against the one who held absolute power over their employment in a private company and this would be the tendency towards their employer if it were a government instead of a company. If this employment of the individual by the state could conceivably be extended until it embraced all toilers, the liberty of the people would be lost and the tyranny of the politicians would be absolute.

If government ownership were to replace individualism in all industries where two or more men are employed as wage-earners, there would still remain a great and important number of people not so employed— notably farmers; but all would be under the control, not of a reasonable and representative government, but of a tyrannical bureaucracy in which small men would obtain and continue the exercise of great powers through their industrial control of the masses.

Under such a general system of government ownership the men who now direct the great affairs of the world would need to be retained at their actual posts, unless society was prepared to suffer the disadvantages inevitable through the withdrawal of the service of those who are best able to direct what they have conceived, created and managed. As the tendency of all government administration is towards mediocrity, routine and red-tape, the services of the most able and creative men could not be retained in administrative positions and it is precisely in such capacity they are most required. Neither could they be induced to struggle for political power or to take any part in governments, as now constituted or as they are likely in future to be formed. Thus an essential element of society would gradually disappear and with it there would be lost those inestimable advantages which may be traced to the spirit of initiative, encouraged by compensation and freedom of action.

An industry run by a government is not only badly and expensively conducted but it would never progress under a government monopoly. New inventions would be discouraged and new appliances and processes ignored, because the great stimulus to which all progress is due would be lacking; and there would be no effective means of forcing affirmative action in anything more important than settled routine and detail. Under such monopolies you may take the products or leave them, without making the slightest difference to the bureaucrats in charge, whose sole attention is directed to playing the flunkey to someone above them in power and kicking someone below them. It should not be necessary to multiply instances to illustrate the dangers involved for mankind if there should be no chance of high favour, or great position, or wealth, or even of a moderate salary and competence, unless they were derived from one or another form of government employment. Under such conditions there would be no liberty and under general and extensive government ownership, such conditions could not possibly be avoided.

As matters now stand there is too great a centralization of power. This should not be further aggravated and consolidated through government ownership. As governments are now constituted and in any other form in which they are likely to be established, they will not be administered by the most capable administrators or by the wisest and greatest men, but rather by those who are able, through shallow and ignorant appeals, to obtain the sentimental following of the thoughtless public, or who are placed in power by the plutocrats, operating through the press. To put into the hands of such men, the direct control of industrialism, and therefore to add the most decisive and arbitrary powers to those already exercised through bureaucracy, would be deliberately to cast aside the small amount of liberty which has been so laboriously and slowly attained.

Politically, government ownership holds only dangers for humanity and economically nothing can be said in its favour.

If a doctor makes a mistake he buries it.

If an editor makes a mistake he publishes it.

If some lawyer talks his way into the position of Chancellor of the Exchequer, where he always muddles his budget and wastes the public money, he covers the deficit by selling treasury bills or bonds. He then squanders the proceeds and is re-elected with great public applause.

He may spend a large part of his life in such notable service and then attain a seat in the House of Lords in recognition of distinguished attainments.

If a business man makes a similar muddle he finds himself in the bankruptcy courts and afterwards out of a job. This is as it should be!

That government is best which least interferes with the legitimate activities of the people and it becomes objectionable and dangerous in proportion to its meddling in the ordered affairs of men and women, or taking direction of anything which they can direct themselves.

The line separating paternalism from despotism is narrow and only most vaguely definable. It is a line easily crossed when the administrative power falls to the lot of ambitious or corrupt men, or when it is wielded by a great administrator, who may be high-minded but who acts upon the conviction that he is a better judge of a people's needs than they are, and who has the sustained energy and organizing genius essential to carry out his designs, even when none but the ordinary powers are nominally confided to him.

If the activities of the people in any great nation should be under the administrative guidance of its government there would inevitably develop expressions of paternalism and governmental interference in private affairs, tending completely to undermine the sentiment of personal independence and responsibility and to destroy all initiative, invention and progress.

One generation of such a policy would render a people unable to prevent the establishment of despotism and would inevitably deprive a succeeding generation of the power to peacefully regain the independence which had been lost.

To attempt to solve the industrial problem through community or government ownership is to throw away the small measure of industrial and political freedom now in the possession of the masses.

It requires almost as great an effort to prevent individuals and nations from degenerating as is necessary for their advancement and ordered progress. This is one reason why any measures that tend to minimize the importance of the individual and release him from any responsibility which he is personally able to bear, are wrong in principle and a menace to his self-reliance, his manhood and his freedom.

In proportion as a man holds the feeling of personal dignity, which belongs to him in his own right, and which he knows cannot be conferred upon him, he ceases to venerate those empty honours which are often bestowed upon the meanest men. He ceases also to feel that he must cling to someone above him or trample upon anyone below him. He thus becomes a man who will not tolerate despotism and who feels no need of paternalism. He rises above the protective spirit because he is able to protect himself. He does not require a government to order his life, control his activities or offer him any artificial support. These feelings so essential to the dignity and progress of man, so important to the maintenance of his intellectual integrity and of such high value in the establishment of a genuine commonwealth, are incompatible with the theory and practice of government ownership and the control which would arise through such ownership and administration of industries upon a general scale.

The controlling power in governments is not exercised by the most numerous class but by the classes which are the best organized and the most economically independent in the state. It is difficult to transfer this power by peaceful means from one class of society to another. So difficult is it that the general experience of man may be said to show that it has not as yet been accomplished by peaceful means. When it is brought about by violence the change is only temporary. One tyranny gives way to another and by slow degrees the pendulum swings back to the opposite side. Gradually the old tendencies reappear and in time either the old tyranny in its old form or one under a new name is again all but supreme.

If the expense of government is borne by taxation

every one has the right to consider that officialdom consists of paid servants, employed by the people, to safeguard the common interests against undue encroachment either from above or below.

If, on the contrary, the state were to embark upon extensive government ownership there would be expressed towards it the sentiments of employees towards their employers, and this — added to the immense hold which governments already have over the thoughtless masses — would in a short time result in the establishment of bureaucratic tyranny.

The industrial master may to an extent be restrained by the government, in so far as he attempts to do more than rob the toilers — but if the government becomes also the industrial master it will have raised itself above restraint. Even when the classes holding political power have interests differing from those of the industrial masters and both are anxious to obtain the goodwill of the masses (if it does not cost too much) the toilers have been unable to attain economic justice, true freedom or any sort of independence corresponding to their numbers and value to society. All hope to realize these natural and legitimate objects would disappear under government ownership.

The last four years have borne tragic witness to the tyranny of small lawyers who obtain absolute powers over the lives and fortunes of nations and destroy both in the name of liberty.

The tyrannies established by the belligerent governments during this war, when the majority of all adults are in the employment of such governments or industrially dependent upon them, should be a stern warning against the extension of governmental functions in any direction or under any pretext whatsoever.

In some eastern and southern nations where industrial

development is almost wholly lacking and where the people are suffering from the evils of ignorance and despotism, I would make a strictly temporary exception to the definite and general principles which I have urged against government ownership.

The industrial development in those exceptional nations must either be undertaken by their local governments or in the alternative entrusted to private international finance, because the governing classes in those nations lack both the initiative and experience essential to the direction of industrialism on a national scale.

If the development is undertaken by private foreign capital the nations will be exploited for the profit of international high finance. This is wholly against the interests of the people concerned and contrary to the future welfare of the backward nations and would tend to augment international issues and jealousies, which have been the cause of all modern wars.

In the interests of world peace and of those peoples who constitute the non-industrial nations, the development of their resources might be properly undertaken by their respective governments provided the principles of personal self-government outlined in these pages were at the same time systematically and thoroughly instilled among the masses, and on condition that the basis of payment for labour should be established in accordance with the principles set out in this book.

Concurrently with this development upon the basis I have outlined there should also be established a general system of free public schools in which the present and future generations of boys and girls would receive a sound and thorough education, along the lines and upon the principles set out in these pages.

All the reasons which operate in favour of the industrial

development of such countries as Turkey and Mexico being undertaken by the governments of these countries, are applicable only to such civilizations, while they are in no sense properly adapted to a similar activity in great nations such as Germany, France, England and the United States, where through generations of political, intellectual and industrial evolution, conditions have been created which would make government ownership of industries a menace to the economic and political freedom of the masses.

As all institutions must be made by man, there will never be any perfect institutions. That is also why institutions will never be permanent. To advance any theory as the final solution of the great and complicated problems involved in our modern societies would be an attempt to set a limit to what may be achieved by man; and this has no limit *which man himself may set*. All that any man may hope to do is to devise general measures which can be applied without involving any change in human nature or any alteration of the motives which control and determine all human conduct, because these will not change. Man's measures must be adaptable to the conditions they seek to reform. They must not be measures which are either visionary, and therefore only applicable in some distant civilization and they must not be strictly temporary.

The tendencies of civilization clearly indicate the large lines along which society is destined to move for some generations. They also furnish the occasion to apply such measures as may use the great forces of civilization for the liberation of mankind, rather than to permit their use towards the continued enslavement of men and extend it to the general industrial enslavement of women and children.

We have had sufficient time in which to observe the

good and evil attendant upon the practical application of machinery to life upon a vast scale, also to weigh the claims of the man and the machine and to know what part of production to allot to each. We have seen why it is that combinations of capital have attained their present proportions, and world character and we can safely indicate what should be the next and succeeding steps in this movement.

We have arrived at an exact understanding as to why products and toil are international commodities and why both are bought and sold upon world markets, and the steps by which one class in society is now able to determine at what price and upon what basis all other classes shall be employed and in what surroundings their lives shall be spent. These are set out in detail in my books.

With the advantage of this plane of observation I have considered it possible to indicate the lines along which the most numerous and oppressed portion of mankind may now proceed in all assurance, to attain for themselves and their descendants those great and legitimate objects which have so long remained beyond their reach. I believe the course I have set out is adapted to the evolution of society for a period more remote than we are now able to predict.

When one takes account of the inertia of the masses, of their economic helplessness, of their ceaseless toil and of the devices which have been used in all times and which are still employed to keep them poor, ignorant and superstitious, he realizes why it is that at this late date it is necessary to state and reinforce by arguments, the steps which are so vital to the interest of the masses.

It is for this reason that one speculates as to the future of these masses with feelings of profound melancholy amounting often to despair.

CHAPTER IX.

THE PRACTICAL STEPS TOWARDS SOCIALIZATION.

As I am opposed to government ownership and mismanagement of industries for the reasons set out in preceding chapters and am not in favour of any extension of the powers of bureaucracy, it follows that I must have other and better means of arriving at the socialization of property.

I have such means and set forth in this chapter the practical measures which may now be taken to attain this goal. They are adapted to the world as it stands rather than to some vague world which does not exist except in the conception of some philosopher.

In the literature of socialism and trade-unionism one has sought in vain for any precise and tangible plan through which the objects desired by the great leaders and philosophers of these movements could in practice be attained.

I hope these pages will supply what has been lacking on the constructive side of these great human movements and that my views express not only a true social conception, but also indicate the tangible and sure means by which the ideal may become a world reality, beginning in the year *1919*.

The measures for immediate and universal application are:

(1) Require the registration of all property owned

by persons, corporations or societies 1st July 1914 and now, together with details as to the property and income disposed of in the interval, and in what ways it was acquired. The registers should be open to public inspection and all property not registered should be forfeited to the state.

(2) All banknotes, treasury bills, notes, bonds, shares or other obligations issued by governments or by corporations or individuals, to be presented within a fixed and brief delay at offices designated by the governments and registered in public registers. The owner's name should be inscribed on the securities. In dealing with banknotes the old ones could be cancelled and a new series issued in exchange and registered by number. All securities not presented for registration within the time stipulated would become void.

No exportation or exchange of securities or values from one nation to another should be allowed pending the registration above outlined.

(3) There must be no repudiation of the principal or interest of the debts which pledge the good faith and honour of nations, but the burden involved in such payments would result in the social and industrial degradation of generations of men, women and children unless a comprehensive system is universally adopted through which every penny of profit made directly or indirectly during the war is applied to the cancellation of the municipal and national debts.

(4) A graduated capital tax payable in the property or securities of the persons taxed and in the event of property which cannot be divided, the levy to be paid in semi-annual instalments upon the basis of interest and amortization of a capital debt. Inherited fortunes to be the

most heavily taxed and the rate to rise progressively above a small minimum fortune. All land not cultivated or put to other productive use to be taxed upon the basis of its productive capacity.

The first of these two measures should be imposed because it is morally an outrage for any man to make a penny of profit through the suffering and destruction of his fellow-men. The second measure is an economic necessity and is a slight tribute to levy in comparison to the sacrifice of the lives of millions of deluded and homeless men. The new basis of land taxes above indicated would force the division and cultivation of unused estates and in so far as these estates were cultivated by wage-earners they should come under the same economic measures as those I indicate for industrial toilers and through which the possession of the land could pass to those who cultivate it—for the time being.

This should be accompanied by village, state and world-organization of scientific agriculture and attended, on its industrial side, by a co-operative system of collection and distribution. Under such a comprehensive plan the local, national and world production of all the principal articles required in the activities of mankind, could be so regulated as to avoid waste, loss, and either underproduction or unusable surpluses.

Where the state is the proprietor of land it should be developed upon the industrial system indicated in this chapter in so far as expensive machinery could be the most economically used.

In so far as there was a division into small tracts, to be cultivated without great outlay on machinery, the same principle of payment to labour could also apply. Where extensive tracts are devoted to the production of cereals and where great works of irrigation or drainage are necessary, the undertaking could be conducted for the account of the whole people with better results under my system than could be attained in any other way.

The millions who now demand a chance to live on the land could become small farmers, having the benefit of what their own toil produced, or receiving a salary and profit in the great agricultural enterprises, upon the same basis as applies to industrial labour. The principle of my system of payment to labour and the steps necessary to universal socialization, must from the beginning be applied to all communal and state undertakings exactly as in the case of private capitalism, until this latter shall have effectively and forever disappeared.

These measures would discharge all national and municipal debts and leave a fund in the hands of the various states and municipalities which would enable governments to commence to redeem some of the extravagant promises they made to the common men and which they have neither the intention nor the resources to fulfill.

(5) In order that men and women may accomplish their obligations towards society, upon a basis which will guarantee the material and spiritual well-being of all who toil and without which organized society cannot longer endure—it is essential to establish compensation to labour upon the basis of its productive value and sacred human rights, rather than upon the present basis of its competitive necessities as a commodity. Starting with a minimum wage, which must have a higher purchasing value than any wages heretofore paid to labour, and rising steadily with efficiency and production until they are upon a basis creating not only entirely new conditions of life for all labourers, but also upon such a basis as will enable the masses who toil to realize the general socialization of the

means of production, upon sound and ethical principles and without violence.

(6) There should be established a minimum return to capital actually engaged in the employment of labour and all surplus resulting from such employment should be divided between capital and labour, upon the basis hereinafter set out.

(7) All capital invested or used directly or indirectly in the employment of labour should be appraised in order to establish the new basis of a minimum return for capital, a minimum wage for labour and the gradual and complete socialization of all capital and labour.

(8) This appraisement of capital and the establishment of a minimum wage for both capital and labour, should be carried out upon a national and universal scale by commissions appointed with respect to every branch of industrial activity and dealing with the local, national and world positions of labour.

(9) Agricultural commissions similarly composed and working to similar ends, should deal with the whole question of agricultural production, the cultivation of state lands and the division of great and small estates.

(10) The minimum return to capital must be based upon the actual value of the property and credits employed in each instance and must take into account the basis of the minimum wage. In principle the minimum return to capital might be taken at 4 per cent per year.

(11) The value of each enterprise howsoever great or small, in which any men were employed as wage earners, would be determined by the commissions. Shares of capital stock to the amount stipulated, would be issued to the actual owners, and would represent the ownership of the undertaking in the same effective way as it is now represented by shares and bonds. Against the issue

and delivery of these new shares the whole of the then outstanding securities would be surrendered to the public trustee and cancelled.

This would completely and finally obliterate all fictitious capital which now levies such astounding tribute upon industry and the entire burden of which has been borne by labour, while on the other hand this fictitious capital has furnished the basis of exploiting the producers of raw material, robbing the consuming public and expropriating the savings of the frugal.[1]

(12) The certificates of stock would state that after receiving the minimum cumulative dividend specified, the balance of the profits would be distributed as follows:

(a) 25 per cent to the toilers engaged in the enterprise in question, in proportion as the wages or salary of each bore relation to the total paid as wages and salaries each year. This would protect anyone who might be employed in a given enterprise for only a few hours or days in a year.

(b) 25 per cent to the registered holders of the certificates of stock in proportion to their holdings. The payments both to capital and labour to be free from taxes of any sort.

(c) 50 per cent into a national fund to be applied for the socialization of the enterprise.

The toilers in every enterprise to have the right, but not the obligation, to invest all or any part of their income in purchasing at par, the certificates of stock of the enterprise in which they were engaged.

(13) The whole of the earnings of every enterprise should be deposited with a national public trustee, to be

---

[1] This entire system is exposed to a critical analysis in my book: "*The World Allies*" Chapters V. VII. VIII. IX. XI. XVI.

administered by him in trust for the capital and labour directly concerned and for the people as a whole.

The public trustee should be chosen by the voters of the nation, by general secret ballot, under an electoral system such as outlined in chapters VI and VII of this volume and entirely outside all government interference. His term of service should be one or two years and all his appointments should be non-political and subject to revision by the commission of experts and toilers.

(14) In so far as the toilers did not exercise their right to purchase the certificates of stock representing the ownership of all enterprises, the public trustee would have the right and also the obligation to invest the 50 per cent paid to him under "C" above, in the purchase of such stocks at par.

The principle to be followed in such purchase would be to acquire the shares in every enterprise in the proportion which they bore to the total shares outstanding, in order that the socialization of all enterprises might be carried out concurrently.

(15) Employees would in the beginning have the right to choose a director in every enterprise, the choice to be made by secret ballot. Their further representation on the board to be in proportion to their holding of shares. All meetings of the shareholders to be open to the public, instead of being guarded as they now are by stringent regulations excluding the public and misrepresented to the public as they now are by paid reports in all newspapers. This polite form of newspaper blackmail costs a great company from £ 1000 to £ 5000 for each meeting of its shareholders—especially if it requires more funds or patronage from the public.

(16) In order that my system may render its maximum service to labour and to society, it would be desirable

for the toilers to devote a great part of their surplus to the purchase of the stock, rather than to hoard or spend it. The share capital could not be increased against any surplus or reserves accumulated from earnings and which if permitted would result in setting aside excessive reserves and correspondingly reducing the income to labour.

Auditors appointed by the government should supervise accounts and be able to check outlays on plant, in order to safeguard the interests of the toilers and the general public.

As this system would put an end to strikes and to all industrial disorganization, the trade unions would be free to devote the funds they have already accumulated, to educational and other social objects.

(17) A part of the 50 per cent paid to the trustee under "C" above should be devoted to educational purposes, because any socialization of property which is not accompanied by a socialization of people will do nothing more useful in an ethical sense, than to multiply the number of people who will use an increased income for unsocial ends.

(18) The organizations of labour in all nations should be federalized and their federation could determine, in annual meetings, the headings under which one fourth of the fund "C" might be expended in educational and social reforms.

As the interests of all labour in every nation are identical and as all who usefully labour with their hands and brains should progress together towards a universal goal, one of the inevitable accompaniments of this movement should be a WORLD PARLIAMENT OF LABOUR, which should hold quarterly sessions in the various capitals of the world, create its own council of ministers and boards of enquiry, engage its experts and specialists and draft comprehensive world measures, designed to be presented to the various national political parliaments as the basis of all legislation affecting labour and there can never be any legislation which does not affect labour.

It is to be hoped that the International Labour and Socialist organizations will create this world parliament without delay and that it will stand solidly upon the platform of socialization I have outlined, or upon a better plan if one can be found; that it will commence its labours in the year 1919 and work for the social welfare, without distinction as to race, nationality or religion. Such a world parliament should be provided from the general funds with its own parliament buildings and expenses, it should confide to its cabinet the powers to carry out decisions, summon the parliament in the event of a crisis and by the decisions of such a parliament, the labour and socialism of the whole world should abide and upon its mandate they should act.

(19) Commencing with the twenty-fifth year after the adoption of my system to each industry, the payments by the public trustee would be decreased two and a half per cent per year, under headings "A" and "B", one half being deducted from each of the payments and added to the fund under heading "C."

(20) When this reached the total of 100 per cent, the whole of the payments subsequently made to the trustee would be applied to the retirement of whatever remained of the outstanding certificates of stock and the private ownership of all industries would have passed out of the hands of both capital and labour and would be effectively socialized.

During the progress of this evolution the slums would disappear. There would be an end to crowded tenement houses and a decentralization of population generally. There would be a steady trend away from great cities, and an ever increasing tendency to combine industrial employment with work on the land. As the prosperity of the toilers increased they would become the possessors of small allotments, which would remain for the use of themselves and their descendants, only so long as the cultivation was continued, after which the property would pass to the public trustee for communal use.

(21) All buildings rented wholly or in part as shops, apartments, tenements or for other purposes, would be subjected to an appraisement similar to that applied to land and industries. Upon that appraisement the rent would be established to return the same minimum income to capital as is provided in the industrial scheme and the capital would be represented by certificates of stock, delivered to the owners of the property.

(22) In order that this important drain upon labour might cease concurrently with capitalistic industrialism, the public trustee would include in his stock purchases, the stocks which represented landlordism, and upon a proportionate basis.

The principle should then be followed universally, in all villages and cities that, so far as possible, small shopkeeping should be abolished and give place to centralized public markets conveniently distributed and conducted for the benefit of the public and freed from the slightest profiteering or waste in the collection and deliveries of all articles.[1]

The socialization of production would thus be accompanied by a socialized or co-operative distribution in the most ample and effective sense.

The burdens placed upon humanity by landlordism and small shopkeepers are enormous and represent the

---

[1] This would automatically dispose of all middlemen and establish a direct relation between the producer and consumer.

maximum of disorganization, waste, parasitism and unsocial activity.

The present system of retail distribution is so hopelessly unsound that in some of the most important articles of human consumption the cost of retailing the goods is more than the cost of production and transportation. I state it upon my own experience that I shipped great quantities of food products more than seven thousand miles to the wholesale centres of London and that the selling price of the goods delivered was less than one-half their retail selling price at a small shop one hundred yards from the central market. This is not an isolated but a general experience.

Notwithstanding the immense tribute levied upon society by small shopkeepers their own existence is nearly everywhere precarious. Through rent, small turnover, anarchy in distribution and senseless competition rather than co-operation, the burden imposed upon society by small shopkeepers is a great and unnecessary load.

One of the most important results of my financial measures would be the closing of all stock-exchanges and the forcing of one of the most parasitical and dangerous elements of society to find other means of support. There should be an end to all purchase or sale of stocks upon margin and there would be no financial speculation in a world in which all the capital was real and under permanent option to the toilers and collectivity at par. Along with this stock-exchange rubbish, would also disappear hundreds of thousands of expensive and contentious lawyers, who are the sinister tools of high and low finance.

The control of banking and credit would also pass from the hands of those who now dominate the life of the world, into the hands of those who should own and run the world's industries. Gold would take its proper place as a commodity, along with iron, wood and coal, which is to say, that it would cease to be the god before which humanity stands in wonder and worship.

(23) All insurance organizations whether based upon the employment of private capital or conducted upon the so-called co-operative system, should pass to the public trustee as a social activity. Where capital was employed it would be appraised and dealt with as the landlord capital under article 21.

There are many reasons why these insurance funds should not longer be under the existing control. The whole system of both life and fire insurance is a distinctly anti-social undertaking and the compensation of all employees rises automatically in proportion as they serve the profit-making aims of their employers, in ways which are totally opposed to the public interest.

The power which the control of insurance company funds places in the hands of the directors of insurance companies is not in the least realized by the public, whose funds are the basis of that power. It is a power well understood, feared and respected among bankers and furnishes the basis of a special type of high finance and control over credit, which no men should be able to manipulate to serve their personal interests and increase their private fortunes and general arrogance.

The great joint-stock companies now dominating the life of the world have been financed upon a basis which enables them to exploit the public and rob the toilers, and consequently the capitalization of the incorporated societies would in future stand at its actual figures only in the companies whose issued capital did not exceed their tangible assets. The various classes of securities issued by most of the great companies have been created upon the basis that the rate of interest promised and the rights and privileges accorded to the securities were high and attractive in proportion as the tangible security was unattractive. The whole of the disorganization, capital losses, and financial anarchy involved in the present system of corporate organization and finance and designed to exploit the public, plunder the credulous and rob the toilers, would under my system be substituted by organizations in which there would be no fictitious capital, no discrimination amongst investors, no exploitation of the public and no longer any robbery of labour.

It should be made quite clear that while high finance is international, with a world understanding as to the terms upon which the great enterprises can be financed internationally and in this sense there is little or no competition of high finance with itself—once the enterprise is presented—there is great rivalry among international banking and financial groups as to who shall control the development, establish the "ground floor" participations and benefit from the pressure which finance puts upon politics. All this leads to the use of secret diplomacy, the interference of great governments in weaker states, the struggle for routes of communication, and spheres of influence, and necessitates militarism, imperialism and finally international wars.

The whole of this monstrous business will be augmented through the creation of a number of new states in the undeveloped parts of earth and in the struggles as to the finance, industry and trade of Mexico, South America, China, Turkey and elsewhere. All this is against the interests of the borrowing states and also against the security and ultimate interests of the international investing public, as distinguished from the totally different interests of parasitical high finance.

If a proper League of Nations existed it could and

should put international finance upon a totally different footing. This could be realized upon the following basis:
- (a) All states or enterprises within any state desiring outside capital for development, should be compelled to make application to the Industrial Commission of the League. This commission would study the project and investigate the matter through experts employed by it in the country in question.
- (b) If approved by the Industrial Commission it would be referred to the Finance Commission which would make its independent enquiry. Care to be exercised, upon a world-scale, to avoid over-development in any line and to stabilize all industrial activities of production and distribution; also to guarantee that the development best suited to a given country should be carried out with reference to local needs, but also with the larger object of serving the social and economic interests of the world of nations and of all productive classes.
- (c) Pursuing these principles the Finance Commission would appropriate the sums necessary to carry out all projects. The international credits required for the purpose would be drawn upon and applied under supervision of the Finance Commission and the securities would be issued upon the basis set out in this chapter, thus applying to all industrialism the universal principle both as regards finance and labour, and leading by sure and simple steps to universal socialization.

The Finance Commission would nominate an auditor for the accounts of all states and enterprises to which it had extended credits. This control in accounting would continue until credits had been discharged. At any time upon default of any borrower the Finance Commission would be able to assume entire control of the revenues, in case the defaulter were a state, and the management of the enterprise in cases other than states.

This would involve the abolition of all private control over banks issuing paper money, and it would eliminate all banks from directly participating in international finance, through the manipulation of securities, credits or otherwise. The League of Nations would be the only international borrower and if such a League were properly constituted it would be able to pledge the good faith of humanity and therefore to aid world development upon a basis raised entirely above risks, manipulations and high finance.

The money of the future should be an international currency, issued under the supervision of the Finance Commission. The amount and terms of issue and distribution among the nations would be controlled by the League. The notes would take the form of the ordinary bank notes and on the margin, the equivalent in the various countries would be stated. This would put an end to the bankers' exploitation of foreign money, abolish their arbitrary dictatorship of national and world credit and destroy the supremacy of gold and silver.

The socialization of people must accompany the socialization of property. This is a slow process and under our present capitalistic system it could never be accomplished. Under my system which will create a new world economically and socially, the progress of humanity towards a new world ethically will surpass our most sanguine hopes. The masses have never been given a chance in this world. I propose they shall have that chance. My system will open the way along which new steps may be taken in the certainty that they will never need to be retraced.

The adoption of the system I have outlined would constitute a bridge over which humanity might safely pass from the actual exploitation, violence and anarchy to a universal co-operative commonwealth, in which the existing evils would be unknown.

The more intelligent among the industrial masters realize that they can no longer exercise their old powers. They are prepared to offer the toilers a participation in management, but the toilers must have a participation in profits upon a basis which will transfer the mastery and ownership of industrialism to those who toil with their hands and brains and which will lead by certain steps to a complete socialization.

The toilers should be prepared to compromise—not upon the principle involved and which does not admit of compromise—but only as to the immediate method and extent of its application. This method I consider to be fairly and scientifically outlined above. It is practically workable in our actual civilization and can be applied immediately, without any disorganization of society and keeping in active employment all the useful elements now engaged in production and exchange. This is an essential condition of any useful social reform.

The transition must in any event be gradual. It cannot be finally and *universally* accomplished in one or in several generations, but it can be undertaken without delay and the benefits to humanity would be great and ever increasing as regards the masses in whose interest the measures have been conceived.

There has been too little emphasis laid upon the sound intellectual and ethical evolution of men and women and perhaps too much importance attached to a mere increase in the physical comfort of life. I do not minimize the value of the latter, but it should be considered important only if it is attended by an ethical evolution. This is indispensable, if humanity is to rise to a civilization which will not merely increase the number of people who think and live unsocially, rather than prepare the way for a real and enduring social commonwealth.[1]

The appraisement of all property which employs labour would be the first practical step towards the establishment of industry upon a basis which will enable the toilers to improve their material and social surroundings.

The value of any enterprise is not enhanced by issuing millions of watered securities against it and its value remains the same when the watered securities cease to exist. No real value is to be altered or destroyed but it is to be fairly stated and capitalized upon the new basis. The effect of a general application of this system would be immediately to alter the distribution of the products of all toil and this is an essential requisite to any amelioration of the conditions of the toilers. Production would be greatly increased because the toilers would at once become members of a co-operative undertaking, in which all would have a common and identical interest.

The guiding brains of industry and trade cannot be dispensed with, but in a few years the most industrious,

---

[1] The diagram printed as Appendix "A" to this volume indicates the lines upon which such an intellectual, social and spiritual evolution may in time be universally realized. It was prepared in colaboration with Dr. Nicholas Roubakine, whose great labours may raise his theories of bibliological psychology to a science. His work on the practical side of this important research was begun in 1889. In 1911—15 he published in Russian his first books dealing with this enquiry and his comprehensive survey of the problem is being translated from the Russian for early publication in English and French. The activities grouped under number 1 of the diagram embody the aims which Mr. Paul Birukoff considers fundamental in the work of universal regeneration. The diagram as it stands was intended to indicate graphically the scope of a Federation which we hope may be founded within a reasonable time.

frugal and efficient toilers would occupy the best positions in industry and enjoy the most independence in the state and by the time the socialization of capital had been achieved, the ones under whose guidance it would then be, would be qualified to direct the world.

There is no enterprise, great or small, to which this system may not be applied. It offers what appears to me to be the only solution compatible with the rights of labour and capital, which humanity is now able to adopt.

It would abolish exploitation and anarchy in production, distribution and sale and lead by peaceful means to universal socialization.

It is the alternative of confiscation, universal violence and civil wars.

The one or the other course is likely to be followed upon a vast scale. The horrors which imperialism and high finance have brought upon mankind and the actual blindness of the ruling castes render the situation dangerous in the extreme.

Unless moderation is shown among all classes the situation will pass beyond peaceful remedy.

There is no remedy in violence because like begets like in the material and moral world.

The remedy must be such a peaceful evolution of the manual and intellectual toilers, in morals and in administrative capacity, as will in time qualify men and women to establish and maintain a genuine social state.

CHAPTER X.

THOUGHTS CONCERNING PHILOSOPHY AND CHRISTIANITY.

There is in every human breast a longing that its conscious life may be continued beyond the time which marks the ordinary career of man. This is the natural desire for personal immortality as distinguished from the permanence of what man may create. We cherish the constant hope that we possess, or have become something, which will not pass from the struggle, the beauty, the pain and the prayers of our few days on earth into complete and lifeless oblivion. Philosophers and poets speak to future ages only because they have recorded something which forms the most profound part of the contemplation, the hope, the joys and the despair of mankind. The philosophy and the songs which live through the ages represent what some men were compelled to write or to sing not for others—but for themselves.

It is because the poet and philosopher belong to realms higher than any form of action, that they link their lives to ages other than their own, in ways which are denied to men who may be masters for a little time in achieving what is apparently great because it is close at hand and tangible; whereas it requires generations and the enthusiasm of men who may be uncreative to bring great ideals within the reach of the masses.

The ones to whom the world is most indebted were not

men of action and did not receive the honours of their age, but all evolution and most revolutions may be traced to the teaching of those who usually took no part in the active affairs of their time. The noble inscriptions written upon the banners which are followed by humanity, did not come from the hands of political leaders who controlled the lives of men, but rather from those who, in comparative obscurity, were able to trace the path along which humanity was destined to move in search of truth and in the endeavour to attain its ideals of happiness and liberty. The most enduring places among men are and always will be occupied by those who inspire, rather than by the ones who perform the most noble and altruistic service for mankind.

The story of man's progress is written in the hostility of each generation toward all endeavours to alter existing institutions howsoever oppressive and odious they might be; or to change existing faiths, howsoever benighted and horrible; or to overthrow social prejudices which were an outrage to the dignity of man. The men who are now remembered with the greatest affection or veneration were regarded by their contemporaries as fanatics or blasphemers. The tyranny of public opinion is one of the most potent forces in suppressing those who might be great benefactors of their race. This is the more to be regretted because it is one of the chief obstacles in the path of human progress and its effect is to retard the rise of the multitude whom the ruling castes wish to keep in mental and economic bondage and whose elevation and freedom have been the principal concern of the illustrious men who where persecuted by their own generation and worshipped by succeeding generations.

There is no institution free from defects and no social system which adequately meets the most fundamental requirements of a well ordered world. No religions respond to the reason or satisfy the most noble aspirations of the greatest minds and yet the existing institutions and systems are regarded with such unthinking awe, that it would be considered more than an impertinence to suggest that they must be replaced by others which are in accord with the nature and the needs of mankind.

It would be without purpose unduly to dwell upon the fact that religions in general are merely blind professions of faith in something incomprehensible and which in fact may exist only in our imagination.

If we contemplate the philosophy which has held almost undisputed sway among thinking men for thousands of years, we see how prone man is to accept as truth a series of conclusions which are based upon principles assumed but which do not have the slightest importance if the assumption is not true.

Into man's most profound and important speculation there enter not only many unexplainable quantities but also an unknowable quantity which man must assume as the great Cause, to which all that is may be traced, but which can be pursued only into an obscurity where the thread is lost. It may well be doubted if the intellect of man can rise to the sublime height where it will ever be able to say in all assurance "I am at the fountain of life."

In an enlarged edition of my work on "Immortality" now in preparation, I examine what appear to be the defects in some of the conclusions of the most celebrated philosophers and seek to show how far man is justified in assuming the existence of an ethical aim in nature.

The most renowned philosophers, whose reasoning stands at the summit of man's contemplation, have assumed and endeavoured to show, that the operations of nature are directed towards moral aims; whereas it appears only that man hopes this may be so; and this hope is based upon his feeling that purely physical ends can in no way respond to the most important part of his being—which is spiritual.

In proportion as philosophers have also been scientists and naturalists their research in the material world has caused them to dwell upon the justice and the inflexibility of nature and the tendency to pass from the simple to the varied and complex, arising from what must be assumed as a common Cause—but they have not been able to see in all the marvelous manifestations of this Cause any clear evidence that its operations are towards moral ends. In physical, intellectual and social evolutions an apparently simple cause leads to a great variety and complexity of results, that which may be regarded as concrete becomes ever more widely diffused and changed. Perhaps in the evolution of man this is most strikingly illustrated and to it may be traced one of the most important of all the natural sources of inequality, which is more emphasized among men than in any other realm.

Man assumes the existence and purposes of a moral principle because he cannot believe there is no meaning in all the glory and tragedy of time. He must not however, hope to arrive at any conclusions which may be dignified by the name of logic until he lays aside all faith, because this is not the concern of philosophy. Faith will depend upon the time and place in which a man may live and is constantly changing, whereas what concerns the philosopher must be universal and changeless. He will not therefore assume to know the existence of a God, much less will he seek to assign attributes to what he sets up in his own mind as a divine image. He will not assume that man has a soul, or that because there is a God and He is good, and man's soul appears to render him capable of perfection, there exists the basis upon which he may build an incontestable system of morals. Man will, on the contrary, assume the existence of nothing of which he is unable to prove the existence. He can say of himself no more than "I am" and seek to interpret what may be shown to have preceded that and also what should logically follow it.

One turns from the philosophy of the ages with the oppressive certainty, that no two philosophers have been able to agree, that all philosophy dealing with the mystery of life begins with an assumption and ends in a speculation and that it is beyond the intellect of man in its present state, to establish a system which is in itself perfect and which at no point must rest upon mere assumption.

It has been the great design of science and philosophy, each in its own and distinct way to trace life to its origin, but neither the one nor the other has done more than follow life backward to the point where we must say it has emerged from a mystery and to follow it forward to another point where it is again lost in mystery. Our positive knowledge upon this subject is confined to experience which, for science and philosophy, is at an end when the torch of life is blown out as a candle in the wind.

This means that the most essential field of enquiry is excluded from the range of experience, not only of personal experience but of all life experience. To what length man may sometime extend the boundary of positive knowledge towards what now appears to be unknowable, can at best be nothing more than a speculation, and therefore beyond the actual reach of positive knowledge. We can only speculate from a theory without being able to prove that our assumption is true and we cannot do more than erect a structure which rests upon an hypothesis.

Philosophy reasons to or from what is at present an

unknowable quantity. Its logic is a circle from which
there is no exit. It does not lead to the beginning or to
the end and assuredly the wisest man is the one who
knows that he does not know.

If man knew anything as to the "First Cause" or the
"Last Effect" he might solve the mystery of life, but
as at present he knows nothing about either, there is a
well-defined limit beyond which he cannot go if he
would take each step upon ground which cannot be
disputed.

In my meditations on Immortality I seek to indicate
what appears to me the present boundary to which man
may go in all assurance of his ground and some of the
reasons why he is justified in the conviction that his present
experience does not represent either the beginning or the
end of his existence. I show that it is necessary to look
away from conscious experience to something which is
equally certain for each individual in order to determine
the relative importance of our present life, in the same
way that it is possible for us to realize the motion of our
earth—not by looking at it—but by looking away
from it to objects at a remote distance in the heavens.
Also why we may ascribe to man a universality in his
own right.

The lines of this enquiry are projected beyond all the
limits possible to faith or to any form of paternalism in
a natural or moral world and that "something" which
man feels to be "himself" is followed in its natural course
as one might follow a river which finds its way to the universal sea. This river, like the tide of man's genius passes
over and around all obstacles. It enriches and makes
beautiful the earth. It is bridged and diverted in its course
and bears upon its tranquil bosom the burdens of men,
but these are all incidental. The river took its own way

towards the sea for reasons wholly independent of its uses, for reasons which had their origin and were to realize their fulfillment within itself. It did not pass over the earth to bear our burdens or to carve its image on the mountain rocks, but rather to find its own way to the great depths where it might once again be free.

We may follow the river to the spot where it traces its last figures in the sand as we would follow a path or light from some great human genius to the end of his fleeting life, only to find that as we pass away, the path leads on, and that the source of our light, even if lost to us, is not in fact lost.

These reasons followed to their possible end, show why we may regard our life here as merely incidental, as only a dream and a shadow, and also why we may expect to evolve into a state which is not made up of impressions and sensations and is not subject to the restrictions arising from physical organs. Here we stand with the feeling that there are no limits of time prescribed for our nature, as distinguished from our body and that it is in that nature our real life abides, rather than in our body which soon becomes dust. In this connection I would briefly refer to a phase of this subject which is considered at length in my "Immortality" and that is, as the physical pleasures are increasingly experienced they are in a corresponding ratio less pleasurable and finally cease altogether; whereas the intellectual pleasures increase as they are extended and repeated, until they become towards the close of life, the source of a noble joy which exceeds all the expectations of youth and all the bounds of physical pleasure as experienced either in youth, maturity or age.

If then we pass to that still higher realm of spiritual happiness which is only partly intellectual and not in the least physical, we enter into an increasing area of peaceful charm, which brings impressions of a conscious grandeur and leaves us with an ever increasing sense of dignity and power, from which all intellectual fatigue is banished, and in which the body is in no sense concerned. It is at such times man feels that the meaning of immortality is to be found in an ever recurring youth which can only be attained through death. Man is not concerned with what may come in that unknown state where all our gold of truth may be refined and all the dross of life be left behind, where also we lose all hate and fear. There perhaps we will learn to care for only what is beautiful and if we come again to earth it will be in such a spirit of gentleness and love as will carry to the humblest and the greatest minds, the message that in their origin and ways there may be something quite divine.

Even the greatest intellects, inspired by the most profound sense of the spiritual significance which attaches to the manifestations of material forces, are baffled when they arrive at the line which divides and which I believe forever separates the known from that vast realm which is not only unknown but unknowable. I would attach to the material realm only a relative importance, but I find in it so much that leads me to a point which is itself spiritual and beyond which all must be spiritual, I am compelled to feel that the true mystery of life lies in realms which we cannot now fathom and which will never be fathomed. Looked at from the point of view of an infinite progression, resting as a possibility of the human understanding and inherent in our nature—it follows that we shall forever seek what we can never find. Were it otherwise there would be no infinity to man's progress and there would be a clear and definite limit beyond which he could never pass, howsoever he might progress through thousands of years, towards his possible attainment, whereas I would assign to man so grand a role, as to place his highest possibility perpetually beyond his reach. There is in this the great advantage that when it is understood no one will pretend to believe that he has touched the limits of his possibility, because he will realize that beyond all that he can ever know, there lies the true mystery of life which he can never know and that it is solely upon this basis that immortality or infinite progress can rest.

How far this may be tangibly followed in the contemplation of man's possible destiny is regarded in some of its varied aspects in my book on "Immortality" and will not here be further pursued.

If it may be said that many men do not desire immortality I do not believe there is any man who has no desire to realize a higher and more perfect form of existence. Even those who would escape this life do not seek oblivion, but rather only freedom from conditions with which they are unable longer to cope, while they cherish the hope that there may be a future in which they are to be more free. I would not attach undue importance to the hopes of man, but I find in this life they are so closely related to his achievements that it is natural he should believe they may have a genuine significance in their relation to a future state.

All achievement is in the direction of our hopes and some of the most important of these hopes are realized, although their realization would at one time have appeared impossible. It is difficult to set a limit as to what man may reasonably hope to accomplish and in no realm is this so essentially and naturally true as in our moral life, since in that realm we are less dependent upon environment and the will of others than in the material phases of our existence. What we may accomplish materially may depend upon a variety of circumstances and be determined to an extent by others, but what we may become spiritually depends upon ourselves and may be only remotely related to our tangible achievements, and almost wholly uninfluenced by our surroundings. It is in this sense that the hopes of man, as regards his possible attainments in the moral realm, may have a high significance. In considering the importance of man's hopes I attach weight only to what he steadfastly determines to accomplish by his own endeavours. I do not take into account the miserable attitude which causes most people to hope that they may obtain important objects in this life and immortality in another life as the gifts from either God or man. I speak of hope in the sense of a sustained reliance that one may achieve the large material or moral ends which he feels rightfully correspond to his nature and capacities, and which makes it unthinkable for him to seek gifts or favours either in this world or the next. Man has the power to stand upon his own feet and create his own material and moral world from which every form of paternalism is excluded. If this were not so, then man is no more than a moral mendicant on the paths of time. All that one seeks to obtain as gifts or favours is worthless to him morally and is destructive of the noble sentiments which alone can attach value and dignity to manhood.

It is for these reasons I am opposed to every form of paternalism in dealing with material affairs in this world and that I reject all proposals based upon any form of paternalism or charity as regards a possible future state. Both are against the personal dignity and the material and moral progress of mankind and contrary to the principles of a universal nature which renders unto every men according as he sows and nothing unto him who does not sow.

In the first chapter I set out at some length the basis upon which children may be imbued with the principles of self-government as it relates to their conduct and affects their moral and general attitude towards others and it is not amiss to mention here that the same principles should be applied to all the institutions which exercise an influence over the most important concerns of men and women of mature years.

If this principle is to be thus applied it follows that there must be an end to the attempts to control matured human beings by constantly imposing upon them a doctrine of "thou shalt not." Those who attach importance to intellectual liberty and who would uphold the dignity of human reason will not deny to any system of teaching its full value or withhold any recognition of its merits. It is in this spirit that reference is here made to the ethical claims of Christianity, which for centuries has exercised so profound an influence upon mankind and whose founder has had, and will long have the highest place in the homage of men as the one who among all others has borne the highest and most hallowed name.

There are many and dangerous tendencies in modern society to submit to a rule of brute force and tyranny without protest or moral courage. While men's most precious rights are ignored they do not resent the most flagrant injustice and do not realize that never were their liberties so much in danger of being crushed under institutions as at present and never were the institutions so little deserving of esteem— much less of veneration and worship. To such an extent is this now carried in all belligerent nations that a man may not criticize some mediocre politician, without being accused of disloyalty to his country, whatever that may mean, nor can he lift his voice against the tyranny and pretension of priests without incurring the charge that he is rejecting religion, morality and God.

Let it be stated directly that if Christianity had any deep and genuine ethical significance for the millions who profess it, there would be no war. When people love their neighbours as themselves they do not kill them and yet the ones who for fifteen centuries have kept humanity at war were those who most strongly protested their adherence to the gospel of peace.

If we pass from the dismal teaching and the more dismal practice of the clergy, to the fountain of Christianity and examine what it was that Christ actually taught so far as it can be known from the New Testament, it is quite clear that it does not constitute a code of morals upon which society could ever securely rest in this world. If such society could exist it would not be adapted to any conditions which man can here create or which he can reasonably conceive and in any event it could never result from any conduct influenced by promises of rewards or threats of punishment.

Perhaps it is for this reason among others, that the great and universal nature which is over all the acts of its creatures, permanently bars the way to the creation of such a society in any material form on earth and that the symbolic significance of Christ's nature, is that it was not of this world.

That Christ conceived his ideal state as a spiritual kingdom I do not doubt and it is only because the masses are too unspiritual to realize that there is any definite existence beyond what they are able to see, that they attempt to apply literally what must only be contemplated spiritually, and which will never be applicable to man in any stage of his development until he has by his own self-control, justice and pure ethics raised himself above all need for laws, restrictions, prohibitions, promises or threats of any sort—either as applied to this life, or to a possible future state.

The great and exalted Nazarene taught submission to all authority whether it was good or bad, and loyalty to whatever government might exist, even if it did not deserve loyalty. He constantly referred to and drew from the Old Testament as a code of moral law and yet the Old Testament was devoid of the great ethical teaching which the Greeks and Indians had proclaimed and which included the hope of immortality; a faith not contemplated by the Old Testament. Moses and the Prophets taught that God was petty and revengeful, that he punished His enemies and rewarded His friends, and that these punishments and rewards were in the form of property, personal honours and power—three things to which high-minded men will not attach any importance—and certainly would never regard as the ultimate worthy objects of life.

In so far as Christ rose above this class of teaching he altered the *object* for which men were to strive, but the interpretation of his teaching from first to last ascribed to it the character of a gospel of rewards and punishments. In so far as such teaching becomes the motive force or the restraining influence in the life of any man— just so far does he cease to be a social being, who will regard the interests of others without reference to any benefit or loss which he may himself incur. To make the hope of rewards or the fear of punishment in any way incentives to conduct is to appeal to the lowest instinct in human nature. It is an instinct above which all men must rise before they can render any great and lasting service to mankind and above which the Christ himself had assuredly risen.

There is another and important phase of this religious teaching in its bearing upon sound morals and the principles essential to genuine self-government, as it applies to the individual and through him to society as a whole, and that is what must follow from any gospel of "Thou shalt not" and which is suited only to slaves. So long as men must be governed by constant prohibitions, and interferences in their lives through negative commands, they cannot attain that independence and reliability of character upon which alone the institutions of genuine freedom may be founded. All such teaching, whether by the church in matters of religion, or by governments in the social relations is wrong and constitutes one of the principal obstacles on the path of human progress. It is therefore no occasion for wonder on my part, having regard to the conditions essential to large freedom and finality in human reasoning, that from the days of the great and benevolent Marcus Aurelius, down to our time, the philosophy which has done the most to elevate and ennoble human reason and exalt the mind of man has come from those who had studied and rejected Christianity and who could not accept it even as it is set forth in the New Testament and much less could they accept the dogmas of the church.

Considering the form in which this teaching is now presented to mankind there need be no occasion for wonder that it has lost all vital power to influence the most consequential acts of men and that its original dignity and beauty have been lost. Beginning with the jangling bells and ending with its manifold idolatry, the church as an institution, especially the Roman church, pursues a course which is designed to impose an unreasoning and slavish respect for all arbitrary authority and a submission to all existing social and religious prejudices. To such an extent is this now carried that men and women are lead to believe that those teachings which would in reality be for their freedom and highest good are in fact a danger to human happiness and true religion. All such teaching must permanently tend to prevent mankind from becoming truly self-governing and in any high sense ethical beings.

I have no doubt that a great part of the teachings of the Christ are to be taken only in their mystic sense, and that it is only in such a realm that their significance can be realized. It is due to the low level of man's spiritual attainments that nearly all men fail to understand the sense in which this exalted nature sought to impress upon those around him the beauty and the reality of what was termed the Divine love for man.

Instead of realizing that this love had been shown in the vast and wonderful universe given to man and in which man must work out his own destiny and expect to reap only what he sows, humanity is so weak, ignorant and unspiritual that it took the assurance of this love as an indication and promise that what man failed to do for himself would be done for him by a Creator through prayers uttered in adoration and fear. All gifts are contrary to the laws of Nature, which is to say that they are contrary to the universal law. It is this reliance upon Divine aid to violate its own laws, that has stood as a barrier on the path of man's highest progress.

It was in the interest of the clergy to keep humanity in ignorance and infantile helplessness as long and effectively as possible, in order the more readily to impose its temporal power as an agency which assumes to represent the Creator and to speak to humanity in His name and with the pretence that it could bestow blessings, avoid the natural and inevitable consequences which must follow every act, that it could grant or withhold God's favour or protection and that it could give, not only His forgiveness, but grant free licence to commit again and again the acts which seemed to necessitate forgiveness. That all this monstrous pretence would be repugnant to the Christ I do not in the least doubt and that it is in the worst sense harmful to mankind is abundantly proved, but that it is possible seriously to be put forward and blindly believed illustrates how unworthy mankind was of the Christ and how unprepared it was and is to understand his teachings aright or to follow in his steps.

Mankind reads into Christianity a paternalism which is foreign to the mystic teachings of the Christ as they apply to this world and which were intended to indicate a possible higher spiritual state for humanity, up to that vast and remote exaltation, where man may attain a complete harmony with his Creator and enter into the Divinity itself.

It is for these reasons, among others, man should be taught that the possibilities of a future state, which he regards as immortality, rest exclusively with the individual, to be realized or lost according as he uses the gifts of an all-wise Creator, who cannot do more for man than has been done, in bestowing upon him the gift of life in an infinite and wonderful universe, where all is within the scope of man's proper nature and where nothing depends upon favouritism, accident or chance and in which as the Christ said: "Whatsoever a man soweth—that shall he also reap."

So much importance do I attach to this principle that I believe it can be followed by humanity to a destiny so high as to abolish laws of every sort, in the same sense

that as soon as the earliest stages in a child's life have
been passed, the child must not be controlled or governed
by prohibitions and under wise policy these become at
last entirely unnecessary and threats are at all times
wrong. Unless this is in fact so, there can be no moral
progress or true freedom for the individual. That there
is now among men so little of both these great and priceless
attainments, is to be attributed in a large measure to
the artificial restraints, the false hopes, the threats, the
promises, the pretence and the oppressive tyranny
expressed towards mankind through its unspeakable
institutions and its immoral creeds.

Humanity is only in the beginning of its development.
Vast and varied as are man's actual achievements they
serve only as an indication of what he has not achieved.
At every step in his local conquests of nature through
the use of its own laws, and in every phase through which
he passes in the conquest and higher expression of himself, he has unmistakable tokens of capacities and possibilities which all but baffle his understanding and which
cannot fail to be pursued by him to ends which are now
beyond his imagination. In proportion as man can be
led to feel that his destiny here and everywhere and now
and forever depends upon *himself* and that it is only
through a process of evolution, ever towards a higher
being that there is any occasion for, or possibility of what
he terms immortality—in just that degree will he attach
such dignity to his own being that he could not ask and
would not expect to receive any favouritism, either from
God or man. Neither could he then inflict injury upon
any other being. Man is here as one of the manifold
expressions of an unknowable mystery, but what he is, he
is in his own right and what he may become must be an
inevitable sequence in the ordered relation of events

which flow from a certain cause. The effects of this cause can never be averted or in the least degree altered in kind and it is only when man has learned that he must look within himself for all that is to free and ennoble life that he can take sure steps in which he will not have to rely upon either God or man, to do for him what only he alone can and should do for himself.

It is for this reason solely I have considered it a duty to draw attention to what is now the most dangerous aspect of ecclesiastical authority, coupled as it is with political power and to emphasize that it is because of man's unthinking acceptance of what is in fact not true to his nature or in harmony with his interest and reason, that he has brought upon himself such disastrous evils in the material, intellectual and moral realms.

The attitude of submission to one or another institution tends towards submission to everything to which man should never submit. Some of the most melancholy pages in history attest how terribly true this is and also that it was only after a sufficient number of men had thrown off the pall of superstition and had rejected religion altogether that they were able or that it occurred to them to overthrow the institutions which joined with the church to keep them in bondage.

It is due to man's pretended acceptance of something which has been to him only an empty symbol, that he is without protection against the terrible storm in which his civilization and religions are being wrecked.

It is in the name and under the sanction of religion that war is made, that alien races are enslaved, that the toil of the world is exploited, that women are degraded and children deprived of all that should be the sacred rights of childhood.

The whole of this shameful business may be traced to

the pretention and superstition which men tolerate when these should instead, be completely repudiated and in their place should be an ethic which would elevate, ennoble and free the human reason and give homage to all that lends independence, moral courage and dignity to life.

CHAPTER XI.

THE NEW MARRIAGE SYSTEM.

I wish not to leave open to any possible misconception what appears to me both the highest and the inevitable social relation for men and women. This is indicated on page XI of the preface, in which I venture to forecast what is to be the remote goal of man's relations with woman, following sound biological and ethical principles.

It will not be amiss briefly to observe some of the tendencies towards polygamy and the forces which must constantly counteract these tendencies and why in the end these forces are destined to triumph. Regardless of all temporary counterbalancing influences it is true in principle that only those who are most fit may survive. Any thing which tends towards unfitness is doomed to disappear. When this is applied to the physical aspect of promiscuous sexual relations it means that such relations increase the liability of both men and women to contract diseases which are in themselves fatal to the physical wellbeing of the persons involved and tend to exteal minate the race.

Polygamy and promiscuous sexual relations are totally unalike. This is one of the reasons why I consider polygamy to be the only honourable and scientifically sound method of dealing with the great and pressing evil of promiscuous sexual relations now existing upon a scale unequalled at any other period in history.'

As humanity progresses towards universal socialization

there will be less opportunity for the unfit to survive, because the position of every member of society will more and more depend upon his personal qualities, rather than upon any of the accidents of birth or fortune, since nearly all such favoritism rests upon an unsound and unmoral usurpation of political privileges and property. The demands of this movement are that what is best in men and women shall be ever augmented and what is not suited to a true social state shall disappear. From this aspect the ones who have the benefit of the love and care of both parents will, in the natural course, be the best equipped for the great days when all men and women must stand upon their own foundation and create their own place in a proper commonwealth.

As society emerges from the horrors of over-centralization of underpaid men and women and returns more and more to the village and communal life, which is to be a part of future industrialism, there will be a decreasing tendency towards all the vices which are now the plague of our disordered and unsocial system. This will be another and important step towards monogamy because it will bring an ever increasing number of people under what may be termed local social restraint, which is more potent for the average person than all other forms of restraint. In principle I am opposed to all tyranny of public opinion, but the time is still remote when man may be properly freed from such restraint, through self-culture, altruism and sound ethics. It is a moral state at which the masses must arrive before they will feel that no restraint is necessary. It is at all times difficult to draw the line where it should be drawn against the arrogance of public opinion, but so long as any line must be drawn, it should be in the interests of the material and social wellbeing of the people—although it may inflict undeserved restraint

or hardship upon exceptional members of society. The
principle applies to the mass and the few will always
be judged by the standards of the mass, rather than by
their own standards, which may be in conflict with the
sentiment of the mass, even if not opposed to its highest
interest. The mass instinct is often wrong in particular
instances and usually slow to understand even the greatest
projects conceived for the common good, but there is
abundant evidence on all the pages of time that the mass
instinct, when allowed to take its course, is ever tending
to realize the greatest good for the greatest numbers and
is thereby slowly marching towards the highest goal.

There is a solemn duty placed upon all men that this
movement should in no way be retarded, that it should
be steadfastly guided towards its largest ends and that
individuals should subordinate their temporary and strictly
personal aims to a realization of the general good.

It is one of the baneful privileges of the aristocrats
and plutocrats that they have the power to dispose of the
lives of men and women in ways which cannot lead to
any high and noble ends and which tend only to increase
the evils which all men of power should unite to suppress.

It is upon this basis that the common good can alone
be realized and it is from this standpoint that I have
considered what should be our attitude towards the ab-
normal situation now existing between men and women
and what are to be the immediate measures to deal with
this situation, *keeping steadily before us the ideal of a monogamous social life and how it may be established among men.*

The fact that it does not exist and that all present
tendencies are in the opposite direction does not in the
least indicate that it is not a desirable goal and one which
can be generally attained.

It will be seen that my suggestions as to a new marriage

system to meet the emergency which has been thrust upon humanity by imperialism and high finance, all tend towards an ideal in which there would be no place for polygamy. They are temporary measures which would enforce upon men a new sense of responsibility in their relations with women and prevent men from exploiting the present and temporary crisis into which women have been so ruthlessly thrown.

By the most stringent measures I seek the protection of women, in the conviction that it is only through such protection they are to find complete emancipation and it is only upon the basis of their complete social and personal emancipation that society can attain its highest ends.

Slowly through the centuries the position of woman has altered as regards her relation to her immediate family and towards the state. Upon its large lines this alteration has been in the interests of women and therefore of humanity, but the problems created by the infamous war must be met upon a basis that will enable women to consolidate the progress they have made and guard the advantages they have won.

These advantages are now in danger of being neutralized or perhaps even lost for some generations, if women continue the victims of promiscuous sexual intercourse and enter generally into industrial competition with men. For biological and social reasons, apart from ethical considerations, this must be avoided. Promiscuous relations result in diseases which exterminate those involved and so long as we continue our scandalous waste of men through exploitation and wars there will be either legalized polygamy or promiscuity and the latter leads by sure steps to a wholesale waste of life and will inflict untold misery upon millions of defenseless children. If monogamy is, as I believe it to be, the only system which will survive or which is fit to survive, it is a system which can be firmly, generally and truly established only in a society which is itself fit to survive. As society now stands it is not fit to survive and it cannot endure upon its present basis and it will not survive, unless its fatal tendencies are abolished and the great evils now inflicted upon the masses are remedied without too much delay.

All the measures indicated in these pages lead surely towards a better future for humanity and they should be applied to the various phases of human activity as concurrent and related measures. They do not seek merely temporary ends, but indicate a remote goal which can be reached only through the passing of generations, and which cannot be reached at all on the lines now being followed by a blind humanity, which allows itself to be led by men who are equally blind.

Slowly the universal socialization will abolish the evils of exploitation, decentralize the great populations, emancipate the ones who toil with their brains, and hands, and make the way clear for the survival of all that is in harmony with the universal principle of the greatest good for the greatest number. And when that day comes, men and women will have risen above all the monstrous wrongs which now beset them and they will have risen in their family relations to effective monogamy.

It should be one of the most constant and general aims of women to seek a sound education upon the principles I have indicated and when this is pursued by women until they attain the age of twenty-five, they will become a new force in the world, tending to elevate humanity, and requiring more and more from men in social and cultural attainments.

If the men pursue a similar course until they are twenty-five, and if through my system of marriage the evils of promiscuity could be ultimately abolished, these new generations of free, clean and intelligent men and women comrades, each occupying their co-operative sphere, rather than entering a competitive struggle, would create a civilization, which is to-day beyond the most extravagant imagination of any man.

As it is the desire of all persons to realize their own happiness they must be prepared to express such social ethics as will tend to the realization of general happiness, if such a state were possible of attainment. It will be admitted that only a few ever achieve happiness. By this is meant the realization of the highest joys which we seek or wish in life. To the extent that man's capacities are complex, great and varied, the difficulty of accomplishing their fulfillment is obviously increased and man is unhappy in proportion to the things demanded by his nature and unattainable by him; also in proportion as he ignores the moral and social obligations which rest upon every man howsoever great or obscure his lot may be.

As society increases in complexity and as the area of individual influence arising from all actions is constantly enlarging its effects as well as its scope, there are increasing reasons why this tendency should be accompanied by a corresponding effort to establish individual relations upon the most simple as well as the most natural possible basis. Instead of this being in fact the trend of society, men and women have steadily multiplied their difficulties through an ever increasing interference with all that is most natural and beautiful in an ordered life between them and have constantly acted as if it were their chief concern to make the life of each as complicated, troubled and unhappy as possible. The result is that what all seek none are able to find. The world is bereft of song for men and women because the joy of life is buried under mountains of institutions, all founded upon pretentious appearances and unreality and at every turn we are greeted with some grotesque horror for which we alone are responsible and which we had no interest to create and less to maintain.

The strongest influence which exercises power over the average man or woman is the desire to obtain that which will be of the most use as a means to a given end, rather than that which is in itself most desirable as an end, without regard to any ulterior considerations. If we place in this category the acquisition of money and power we find that the reasons for which they are generally sought are such as to preclude their wisest use in cases where they are attained and so high a value is placed upon them by mankind as a means to many ends, that nearly all who set out in the scramble for money and power are in advance destined to fail. As men have at the outset given an entirely false and exaggerated importance to these non-essentials, humanity presents the melancholy spectacle of adding disappointment, regrets and remorse to its material and moral failures.

There arise out of this false standard of values all those evils which must ever follow in the train of wrong principles, adopted from unworthy motives and held in sufficient regard to dominate the pretensions as well as the acts of men and women through the greater part or the whole of their lives.

It would be regrettable enough if such moral failure were to involve only a minor phase of man's activities, but when it involves all that is most essential in the whole range of human relations, it is necessary to look to a remote future in order reasonably to hope for the existence of a humanity which will regard the most important concerns of life in their true proportions and thereby establish a standard of morals freed from all the baneful effect of punishments and rewards as the motive force of human conduct.

It will be urged that there are some minds of so large a grasp, directed by a will so inflexible, that they ignore what may give them the highest amount of happiness in order to attain ends deemed more important for others, rather than anything which life might otherwise offer to themselves. This is a consideration which can be weighed only by experience and observation. The testimony of everyone upon so intimate a motive of action is of great importance, not in establishing the general principle of conduct that happiness, or the avoidance of pain is the ultimate object of all endeavour, but rather as indicating that it is only in the achievement of what man feels to be his highest purposes, that true happiness is in fact to be found.

I believe this to be a dominant necessity of the most elevated minds in pursuit of what they regard as their greatest happiness or ultimate good. Nothing less than the feeling that they are progressing towards their largest destiny, and that they are helping others towards a higher goal, will satisfy the conscience of men and women who have attained the sense of moral responsibility which should rest upon each member of society. So natural is this feeling of relationship to other human beings that it logically carries with it a keen susceptibility to the opinion of others. It is precisely at this point that those who are not at all in accord with the prevailing notions of others, and who are also conscious of the value of their own convictions, are prepared to surrender to popular prejudice those feelings which should be maintained to combat and destroy all prejudice.

I have endeavoured to indicate with some precision in preceding chapters that what appears to be simple or even accidental in the intellectual, material and moral world, is in fact an essential sequence in the ordered nature of a universe in which nothing is left to chance and in which everything that now is, may be traced to something which has necessarily preceded it. In this view I have considered the past and present position of women as it relates to and must arise from their most enduring traits, expressed in general tendencies, in order that the conclusions reached may indicate a solution of the great problems under review.

Women are entitled grievously to complain of their present lot. It is a complaint with which I am in complete accord, but I feel most earnestly that their highest happiness and the good of posterity, which involve women's most noble and natural occupation, with true freedom for the display of their greatest faculties, cannot be realized if they continue to be led along the unfortunate paths they are now following.

I regard it a solemn duty to indicate what I am definitely convinced is the only effective and honourable solution of the existing economic and social problems and to state the considerations upon which my views are founded.

Women are more than ever being flattered into slavery. It is through well-disguised flattery that peoples, nations and individuals have usually lost their freedom and that they will always be in danger of losing it, because pride and vanity are the most general and lamentable defects of mankind.

The most dangerous flattery of women now takes the form of giving them the ballot and urging them generally to become competitors of men in the professions, industry and trade. They are told that they can do man's job quite as well or better than he can and that they should show men there is nothing which women cannot or should not do. No advice ever given to women was so contrary to their highest interest or so much against the welfare of mankind and if extensively and generally followed it will result in the complete industrial enslavement of men, women and children. Women are told they should have equal pay for equal work and that is quite true, but if they could understand what this means they would discover one of the vital dangers they incur through industrial employment.

From my position as an employer I will briefly set forth what is hidden in the necessity that this suggestion should be made at all. It is this: Men are employed upon the basis of their competitive necessities, without regard to the value of what they create and based upon the minimum wages at which they can exist and propagate more toilers. The men are bought and sold in a competitive market along with cattle and corn and as a world commodity. Their bare necessities are the measure of their value, even when there is not excessive competition and great unemployment.

The women have been bought upon the same shameful basis and as they had fewer necessities, they could be purchased at a lower price. As they are entirely unorganized they are a cheaper industrial commodity. Their necessities are less, usually because they are the supplemental supporters of a family, rather than its only support. To just the extent that the number of women toilers increases in trades and industry, the wages of men and women will be reduced and equal pay for equal work, if accorded to these deluded women, will mean nothing more important than the further enslavement of men and a more oppressive slavery of women. This will result because women will never upon any basis, be able generally to earn as much as men, for the simple reason that they cannot do an equivalent amount of work. They are by nature, temperament and constitution disqualified to compete upon equal terms with men in trade and industry. Under the pressure of sentiment which makes its most effective plea to women, they have for a brief time, performed arduous work with great enthusiasm and devotion. It is precisely their emotional qualities, which temporarily sustain women beyond their normal strength to do a work they should never have been forced to perform and which they cannot indefinitely continue without incurring consequences of a general and disastrous character.

Women should be told that the men have never had any incentive to do their best or to perform the amount of labour of which they are readily capable. Men have been injudiciously advised to reduce their output in order to increase wages, whereas such a policy can only have the contrary effect. The only thing that may be said in justification of a policy so unsound on the part of labour is that under the plutocratic principle of employing men on the basis of their necessities they would only be paid enough to meet such necessities and as they increased the number of units of production per day their masters decreased the per unit payment as wages. I do not here go more exhaustively into this important phase of the economic side of this question because it has been considered in its various bearings in *"The World Allies."*

Not only in its economic aspects, but in other ways this competition will prove a calamity to mankind, because in proportion as women reduce the wages of men and as there are now millions more women than men, there will be general and promiscuous relations between men and women and consequently one or more generations of fatherless children to be cared for by the state. Nothing could be more ruinous to men and women in general than deliberately, through ignorance and lack of foresight, to bring this havoc upon themselves.

If this is to be avoided there must be a complete change in the basis of payment of men and no industrial employment of women or children and the present system of marriage must be radically altered.

Men must have the benefit of the fabulous wealth they create and women should be enabled to live their natural lives, freed from economic competition with men and assured the full enjoyment of their rights to home and motherhood.

A right can exist in its most strict and effective sense only when some obligations have been entered into, which definitely establish and define it and which properly impose upon society the duty of safeguarding it.

As matters now stand the protection of women in their relations with men is left to the generosity of the men. Except among those who have titles or money, there is no contract entered into between men and women either through marriage or in sexual relations without marriage, which affords the least protection to women, either in an economic or moral sense. So long as it suits a man to deal justly by his wife or mistress he does so, and when it suits his caprice, he ceases to do so. This is an intolerable and immoral position, from which women must be liberated in the interests of all that is socially the most elemental and ethically the most sacred. A right is only enforceable if recognized in some definite form which admits of clear interpretation. For these and other reasons, in matters having an aspect of permanence or which may involve interpretation after a period of years, it is essential to define the obligations and rights in the precise terms of a written contract. When rights are so defined they cannot be ignored or their enforcement refused, without destroying the foundation upon which society itself is based.

In a consideration of one's rights there is and must be a clear distinction between those arising from obligations created or implied by conduct and those established and defined by contract. The rights of a woman established through intimate relations with a man are moral rights, created by conduct which implied definite and direct obligations in every sense morally binding, but society has not attached any legal value, or given any legal status to such moral obligations and they are consequently not enforceable. There is a further and great distinction to be made between the position of contracting parties when, as in the case of marriage, the consideration upon which the obligations are created towards the woman, is a consideration which she has provided when the contract is signed and she commences her relations in marriage, as distinguished from the ordinary contract in which this unique element is not involved, because a woman gives herself and has nothing more to give.

It is due to the prejudice with which all such relations are generally regarded that there is not even a moral punishment inflicted by reason of any moral injustice which may result through them to women. So prejudiced and perverse are the general notions of propriety and the moral sense of mankind that instead of calling the man to account either for his conduct or for the moral injustice he has inflicted upon another, society does nothing more useful or just than blame and ostracize the woman. This attitude does not arise so much from the instinct of self-defense on the part of society as from the resentment that its whims have not been sufficiently respected—at least in appearances. It is not the thing in itself which is condemned but rather that what is practiced contrary to the pretence of society must be hidden from its view, otherwise society will retaliate. The true interests of society, as a measure of self-defense and disassociated from any higer considerations, would be to so regulate the basis upon which such relations may be entered, as to ensure itself against the transfer of what should be the personal obligations of individuals, to the charge of society as a whole. These are the more direct and primitive results against which society has the right and is under the obligation to protect itself in the general interest, quite independently of any considerations as to its duty towards the helpless individuals involved.

The governing classes, which prescribe the measure of discretion and limit the powers to be vested in any executive or judicial authority to compel a discharge of obligations imposed by duty and morality, have taken special precaution to limit such powers to the right to enforce what may be termed definite legal obligations and only to enforce these at the express request of someone competent to invoke superior aid and demand outside protection. It cannot be seriously urged that this affords any definite or suitable protection to millions of women who through economic pressure and the monstrous crimes of plutocracy, are placed under moral and material handicaps by men. And as it is impossible in practice to clothe any tribunal with discretionary powers, enabling it to interfere in the relations of individuals, to prescribe their moral duties and enforce the observance of obligations which, however sacred they should be considered, are not recognized in law as binding, it is necessary to bring these most important acts of social conduct within the bounds of law and render them illegal, except upon a basis which creates definite legal obligations, capable of being effectively enforced.

This brings us to a consideration as to how such results may be attained and the measures required to give definite and general effect to what will be readily conceded as most desirable in the general interest of society and equitable as regards great numbers of women who are now the victims of our egregious wrongs.

There is no other relation in life from which come such great and important social evils and which results in such monstrous injustice to women as the relations which they form with men. The present standards which enable a man to inflict permanent injury and social ostracism upon one or twenty women, while he escapes a hero and marries some brainless girl, who considers him a sport—is an impressive proof of the low standard of justice and morals now generally sanctioned and a melancholy indictment of the female sex upon both intellectual and moral grounds. Upon intellectual grounds because they have not sufficient sense and too much vanity to understand that they may be only one more addition to his list and not the last number to be added. And upon moral grounds because, instead of condoning and in a way admiring the injustice he has inflicted upon other women and instead of the unconcern they show because they expect to escape that special form of injustice themselves—they should in ethics and justice make such conduct a bar against any man seeking their affections.

Once more there enters into this attitude those considerations inevitably arising from a sense of competition which women naturally feel towards each other and also the sentiment that those who have apparently failed were playing the game of life upon an irregular or unconventional basis, which in the mind of the average woman is unconditionally condemned, especially after she is herself married or before marriage if it happens that she is too timid, cautious or intelligent to risk the game of life upon a basis which does not offer the maximum of security for the minimum of hazard.

It is the injustice and wrong to women that are now associated with man's polygamy which are reprehensible in themselves upon ethical grounds rather than polygamy itself, which in the form set out in this chapter is not to be condemned upon such grounds.

The vast army of women who are either mothers without husbands or who have men without enjoying any stability, protection or security in their relations, or who are vegetating away their lives as old maids with entirely exaggerated notions regarding sexual matters, and also that other vast army of women toilers and helpless women of the street which daily grows larger—these are only a part of the tribute paid to a marriage institution which is contrary to human nature and an outrage upon society.

It has been contended by eminent philosophers and re-echoed by those who advocate the general employment of women, that the greater part of the selfishness and injustice in the world arises from the self-worship involved in the so-called subjection of women by men. I believe on the contrary that the strongest influences towards generosity, the most effective appeals to tenderness and the most ennobling sentiments, which exercise great and constant and permanent influence over the lives of the majority of men of all classes and in all the circumstances of life, arise precisely because of the dependence of women upon men and the feeling that it is upon this basis that women confide their lives to men.

In proportion as women pass from this relation to one of competitive struggle with men, they will be regarded by men as an increasingly competitive element in an already congested and disorganized society. This would in practice mean that so far as women had the power to do so, they would surrender their most effective means of protection and in exchange would receive the right to fight their protectors, to contest with them for the exercise of power through the ballot and in general to enter fields of activity and conflict for which they are disqualified by nature and from which the large interests of humanity can sustain only great and increasing injury. I am not opposed to women having votes or entering into all *intellectual* pursuits, but they must not hope to obtain their economic and social rights except through organization to vote with the men of their own class. They must not do as those men have done, namely to divide their votes among parties controlled by plutocrats and exploiters.

There is a general feeling among women that they are under economic and social subjection to men. To an extent this is quite true and it is in the highest interest of humanity that no members of society should feel that there is any sort of personal or collective tyranny over them, which can in the least repress the complete expression of their powers. So far as such tyranny exists it should be discouraged and as soon as possible destroyed. The division of labour in founding and maintaining a home implies that the man shall produce the means of family support and the woman shall spend it. In this relation the woman should be made to feel that she has earned an income in her toil for husband and children and in sentiment as in fact they are spending what both have earned, each in his most natural sphere. If this were the attitude of men in general, a great part of woman's feeling of subjection would disappear because in an intellectual sense the supremacy of one over the other is not subject to regulations or controlled by sentiment. How far, then, are women under a recognized and avoidable subjection to men?

As this is a matter of first importance to millions of women it should be examined with an impartial desire to ascertain in what ways the subjection of their sex is most unbearable and how it may be abolished. In the first instance it cannot be said that women are in any sense under legal disability arising from their sex. No man has any legal advantage over a woman solely upon the ground of sex in any tribunal where they appear as litigants with respect only to property. Unless there are relations other than those ordinarily existing between litigants, the woman suffers no legal disability. On the contrary, when she is before a jury of men she has a distinct advantage over a man.

If, on the other hand, there is litigation between husband and wife involving an annulment of marriage and if the woman establishes grounds for divorce, she obtains not only the children but a decree which compels the man to support her and the children. He has the alternative of leaving the country or going to prison. If on the other hand the man obtains a decree upon similar grounds he may have the children and support them, while the woman is free to contract other relations relieved of all responsibility. The penalty of losing one's children through a divorce court is severe enough—but it is one which falls with equal weight upon the man and the woman. It will be contended that the legal disability consists in the difference of the grounds upon which divorce may be obtained by men and women. This difference is not so great as it appears. In some countries incompatibility of temper is a mutual ground, in others the desire of both parties is sufficient, but if we take the position as it exists in one of the most advanced, as well as one of the greatest civilizations, namely in England, we find the laws best suited to sustain the contention made by those who hold that women are under legal disabilities in all phases of their relations with men. The grounds of divorce in England are in effect that the man must be proven to have committed adultery and in addition desertion or cruelty must be established, while as regards women it is sufficient if they commit adultery.

There appears in this distinction a greater difference than in fact exists for the fundamental reason that men are naturally polygamists. A man may have an intimate relation with more than one woman without in any way altering his sentiments for either the women or children and without giving occasion for the least discord between them so far as he is concerned. Women, on the contrary are so unlike men in matters of temperament, and such relations have for them a meaning so different from what they can have for the average man, that when a woman becomes polyandrous her attitude towards the association previously in existence is such that it usually cannot continue.

If the fascination for a man outside his home is sufficient and he is quite independent of the opinion of his neighbours and of public sentiment in general—which few men ever are—he will add desertion to adultery, although a gentleman will never add cruelty to it.

If the grounds for divorce do not exist and the basis of mutual happiness has disappeared, the home is no longer a home in any beautiful or noble sense and its reason for existence has ceased, at least so far as concerns the relations of the man and the woman towards each other.

What may be the value of such a home to the children, will depend upon a variety of circumstances which are too special in their application and too transitory to admit of generalization.

As matters now stand the associations a man may form outside his home impose no obligations which can be enforced and the relations may be commenced and terminated upon such slight considerations that instead of desertion (in case the wife objects) the man may apparently accede to her whims by terminating the outside association known to her and almost immediately forming another which he vainly hopes may remain unknown. The extent to which this sort of deception and discord are experienced will depend more upon the economic independence of the man and the size of the city in which he lives, than upon all influences of education, religion and social pretences combined. It is reduced to the minimum in rural communities, towns and small cities, not because the people concerned are in any essentials different from those in the larger cities, but because they do not have the opportunity to conceal what they do not have the courage openly to avow.

Pious people who have their heads in the sand, will strongly object to this as not fairly representing man's attitude towards women and unfortunately married women are the ones who will most strongly object. It is nevertheless the attitude of men in general. The extent to which they put these sentiments into effect will depend, primarily, upon the relations existing between them and their wives. It will be determined apart from this influence, solely by age, climate, surroundings and temperament. We must take men and women as we find them. They do not change greatly from one century to another in what concerns their most pronounced and fundamental tendencies and their nature never changes.

It is far from my thought to suggest that the

unethical animal savagery in man's nature cannot be overcome. It can be and is constantly overcome through the supremacy of the spirit over matter. The progress is, however, so slow and so personal that when humanity is viewed as a whole, it has not in thousands of years recorded anything which establishes a fundamental change in man's nature, as distinguished from changes in his habits, his mode of life and his philosophy.

The most important alterations of sentiment and mode of life may be traced to altered personal environment, arising through general or special changes in the economic and social surroundings, or through the *sacred influence of a love which creates its own and special world.*

The relations men and women establish can be ideal only in so far as the ones who establish them are ideal and it is for this reason that ideal relations rarely exist. Life for humanity is unfortunately and unnecessarily a compromise at all points and in all relations. The more stupid and the meaner people are, the more readily they accept this compromise and all that it implies, and the more difficult it is for them to realize that any compromise is involved. For most people the moral compromise is of much less importance than any compromise which concerns their comfort or passing pleasures.

Quite apart from the direct harm which results to individuals and to particular associations through any form of hypocrisy, its detrimental effects upon society as a whole are almost incalculable. Only children in the first few years of life are like flowers and show us the high possibilities of our nature, not from an ethical or social point of view, because they are usually deficient in both, but from the point of view of candour and instinctive naturalness.

There might be something beautiful in man's pretence to think, feel and live upon a higher basis than he has actually attained, if it arose from a longing really to find within himself and constantly to express those qualities which are regarded as an honour to mankind. The moral value that might arise from such a sentiment is not attained because the individual does not seek to exemplify ideals but only pretends to do so.

If we examine the relations of men and women who are associated in marriage, and consider what are in practice the broad outlines of such associations, we will be obliged to attach less and less importance to the actual or supposed difference in the legal position of the two, as compared to what are in fact their actual relations in the general concerns of life.

It will be conceded as one of the most elemental of all propositions that where radical difference of opinion may arise the final power of decision must somewhere be vested. This is true as regards not only the creation of governments but as to the discharge of all their functions. The same applies to all tribunals which are to pass decisions upon the inevitable differences arising among men. It is a principle which must be applied to the home and it also holds true in the general activities of society. The most independent and enlightened individuals accept the principle that they may properly be compelled to abide by decisions with which they are not in accord and which may in their view be unjust and an infringement upon their most personal rights. That such decisions are constantly made and enforced does not admit of discussion and they arise, not from any defect in the principle involved, but rather in the errors of application which are inseparable from all human decisions. If, therefore, in certain circumstances the law seems to place the woman under disabilities as regards her ultimate rights, when her opinions are in conflict with those entertained by her husband, there is no other relation in life in which this apparent advantage is of so little practical importance to a man. It is never resorted to except in the most extreme cases and then only when the basis upon which home life may properly continue has been destroyed.

The home is the one place in which the average man is disposed to say "yes" and the last place in which he always desires to say "no" to the wishes of others. It is the one place where he is the most reluctant to display those critical and cold judgments, which the stern necessities of life—not tempered by love and tenderness— are constantly imposing upon him in the great and varied concerns of the world.

The point of my contention may perhaps be more clearly illustrated by examining the practice of partnership among men in business and in the experiences of a board of directors in the management of important undertakings. A partnership between supposed equals in business, where the interests and responsibilities are taken as equal, is covered by a formal contract of association, in many respects not unlike that which is expressed or implied in the marriage contract. The duties of each in a business partnership are rarely precisely defined, as is also the case in marriage, although they are usually understood in a manner which implies an agreement— even if it does not in fact constitute one. The differences which may arise in the working of such a partnership are the result of the manner in which the work of the partners is performed, rather than as to what work should be alloted to the several partners. These differences result from events which may be small or great, from defects which may be real or imaginary, but which could not be foreseen and hence could not be provided for, either in the business partnership or in the marriage agreement.

In a business partnership one partner will by common assent be accorded a superior position which in effect amounts to the possession of arbitrary and final power.

This may be so unconsciously exercised in business as to cause no friction among supposed equals, or it may cause constant friction, which ends in a dissolution of the contract.

In the affairs of a great corporation the principle is the same. A board of directors is chosen, consisting perhaps of nine members. In law and in the theory of corporation control, each of these directors has the same powers, each has a vote and all are equally answerable to the shareholders and public. One of the first acts of these directors sitting upon equal terms, is to select a chairman who in theory has no other or additional rights than his colleagues, but in practice—if he is qualified for the position—he will become the actual head of the concern. The policy of the board will be his policy, its decisions his decisions and its mistakes will consist in the board having been parties to or having approved the mistakes of their chairman.

Both in the partnership and in the board there will be consultation, discussion and perhaps differences of opinion as to policy and detail, but in the actual working of the partnership and company the decisions of the strongest man will be final and may in fact be so tactfully put forward that they do not appear to emanate from their real source, but come rather as suggestions from those upon whom the superior will is being unconsciously imposed.

That this is one of the essential requisites to all administrative success, the most powerful and experienced men of business will everywhere agree. The advice of associates may to a degree alter the policy of a leader, but in proportion as he is successful, he follows his own policy. The most conspicuous achievements among men of action in all spheres confirm this principle, whether in war, diplomacy, government, parliamentary leadership or finance.

This is in practice the policy in the best regulated homes and it is in the home where man is supposed to have the most absolute and arbitrary powers that he exercises them the least, or that the occasion for their exercise most seldom arises. There is no other phase of man's activity where he shows so great a regard for advice which he may not highly value as in the home, and there is no other place in which he is so easily persuaded to forego his opinions upon matters in which he has no doubt as to what his opinions should be. This arises from the feeling which man entertains for those who are weaker than himself and who place an undue importance upon what in fact may be trifles. In the home, the same as in the partnership, the company and all other relations, the one who has the right to power and whose decisions are respected is superior to those surrounding him—at least in those natural or acquired powers upon which all intellectual and moral authority must rest. It is only upon that basis that men of attainments and character are interested in the acquisition or exercise of authority and it is only by such men that great powers can be secured and maintained for any considerable time.

Instead of women being excluded upon the ground of sex from the activities of men, so far as history and experience may be consulted, we know that the greatest and most humble men have made women their principal or only confidants, with whom they have discussed their hopes, their achievements, their ambitions, their failures and their glory.

The influence which women exercise over men through their teachings in childhood is great and important, but it leaves the most lasting impressions upon the sentiment rather than the reason of men. Nearly all mothers cause their children to believe in religion for a little while, but it is a sentiment which may not extend beyond childhood because it is accepted without reason and may therefore be set aside if it is ever brought under the scrutiny of reason.

The teaching which men and women receive in childhood is nevertheless of the highest importance and exercises a great and permanent influence over their most consequential acts. This is especially true with reference to man's relations to the opposite sex. It also applies generally to all concerns in which sentiment is an important or decisive factor and it is difficult to disassociate sentiment from the smallest or the greatest affairs of life.

If a particular sentiment which does not subsequently do violence to reason is strongly impressed upon a man in his infancy and is associated with one who was the object of his devotion and his affections, it is rarely ever obliterated and it may—in its own sphere—become a governing principle during the whole course of his life.

It is therefore of the highest importance that children should not be taught to hold as true in childhood what they may be compelled to abandon as false when they attain an age of intelligent discretion.

They must not be taught that there should be any escape from the consequences of their own acts, that there is any paternalism in nature or any mercy shown to a fool. They should be taught that it is natural and just to be prepared to respond to all that may result from their own conduct and that they should so regard life, and so act, that they would not object if all men thought and acted in the same way.

Howsoever sound and thorough any instruction may

be there are some respects in which society will never change in so far as it reflects the natural acts of men because the nature of men does not change. Only such changes are possible as may be realized through altered economic environment, affording time for self-improvement and freeing women and children from drudgery, also the lessening and final destruction of superstition through science and the increase of useful instruction in the principles and application of a sound and comprehensive social and spiritual education.

One of the reforms most essential involves the complete alteration in the education now given to girls in the middle and lower classes. They are destined to work either at home or in industry. At present they are not trained for either. If they are children of the underpaid toilers they are forced to enter the ranks of the wage-slaves at an early age in spite of all compulsory education laws. So long as the earnings of children must supplement those of the father in order to maintain the family, all compulsory education laws are a farce. The average young woman in the industrial classes, especially in England, has no idea as to cooking or the management of a home and children. She has no trade or useful training for any pursuit outside a home and she enters maturity upon the lowest possible basis of usefulness to society, either as a prospective mother or as a productive unit of industrialism.

The responsibility for this shocking waste of womanhood rests chiefly upon those who dominate industrialism and those who guide the church and the educational institutions and upon the small and vain politicians who are too blind to the welfare of their country, to do anything useful for the millions upon whom all national greatness must rest.

Among the daughters of highly skilled artisans we

find a class which is not forced to seek paid employment at an early age and through the instruction acquired from their mothers they are trained to care for children and the home. They and the daughters of small farmers are the most efficiently trained for the positions they are destined to occupy.

In the more prosperous classes of society, where the daughters do not work in the home but attend school until maturity they have no useful education of any sort. They know nothing about the management of a home or the care of children, nothing about the great and important problem of working girls and yet they hope to have a home which they will not know how to regulate or care for. They have learned a little about many things, mostly useless—but they have learned nothing of importance about anything. They learn a little music which they forget immediately after marriage. They read the novels read by everybody else in order that they may find common ground for conversation with people whose heads are as empty as their own, or filled with intellectual rubbish which it is useless to gather and impossible to cast aside.

They are blind to the realities of life outside their own circle and are the most reactionary class of society. They are even a stronger force in the maintenance of plutocracy, than the men of their own class. This is partly because of their instinctive conservatism as women and also because they are less in contact with our submerged, struggling and aspiring humanity.

Some of the results of this fallacious system are exhibited in the mismanaged homes, the uneatable food and the negligence and sloth which fill the public houses as they stand with open doors on the toilers' road to despair. The happiness of mankind is in the keeping of women.

They are the fountain to which the toiler and the dreamer must go to fill the pitchers of their earthly joy. Women are in their natural and rightful place only when they are in a home which they know how to manage and to make attractive even in the most simple and humble ways. In countries like England where among the middle classes, snobbishness is exalted to the level of a religion, in all instances where circumstances permit, the girls are taught that the care of the home and children are to be confided to servants with the result that neither are cared for.

It will require a long time, more economic independence and truer notions as to education and ethics to remedy these grave evils. They are only some of the inevitable results of the deep-seated wrongs which underlie the modern brigandage of exploitation and the slavish respect for authority whether it be good or bad; also the undue regard bestowed upon institutions and prejudices which could never have obtained a shadow of existence among free and enlightened men.

I look to the year 2500 and onward into a future too remote and too dim in its outlines to be discernible to our age and I see even at that distant time humanity still struggling towards the realization of some of its most natural and important ideals. I believe these are to be brought within the reach of future generations through the measures I have put forward and which appear adapted to the well-ordered life of mankind and to its freedom and happiness.

There is no short or easy road which humanity can follow to the attainment of high ends. That nature of which we are the children is never in a hurry. It has an abundance of time. It takes sure steps and moves only in ways which it need not retrace. It finishes one task before it begins another and it never compromises. Its measures are general, inflexible and final. We witness this upon every hand and yet it is lost upon us. It has a language which we have not had the patience to understand or the courage to use and there is little indication that either to-morrow or a thousand years after to-morrow we will follow the principles upon which alone humanity may hope to take definite and constantly progressive steps towards the high destiny of which it is capable.

The way which lies immediately before us is beset with difficulties more grave than any which have marked the history of man. It is hedged about by superstitions, prejudices and hypocrisy which must be surmounted for the attainment of freedom and economic independence, from which alone may come security, enlightenment and peace to mankind.

It is a fundamental necessity that men shall be emancipated from industrial exploitation and women relieved from the burden of all industrial toil.

When men are fairly paid and the rights and obligations involved in marriage are placed upon a natural and honest footing there will be an end to the present economic and social anarchy which threaten to result either in the complete subjection of the masses or in general violence and civil wars. Either the one or the other would be a world calamity.

The reasons why a new system of marriage is a moral and economic necessity are shown in the preceding chapters and it is the purpose of the concluding pages of this chapter to sketch the outlines of this new system as I conceive it and to indicate upon what basis it should rest.

All evolution towards large and beneficial ends in the life of nations must follow a principle which runs parallel to the dominant and changeless traits of human nature and all measures destined to contribute to these ends must be suited to the state of society in which they are to be applied. Considered in this aspect and holding strongly to the conviction that there has been too much compromise and hypocrisy in all the relations and activities of life, the system proposed by me is not founded upon expediency, but rather upon what is honourable and practicable in the actual condition of society and as one of the essential measures required to remedy ancient evils which have grown to almost unbelievable proportions in recent years and which cannot be eradicated by any of the old means of exploitation, oppression and compromise.

Humanity has too long compromised its greatest problems, partly because it is natural to postpone what is difficult or disagreable of solution and partly due to the strong pressure exercised by ruling castes, which from the most remote times have seen in any rise of the masses a corresponding decline in their own favoured positions. The more remote may be the future to which great reforms can be postponed, the more contented are they who oppose such reforms. We look back upon the religious tyrannies of the past with indignation and shame and to the recent institutions of slavery with horror, but these were once supported by the opinion and sanction of the masses, the same as they now sustain the equally horrible injustice imposed upon women through capitalistic exploitation and in the relation of the sexes.

Some of the results of these monstrous wrongs are millions of disinherited toilers, other millions of homeless, over-worked and unprotected women and a disorganized and shattered world, in which the most fundamental and sacred rights of humanity have no existence.

It would be an unforgivable crime to transfer the whole of this wreckage to posterity. Howsoever well conceived in principle, the success of measures depends upon the opportuneness with which they are applied and the extent to which they do not need to rest upon the altruism or disinterested action of any considerable or powerful portion of society.

For reasons clearly set out in "*The World Allies*," the toilers are warned that the most solemn hour in history will strike when the treaty of peace is signed and plutocracy sets in motion the vast machinery it has perfected to complete the industrial enslavement of men and entrap the women of their class. It is then that the great and peaceful movement which means a new era, freed from wage slavery and war, may take its first effective step. If the toilers allow this opportunity to pass they will loose an advantage which will not be regained and the clock of time may be turned backward for generations. Through conditions imposed by plutocracy and its ghastly war, the toilers may become masters of the industrial world, not in the sense that they can replace the controlling brains in the direction of industry, but they can dictate the distribution of future wealth created by machinery and toil. They can do this however only through organization upon a world-scale, for economic action and political pressure.

The relations of women to such a movement and the position they should occupy towards industrialism are clearly set out in "*The World Allies*" and in these pages. In considering these measures it is well to keep in view the gradually changing attitude of the public towards the questions of marriage and divorce which has resulted from the industrial pressure upon men, the ever enlarging sphere of enforced employment for women and the increasing disbelief of the masses in all established religions.

It may be taken as an unfailing principle that the attitude of society toward all economic and social reforms will be more powerfully influenced by the temporary and material interests of its members than by any code of genuine or so-called morals.

Most people refrain from doing what is unpopular, not because it may be wrong, but solely because it is unpopular. Few people are prepared to stand on their own feet and hold any opinions contrary to those professed by the masses who unfortunately are not far-sighted, and who naturally follow those whom fortune or temporary political power bring to the surface. The masses, through which ruling castes exercise potent tyranny, would now be in chains but for the noble and courageous reformers to whose foresight and genius the greater part of all progress is due, but who were compelled to lead the masses against their will and always against their old prejudices and beliefs. It is of incidental importance to note that no matter what they and their neighbours pretend to believe as to conduct, the principal consideration for the majority is, that what is unpopular should not be found out. This is almost a religion in England. The so-called social crimes are not considered disgraceful if they are merely committed, but quite disgraceful if they are discovered.

The whole of this pretence should be cast aside as unworthy of honourable men and women since it is degrading to character and destructive of morals. Any system which makes such a pretence even remotely desirable or apparently necessary should be completely rejected and honourable measures, in accord with human nature and general practice, should be established.

We must take humanity as we find it and this means that any general rules for the regulation of conduct, which imply that men and women are to act contrary to their nature, are destined to complete failure, either in the form of open repudiation or through secret violation by those whose conduct they are supposed to regulate. The marriage laws are not in accord either with the nature or the practice of mankind and the crumbling structure of modern society rests upon a foundation of sand, which has been steadily shifting through industrialism and is now being destroyed by war. It must be rebuilt upon a solid basis, devoid of economic slavery and freed from the necessity of women to forego what would be their highest career in a proper commonwealth and what is also one of their most natural rights.

There must be an end to measures which seek to impose upon the masses a rule of conduct from which the governing castes are everywhere exempt. If in practice the ruling classes were compelled to act towards women as their economic pressure has forced the majority of men to act, the existing regulations as to marriage would not long remain in force, in fact they would never have been devised. It is because the minority of men who control society are exempt from the effects of their unnatural and tyrannical system, or freed from the responsibilities which should be inseparable from their mode of life, that they desire to maintain the existing marriage laws. So far as lies in the power of the ruling castes the actual order of things will not be altered.

The senseless and compromising divorce laws now generally existing would not have been enacted but for the desire of the so-called upper classes to find a way by which their own members might escape intolerable situations. As these wretched laws now stand, their benefits are denied to the masses because the cumbersome machinery of courts, complicated on all sides by hungry lawyers, is too expensive to be invoked by those whose physical toil has created the wealth of the world. The reports of pompous parliamentary commissions have not gotten beyond the stage of recommending legislation to cheapen divorce proceedings, instead of devising measures which would practically abolish the occasion or the desire for divorce, which is at present the only means of escape from situations arising through the operation of natural laws and brought into being by unnatural laws imposed by men. It is man's senseless method to try to cure by wrong legislation a part of an evil created by legislation which was wrong. Society is usually true to its traditions. It imposes upon itself great social afflictions and seeks partial remedies for the evils after they assume their most severe and conspicuous forms.

Some of its laws drive women into the streets and other laws seek to control a small fraction of them by the police. Society employs millions of girls and women at starvation wages to the grievous detriment of humanity. By economic wrongs and laws society prevents the wage-earning men from protecting these women and removing them from factories to homes, instead of competing with them in a senseless struggle for existence from which plutocracy reaps the harvest of the world's toil.

The whole of this shameful system of exploitation, injustice and pretence should be swept away. So long as human life can be bought and sold as a commodity, based not upon its productive value, but upon its competitive necessities, it is the manifest interest of plutocracy constantly to intensify this competition and this it has succeeded in doing through the increasing employment of women and children. As machinery is multiplied and perfected it is increasingly confided to the operation of women and children and this is the deliberate policy of plutocracy as a part of its design to continue and so far as possible extend its enslavement of all toilers.

So long as capitalism can pay toil upon the basis of

its necessities it increases its profits in the ratio in which an ever increasing number in society must toil in order to live. Taking the family as a unit to illustrate this principle it is more profitable to plutocracy if two or four members must earn wages to provide the family necessities, than if their wants were met by the toil of only one member, because the surplus of all production goes to the employer instead of to the toiler. The greater the extent to which this exploitation can be carried, the more profitable it is to the ruling castes.

This basis of payment can be altered only in two ways, both of which are concurrent and essential measures. One is that the employment of women in industries and in all competitive manual labour with men must cease and the other is that, through an economic world-organization of toilers, their compensation must bear fair relation to production rather than, as now, be established upon the basis of their barest necessities. The first of these measures can only be effected by establishing marriage upon a basis which will put an end to industrial competition between men and women and maintain the women in homes where protection is assured to them in their natural order of life.

This necessitates fundamental changes which must rest upon new laws adapted to the present state of society and in accord with the nature and practice of men and women whose relations should be designed to promote their mutual welfare and happiness.

People about to marry are chiefly dominated by the desire to increase their happiness and they are nearly always unmindful of the fact that nature appears to be interested only incidentally in this beautiful sentiment, while it is greatly concerned as to increasing the race. The means which nature adopts may be designed best to serve its principal purpose and its selection is based upon that through which it is most likely to attain its own ends, without reference to whether it attains the objects sought by its instruments.

Some of the most fundamental causes of unhappiness between married people arise precisely from this divergence between the apparent designs of nature and the primary motives of the ones whom nature uses to attain its impersonal ends.

If the marriage relation is regarded from this aspect it may be considered beautiful and honourable only if it is lived in truth, freedom and sincerity and results in mutual confidence, respect and happiness.

It is a relation which men and women should be able to terminate at any time by mutual consent, whereas such a desire now expressed by both parties renders it impossible of realization. If the ones who alone are competent to judge, seek divorce by agreement, it is denied to them, but if it is sought by only one party they are permitted to fight in the courts, for the amusement of the vulgar rabble and the profit of lawyers and to obtain by quarrelling and scandal a decree recording their unhappiness and failure. The results of this divorce are seen in the march of events which cannot fail to have a significance for society and as matters now stand they in turn become the source of more problems and evils than appear on the surface of civilization.

The new system should embody the following essential provisions:

The marriage contract to consist in signing a register to be kept in the local registry office and open to public inspection. A general form of contract to be printed in the register and a certified copy delivered to each of the parties.

All marriages to be reported weekly to the central registry office at the capital of the nation and alphabetically recorded under the names of both contracting parties. Proof to be furnished at the time of marriage that both parties are recording their real, and not assumed names.

Marriage should be permitted only to people who proved by certificate of a registered doctor that they were physically fit to marry.

The age, occupation, income and capital of both parties to be recorded and as regards the capital, of what it consists and where located. The amount which the man agrees to devote to maintain the home should be specified, and in practice it should be paid to the woman regularly through the public trustee, which would be even an improvement upon the custom so generally and wisely prevailing among the best classes of labouring men, who give the greater part of their earnings to their wives. Among others more independent financially this would have an important moral value to the women, because it would relieve them of the necessity of constantly applying to their husbands for money which, even among those who are generous, creates on the part of the woman an atmosphere highly prejudicial to the complete frankness and harmony so essential in maintaining freedom and candour in the most difficult as well as the most beautiful of all human relations. This can never be anticipated by any contracts.

The marriage agreement would stipulate the sum which the man would be obliged to provide for his wife and each child in the event of separation and if he was financially able to do so, the capital required to produce the amount would be deposited with the trustee. So long as the couple lived together the income would be paid to them and in the event of separation it would be paid directly to the woman and similar capital deposits should be made upon the birth of each child.

If the amount agreed to be paid to the woman and

children is to be paid from salary or wages, and if it becomes payable through separation, it should be paid either by the employer direct, or through the public trustee. There should be local and national boards responsible to the locality and nation and in financial and administrative relations with the public trustee. These boards would deal with the whole of the financial questions arising through marriage agreements. The boards would be elected in the same manner as the public trustee and would not be departments of any government or under any bureaucratic control. In no instance should the woman ever be required to feel in any sense dependent upon or obliged to apply to the man from whom she is separated and for whom she may no longer entertain any affection or esteem. There enters into the matter at this point the more intangible but equally important consideration as to whether in ethics and as a matter of moral justice, distinguished as it must usually be from legal justice, the woman has the right to an income from the toil of a man under these circumstances. It may be that through no fault of either the man or woman, they are so temperamentally unsuited to each other as to render marriage a failure, and separation the only honourable alternative. Added to this it may be that the salary or wages of the man are insufficient to maintain another woman and that he is consequently under a permanent hardship. Granting both of these circumstances, I hold that the woman is entitled to this permanent protection, not only upon the legal basis of a right created by contract and which in itself is a sufficient basis—but upon the grounds of ethics and of moral justice.

When the woman enters the relation she justly and naturally abandons all attempt to create her own economic independence and transfers the obligation to the man. This is in the highest sense important to the man as a competitive unit in the field of labour and is an essential condition for the most free and agreable use of the faculties with which nature has endowed both the woman and the man. It is not as it appears to be, an entirely one-sided agreement for the reasons already given and even when it may impose individual hardship upon certain men it will also act as a great incentive for a man to increase his earnings and in this he will be powerfully assisted by the withdrawal, not only of his first wife from competition, but the second wife also, for the support of whom he is striving to improve his economic position. In other cases when the man is independent and is not put to severe financial inconvenience through the loss of his wife, it becomes nothing more to him than the discharge of an engagement which is morally as binding upon his honour, as it is legally a claim upon his fortune.

The capital deposited under all agreements should remain intact and constitute a fund, the interest of which to be applied to the descendants of those who, through illness or death, were unable to meet their engagements.

It will be obvious that the amount of this provision must be the subject of agreement between the parties before marriage and there can be no restriction upon this liberty of contract except a general provision establishing a minimum for the protection of impetuous and ill-informed women who might otherwise be imposed upon. Above this minimum the amount to be agreed between the parties will depend upon the tastes, habits of life and financial position of the parties. I have known girls who toiled for thirty francs a week, who lived in poor lodgings and had no other means of support and these would be contented with a modest allowance, while I know others who would consider themselves poor unless they could spend two hundred thousand francs a year.

In the event of a rich woman marrying a poor man he might be released from any financial responsibility, so long as he was poor, but he should not under any circumstances acquire the slightest rights over any of the woman's property or income and his benefits under this heading should cease in the event of disagreement resulting in separation. This would remove one of the means now employed by unscrupulous men, through flattery and deception to obtain the property of women who are vain, ugly or old and who are brainless enough to believe everything which may be said in praise of their youth, beauty or intelligence.

It follows in the nature of things that women must either be supported by men in the honourable career of wives and mothers or must support themselves in an industrial war of ever increasing horror, waged against one sex by the other to the ultimate ruin of both.

As a transitional measure rendered necessary by a vast surplus of women over men, any man who is able to support more than one wife and their possible children should be allowed to contract plural marriages, each one as binding as the other and imposing in each case similar and permanent obligations on the part of the man. As no house is large enough for two women to live in happiness with the same man upon the same and intimate terms, and as no house is too small in which to make a woman happy if she loves the man, there should be no plurality of wives in the same house.

Either party to a marriage should be allowed to terminate the relation at will, without the consent of the other and without formalities of any sort, except to sign the register kept for such records. If terminated by the woman with or without the consent of the man, she should be free to again marry, but as long as she remained unmarried she should be entitled to receive three fourths of the amount stipulated in the marriage agreement. The remaining fourth should be deposited with the public trustee in the general marriage fund. This would be a slightly restraining influence upon both the man and the woman, as she loses and he would not gain financially from an annulment of marriage.

If the woman again marries, the obligations of the first man should automatically terminate because they must in each instance be assumed by the man before the marriage is allowed.

When such obligations are covered by a deposit of capital with the public trustee, it should be held by him and so long as the man remains unmarried he has no right to touch the income of the deposited capital. If he marries he can use the deposit as the basis of his second marriage and be again able to receive the income. This would be a continuing provision applying to men and women in all subsequent marriages, following separations.

One of the principal reasons why the agreed allowance should remain on deposit in the event of separation is to remove all temptation on the part of the man to terminate a relation and morally force the woman into a second marriage in order to obtain the return of his capital. Also that as it has been set aside for the protection of the women it should remain available for the subsequent woman with whom relations will sooner or later be established and if the man cannot touch either the capital or interest so long as he is unmarried he has no financial incentive to remain in that state and will not incur any new capital obligation if he re-marries. He thus has nothing whatsoever to gain financially from any rupture of relations with his wife and he cannot withdraw from her any of her established protection even if she is separated from him, so long as she does not re-marry.

This follows from one of the general principles which I have constantly in view in these pages and that is that men and women must be responsible to each other and to society for all the consequences of their acts; that no important act is ever without a corresponding consequence, which passes from the individual to society. It is upon this ground only and no farther that society has the right to intervene to the important and yet limited extent herein prescribed. Also that as plural marriages are the only means by which millions of women may now avoid prostitution or industrial slavery, or both, such marriages must elevate and ennoble the position of the women who contract them and must require the men honourably to discharge the obligations which should always be inseparable from relations so important and nearly always so sacred to women.

One of the most difficult of all questions which would arise under plural marriages is that involved in the disposition of the children in the event that the relation between the parents is terminated.

Under our present marriage laws, this difficulty is not solved and in practice it is never possible to render exact justice either to the parents or the children, when the parents are no longer able to live together in harmony and freedom.

It is now generally considered that either the man or woman must be at fault morally or in some other way before a divorce is permitted, whereas it is in the nature of men and women that they may become by slow degrees quite incompatible to each other and yet be in every way people deserving a better fate and having every wish to live in harmony.

This is especially true in the associations formed when

one or the other party was young or inexperienced and in those numerous instances in which one party to the relation experiences a radical alteration of sentiment and development.

Some men and women who are the most conscientious and honourable and who would be incapable of any act of injustice, become so completely estranged that the presence of one is intolerable to the other and yet they feel obliged to continue the appearance of a relation and thus pass at least an important part of their lives in complete unhappiness, which is as unjustifiable as it is unnecessary.

So tyrannical, unjust and immoral are our marriage customs that it is not possible for men and women to retain a friendly feeling for each other and at the same time obtain a divorce. They must now, by slow and pathetic steps, see a relation which once was beautiful beyond all the dreams of beauty, pass gradually down the scale of misunderstanding and contention, until it reaches an abyss of human despair, from which there is no escape but separation, and no release except divorce and no divorce except through recrimination and scandal.

If divorce is resorted to, one or the other is accused of so-called crimes against their honour and these must have been committed with third persons who are likewise accused and the one who has committed the so-called crimes is deprived of the children. If it is the woman she loses her name and her home, with its protection. She loses her income if it was derived from her husband, and she loses him. This last is not usually regarded as a loss. Beyond all this and perhaps more important than all in the affection of a woman, she loses her children and goes a pitiable wreck into a friendless world where she is soon deserted by the man who caused her downfall. Outwardly, if judged by conduct, she may be at fault, but morally she may be without the slightest blame. It is neither prudent nor just to pass judgment by appearances —even if it is ever just to pass judgment at all—and it is only the appearances that come before the court.

The world and its tribunals deal only with consequences and never attempt to trace them to their source, because they flow from the prejudices, the injustice, the bigotry, the pretence and the wrongs of the society which creates them, through bad laws, and punishes them through laws which are horrid. Also it is not practically possible to go beyond appearances to the hidden source of their origin, because that is buried in the secret conscience of each individual and is forever a closed book to all except the person involved. It could not be so much as explained to the comprehension of an outsider, much less to the comprehension of a judge.

In some instances the man may lose his children, when he is judged to be at fault, although the laws at present upon this point, strongly favour the man, arising partly from the fact that he makes the laws and is not a just or generous being and also because experience has shown that a man is generally better able than a woman to provide for children. This is attributable in part to the greater economic freedom of men as compared to women, and also to their more large and varied interests which tend to increase the opportunities for a career on the part of a son and augment the favourable chances of the marriage of a daughter.

Considered as nature no doubt intended it should be, namely with respect primarily as to what is likely to be of the greatest advantage to the offspring, without undue concern for the convenience and still less regard for the happiness of the parent, I believe the principle in the new system of marriage should be that when the father has left the home and the mother and children and terminated the marriage, the wife should be entitled to retain not only the home and children, but also the financial protection which was at marriage agreed. If she again married she would loose nothing, as the financial protection for herself would devolve upon the second husband and she would still retain the home. The protection guaranteed to the children from their father could not be alienated from them even if they remained with their mother and if she again married. The first husband would not lightly incur penalties so great.

If the woman left the man and their children and home, she would be entitled to her income so long as she remained unmarried but she would not be entitled, any more than the man would be entitled, to leave the home and yet take the children, and he would be willing to see transferred from himself to someone else the obligations to protect a wife whom he no longer cared for or of whom he might still be fond but with whom he could not continue to live.

The prospective husband should deposit the capital sum required to protect his wife, since neither she nor the children should ever be subject to the whims or caprice of the man, or their support be left to his good will or generosity, as no man will regard the children of another as he would consider his own.

The protection specified for the children and provided either through the deposit of capital or the periodical payment from income should in every case belong to the children as a permanent right until they attained the age of twenty-one or in the case of daughters until they were married. This protection should be assured to the children quite independently of what may take place between their parents. This would abolish the right of a parent to disinherit any child and it may be taken that among the wealthy the marriage contract would provide a specified minimum fortune as the rightful inheritance of each child when it attained the age of twenty-one, as a capital sum apart from the amount devoted to its maintenance.

Among the poets and the humble classes it may be thought that a wedding which took account of these material considerations would be robbed of its romantic beauty but no material considerations can destroy anything which has the quality of true romantic beauty. I can assure such classes that when an American, British, French or German millionaire is purchasing a title for his daughter, or the children of rich and powerful families are arranging a marriage, the whole matter is placed in the hands of prosaic lawyers and contracts of great length are signed and that these contracts are precise, so far as lawyers have the capacity to make anything precise.

It is not marriage which makes love beautiful, but it is love which can alone make marriage tolerable and therefore the most illegitimate of all children are those who are born to married people who do not want them. Neither love nor anything which arises from it can ever be illegitimate.

It will be conceded that it is impossible for any laws to meet all contingencies which arise without inflicting in special cases undeserved suffering upon someone. The good of the children is the highest consideration to be regarded in all measures relating to marriage and divorce. As society is now constituted and as it will probably evolve through many generations, I believe this can be most effectively and generally realized upon the basis I define.

The law should prohibit any man from having sexual relation with a woman except after marriage, contracted upon the basis I have set out and under a binding, written agreement duly recorded. If this law is violated the man should be given the alternative of immediate marriage with the woman or of losing his liberty. In this latter event he should not be treated in the coarse, brutal and shameful manner that prisoners are now treated and which is an outrage unspeakably insulting to human dignity and honour. He should on the contrary be regarded as one who, having abused his liberty among a free people, was required to forego free association among them until he was willing to discharge the obligations which he incurred in his mode of life. In the meantime the woman involved should receive an allowance from the state and the earnings of the man under restraint should be paid to the state.

The same method would be adopted in dealing with any man who failed at any time to discharge all the obligations incurred towards women and their children. In special circumstances arising through illness or accident, the man would not be held to account so long as the disability lasted. If his dependents were without resources they would be supplied from a fund, contributed upon an actuarial basis and held in trust by the public trustee for the benefit of those temporarily in need. This system would place upon men and women the full responsibility for their conduct, at the same time leaving them all personal liberty, so long as they accepted and discharged the obligations which in honour were imposed upon them as the consequences of their acts. As matters now stand, women are rarely able to avoid such consequences, whereas man's most important acts towards women and society in general, are not followed by any consequences which closely affect him, or which would operate as a just and reasonable restraint upon men who do not exercise self-control or regard the most essential principles of justice in their relations with others.

It may be contended that my suggestions as to a new marriage system are contrary to the sentiment of western peoples, but it must also be said that they are not contrary to the general practice of such peoples. They are contrary to their pretensions — that is all.

It will naturally follow in the adoption of large and general measures designed for millions of people, and the almost countless exigencies arising from the varied aspects of all social intercourse, that individual cases of injustice must result, but the measures here outlined would not perpetuate or involve more than a small fraction of the grave and ever increasing injustice shown in the existing order of society.

General laws governing human conduct must take into account the fact that some people will always act unjustly. There are provisions in the laws for dealing with burglars although only one person in many thousands is a burglar. If men and women were all honourable and endowed with the qualities of judgment, reason, justice and liberality, and if there could be any effective way to make this endowment permanent, there would be no need of laws of any sort — much less for laws respecting the one relation in which these qualities should be the most naturally displayed — namely in the relation of marriage. It is because men and women are not so endowed, and can never be, that it is necessary to set over them some tribunal to which the weak may appeal and which is strong enough to enforce the claims of the weak, without possessing sufficient power to take away the liberty of both the weak and the strong.

As all powers to interfere with individual liberty must

be strictly limited and closely defined, it is necessary to prescribe with more minuteness than would otherwise be admissible, precisely the regulations which may most reasonably be applied to insure the safety and welfare of the masses, while leaving to the individual the largest latitude of personal discretion and liberty compatible with an effective safeguarding of social objects.

How terribly difficult it is to construct a society upon this basis and how remotely in the dim mists of the future such a society may possibly be evolved, is evident to all who have considered the long and tragic struggles of humanity with a mind capable of weighing the importance of tendencies in human evolution and judging as to how far mankind may ever read aright the lessons of history and apply them to personal and general conduct.

Apart from the great economic and moral elevation which would accrue to mankind through my system there can be no doubt that its intellectual and physical advantages would be of incalculable benefit to humanity. In a state of nature uninfluenced by property and castes there is abundant and overwhelming evidence that through a process of natural selection the best males are chosen by the females, with the result that inferior males are denied the opportunity to propagate, and hence the weakest and most inefficient disappear. This principle would apply to a state of society in which men, women and animals were wholly engrossed in the struggle for physical existence and also to such a highly organized and complex civilization as our own; because in each instance preference would be given to the male in proportion as he possessed the qualifications most essential to success in the mastery of his surroundings.

It has been generally observed among singing birds that the females invariably choose the males who sing the sweetest songs. There can be no doubt that through many generations this must have an important effect.

This is one of the most unvarying principles which seems to run as a thread through the great loom of nature, but which man has tried to ignore through laws and institutions and through injustice, oppression and tyranny and in a general scheme of exploitation, suppression and pretence in all the economic and social affairs of life. And that is precisely why the tangled threads in the loom of humanity are filled with breaks and knots and the great skeins of life are caught in the wheels of our modern machine, until they are twisted out of all resemblance to the wonderful and ordered pattern which the hand of God has placed within the reach and spread before the eyes of his children.

We have only to observe the experience of humanity to realize that woman's choice in marriage is closely restricted. Many must marry a type of man who would be unable to marry under my system and there is thus propagated a vast element which would gradually disappear and which society should not longer perpetuate. It is of the highest importance to increase the number of children of the strong, efficient and great and diminish and at last prevent the inefficient, the derelict and the weak from having children at all. I believe this can be accomplished only through the economic liberation of those who toil with their brains and hands, and the adoption of a system of marriage on the lines here indicated.

It should be emphasized that in so far as men and women have found the ideal of happiness, or can find it in monogamy, there is nothing in these suggestions to interfere with such a relation. Instead of my system encouraging polygamy among men now married and having relations only with their wives, it would have the opposite effect, except among men who are too honourable to be polygamists under the existing order, because of the great injustice it involves to unprotected women. Many men who do not hesitate to enter upon temporary relations with several women, without incurring the slightest obligation to support them, would be reluctant to practice polygamy when it involved the honourable protection of the women for the remainder of life. The men for whom my measures are essential, constitute the considerable class which wishes to get something for nothing, whereas the men who would most readily embrace my system are those who have been, who are or who desire to be polygamists, and who are able and willing to respond to all the obligations incurred through their conduct. Such men are incapable of inflicting a certain or possible injury upon a woman whom society does not allow them to protect and for whom mankind will do nothing except further to ostracise and oppress.

The new system would abolish prostitution in its open and thousand hidden forms. It would put an end to the sexual depravity of men and the sexual slavery of women and place upon men the obligation honourably to support every woman with whon he had sexual relations. It would terminate the tragedy of unhappiness among people who should be released from their intolerable marriage bonds and would open the door of home to millions of women who are now the unprotected victims of man's industrial savagery, passions and social wrongs. There is no greater farce than the so-called justice which commits a man to prison because his desire to protect a woman causes him to commit bigamy, while the lawyers who prosecute him, the judge who sentences him and the rude and vulgar jailers who insult him in his living death, are respectable nobodies enjoying liberty and public confidence while they have had relations with two or twenty women for whom they do nothing and to whom they have brought nothing but injury and deception.

In *"The World Allies"* the economic relation of men and women toilers is closely examined and the reasons indicated why it will be the design of plutocracy to multiply the occupations open to women and do what lies in its power to prevent the adoption of any measure calculated to reduce and at last to terminate industrial strife between the sexes.

As there is need of millions of men for wage-slaves and soldiers, it may suit the ruling castes to offer inducements to women to become mothers under a system devised to perpetuate the power of the priests and plutocrats, but no measures less fundamental than those I have indicated will be effective and no remedies less general should satisfy the masses of industrial toilers, in whose hands the most dominant power in the world may now be consolidated. Under my system women would have fewer children but there would not be millions of homeless and childless women.

It is the duty as well as the opportunity of the common men and women now to adopt measures to insure to posterity a complete immunity from wage-slavery, prostitution and war and through an altered economic and social system to establish motherhood upon a basis where it will no longer be an occasion for privation or regarded with dread. Through childhood, maturity and old age those who are born of suffering and pain are permitted to inherit nothing but misery and a ceaseless struggle in order to live. The millions of unprotected women, who must be companions to the toilers and mothers of the race, should unite with their own class among men to free the world from its oppressive and atrocious economic and social wrongs.

The large interests of the human race will be truly served only by a system which will afford economic independence and liberty of choice in companions, in order that the best elements in both sexes may live in relations of security and freedom, upon a basis which will discourage and ultimately put an end to the propagation of the most useless and depraved. This would be one of the most immediate as well as important effects of the system I suggest and under it the propagation of the race would gradually pass from the inefficient, dissolute and ignorant to the strongest, the more intelligent, thrifty and generally efficient.

Women are now forced to marry almost any type of man if they are poor and wish to escape the drudgery and slavery of industrial toil. The ones who leave their hovels for the factory are forced, through the industrial enslavement of men, to earn something to contribute to the family support and that is why they go to the factory. Hardly any women ever go from tolerable surroundings into the roaring grind of the mills, where amid the noise, dirt and drudgery they throw away their lives for a few pennies a day, unless they are compelled to do so, and under my system this would be effectively stopped.

In order to anticipate and answer all the objections which will be urged against the measures set out in these pages and in my other books [1] it would be necessary to extend this volume to a length which might destroy its value among people who think they are too busy to read and to consider even the subjects of greatest human concern, but it may be well to anticipate one more of the economic objections which the political economists and tools of plutocracy will most strongly urge. That is that as they buy toil as a competitive commodity, that as the

---

[1] *"The People's Money"* and *"The World Allies."*

life of the common men and women is an international product, the same as corn and beans, anything which increases the product tends to lessen its value. In "*The World Allies*" this contention is dealt with fundamentally and at length, but I would here point out that when the women are withdrawn from all occupations outside the home, when the toilers cease their senseless economic fight against one another, when they compete, not to decrease wages but to increase production and have a fair share of what they produce, this problem will cease to be of any importance except to the plutocrats who now reap what others sow. This would give new opportunities for the general improvement and education of the masses, the toilers' day would be reduced to a maximum of four hours and men and women would be able to remain in school until they are twenty-one to twenty-five and to retire from hard labour before they are too old to enjoy the tranquility which they have so fairly earned.

In addition to this, the use of machinery to economize and replace human labour has only begun. Men are still in their infancy in the uses of the vast and unapplied forces of nature. Constantly and more rapidly than at any other time in history, the theory upon which society rests is changing and at a time sooner than many now imagine our social structure will either be completely altered or society will be destroyed. It cannot endure upon its present basis of industrial exploitation, imperialism and violation of the sacred rights of those whose toil has enriched everyone except themselves.

Most people now throw away their lives in ways which are ineffective, useless or even worse. Everything is duplication. Waste is everywhere the rule. We march everyone to a different tune, work at cross-purposes and generally struggle against all the great natural currents of life which might bear us in harmony and co-operation along the course of an ordered and reasonable existence.

It is also not sufficiently realized that the development of the great natural resources of earth has only begun and that the larger part and richest sections of earth are entirely untouched or insufficiently used. We get the least imaginable result from the greatest human endeavours —especially on the land. One continent, capable of supporting two thousand million people, has a population of about seventy millions.

The time will come when man cannot endure all the hideous noise which now troubles the whole of his activities. I look to the day when there will be no steam trains, no odious underground railways, no trams and none of that disorder and confusion which now makes human life so complicated, so strained and so miserable. In that great day man will go about his simple and important vocations with the serenity, silence and certainty which the marvellous nature constantly displays in its intricate and wondrous work.

Let it be said with all possible emphasis, that we are only in the infancy of our mechanical, social and spiritual life. Great as have been the dreams of a few men for an ideal commonwealth, even they did not trace the outliness of the wonderful era which awaits humanity when its shackles shall have been cast aside.

It is therefore not to be wondered at that we should stand against the present slavish worship of all that exists, because we look with calm assurance to that better and more perfect day when man shall realize and therefore attain his own divinity in the universal scheme where he now merely gropes in darkness in which the blind are looked upon as the rightful and inspired leaders of others who are equally blind.

If society were to evolve along the lines I have dared

to indicate, as I am sometimes able to hope, and if the development of the resources of earth is once pursued in an ordered and intelligent manner, and the wealth produced by such development fairly distributed among its creators, there would be an abundance for the comfort of ten thousand million people and the question of an overproduction of labour would fade into a future which is so many thousands of years distant as to be of no concern to mankind, since long before then we will have ceased to treat men as a commodity.

It is nothing less than a monstrous outrage that men are now able to so regard human life as to seriously suggest that when a poor man increases his family he decreases his value to society and must pay for his folly by competing with those whose existence should make all men more rich but never more poor.

When a feudal lord or one of the newly created jam-making lords multiplies his progeny he adds to the power and possible fame of his family, but the one difference between a large family of the rich and a large family of the poor is that the rich absorb what they have no power to create and the more there are, the more they absorb, whereas what the poor create passes immediately to nonproductive and exploiting classes. And thus is witnessed the ever increasing tendency to force more and more of the poor to toil in order that they may live at all. This fatal retrogression in the economic life of the masses has now engulfed not only all male toilers, but also millions of women of their own class and additional millions of uneducated, undersized and partly developed children.

It should also be noted that as the means of travel and communication become ever increasingly rapid there will be a growing tendency for people to migrate to distant lands to improve their condition. This opportunity is now denied to the masses because they are economically enslaved and thereby tied to the land and the wheels near the spot of their birth. As they rise out of this slavery they will enjoy the benefits which are now in the exclusive possession of their masters. No feudal lord ever had a more effective mastery over the migration of his serfs than that now enjoyed by the industrial masters whose slaves are tied to their machines, not by law, or by chains, but by an economic bond which is cheaper and more effective and which interferes less with the productive activity of the slaves.

When it is possible for the common man to take his rightful place in society, when transportation in the air enables man to cross the Atlantic in an afternoon, and when the horrors of wars, the snobbery occasioned by kings and plutocracy, the barriers of nationalism and the senseless idolatry of flags are all swept away as the rubbish of a hideous past, there will be a new humanity with standards of life and attainments which are now undreamed of.

This is the goal toward which men's faces should be set with the stern and solemn resolve that no time is to be wasted in taking the firm steps by which alone humanity may pursue the majestic course lying open to it across the centuries. Perhaps a thousand years from now a free and wonderful humanity, will salute our present generation with gratitude and affection, because it laid deep the foundation of a noble structure upon which mankind could create a new world and over which he found also a new and more spiritual heaven.

APPENDIX A.

INTELLECTU

INTERNATIONAL FEDERATION OF WORKERS AND INSTITUTIONS OF INTE
REGENERATION OF HUMANITY WITHOUT DISTINCTION AS TO NATIONAL
WHICH CREATE DIVISIONS

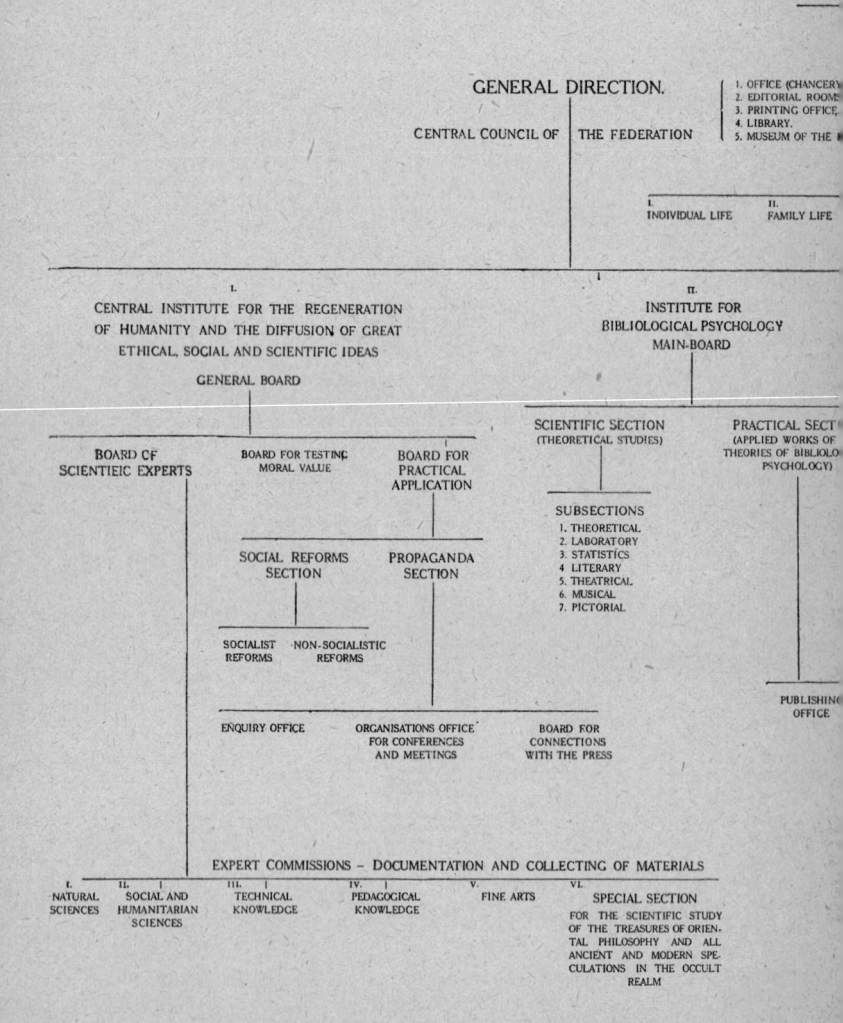

GENERAL DIRECTION.

CENTRAL COUNCIL OF | THE FEDERATION

1. OFFICE (CHANCERY)
2. EDITORIAL ROOMS
3. PRINTING OFFICE
4. LIBRARY.
5. MUSEUM OF THE

I. INDIVIDUAL LIFE   II. FAMILY LIFE

I.
CENTRAL INSTITUTE FOR THE REGENERATION
OF HUMANITY AND THE DIFFUSION OF GREAT
ETHICAL, SOCIAL AND SCIENTIFIC IDEAS

GENERAL BOARD

II.
INSTITUTE FOR
BIBLIOLOGICAL PSYCHOLOGY
MAIN-BOARD

SCIENTIFIC SECTION
(THEORETICAL STUDIES)

PRACTICAL SECT
(APPLIED WORKS OF
THEORIES OF BIBLIOLO
PSYCHOLOGY)

BOARD OF
SCIENTIFIC EXPERTS

BOARD FOR TESTING
MORAL VALUE

BOARD FOR
PRACTICAL
APPLICATION

SUBSECTIONS
1. THEORETICAL
2. LABORATORY
3. STATISTICS
4. LITERARY
5. THEATRICAL
6. MUSICAL
7. PICTORIAL

SOCIAL REFORMS
SECTION

PROPAGANDA
SECTION

SOCIALIST
REFORMS

NON-SOCIALISTIC
REFORMS

PUBLISHING
OFFICE

ENQUIRY OFFICE

ORGANISATIONS OFFICE
FOR CONFERENCES
AND MEETINGS

BOARD FOR
CONNECTIONS
WITH THE PRESS

EXPERT COMMISSIONS – DOCUMENTATION AND COLLECTING OF MATERIALS

| I. NATURAL SCIENCES | II. SOCIAL AND HUMANITARIAN SCIENCES | III. TECHNICAL KNOWLEDGE | IV. PEDAGOGICAL KNOWLEDGE | V. FINE ARTS | VI. SPECIAL SECTION FOR THE SCIENTIFIC STUDY OF THE TREASURES OF ORIENTAL PHILOSOPHY AND ALL ANCIENT AND MODERN SPECULATIONS IN THE OCCULT REALM |

ET LABOR.

CTUAL AND MANUAL WORK CONTRIBUTING TO THE MORAL AND SOCIAL
RACE OR RELIGION AND CONSECRATED TO ABOLISHING ALL SENTIMENTS
O CONFLICTS AMONG MEN.

OCTOBER 21st 1918.

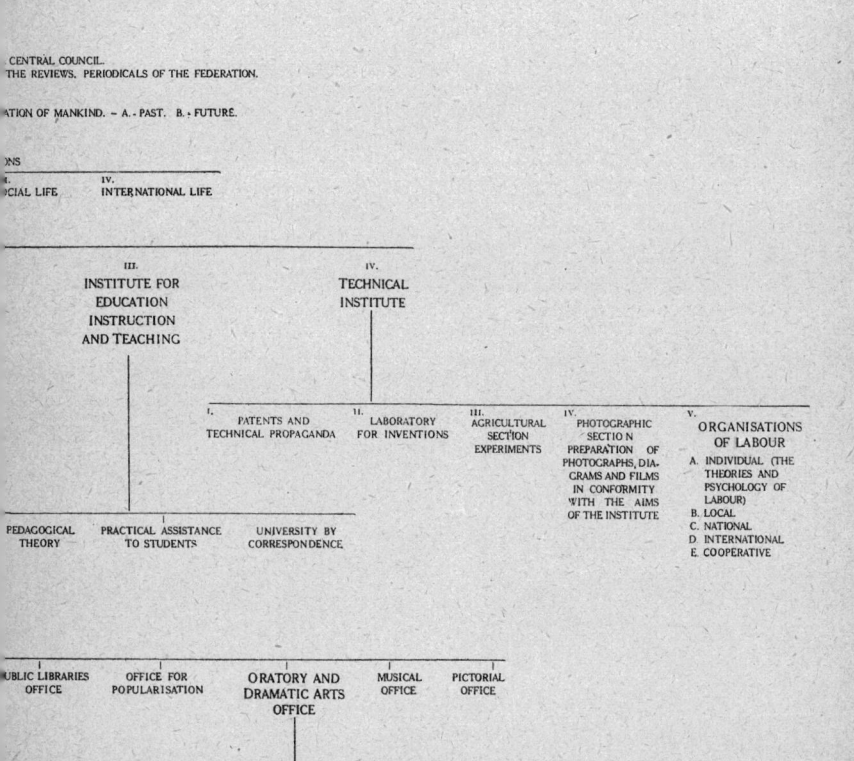

CENTRAL COUNCIL.
THE REVIEWS, PERIODICALS OF THE FEDERATION.

ATION OF MANKIND. – A. - PAST. B. - FUTURE.

ONS
II. IV.
OCIAL LIFE INTERNATIONAL LIFE

III.
INSTITUTE FOR
EDUCATION
INSTRUCTION
AND TEACHING

IV.
TECHNICAL
INSTITUTE

I.
PATENTS AND
TECHNICAL PROPAGANDA

II.
LABORATORY
FOR INVENTIONS

III.
AGRICULTURAL
SECTION
EXPERIMENTS

IV.
PHOTOGRAPHIC
SECTION
PREPARATION OF
PHOTOGRAPHS, DIA-
GRAMS AND FILMS
IN CONFORMITY
WITH THE AIMS
OF THE INSTITUTE

V.
ORGANISATIONS
OF LABOUR
A. INDIVIDUAL (THE
THEORIES AND
PSYCHOLOGY OF
LABOUR)
B. LOCAL
C. NATIONAL
D. INTERNATIONAL
E. COOPERATIVE

PEDAGOGICAL
THEORY

PRACTICAL ASSISTANCE
TO STUDENTS

UNIVERSITY BY
CORRESPONDENCE

UBLIC LIBRARIES
OFFICE

OFFICE FOR
POPULARISATION

ORATORY AND
DRAMATIC ARTS
OFFICE

MUSICAL
OFFICE

PICTORIAL
OFFICE

THEATRE CONCERT HALL CINEMA

FOR PSYCHO-BIBLIOLOGICAL EXPERIMENTS
OF THE INSTITUTE

APPENDIX B.

A SHORT BIBLIOGRAPHICAL REVIEW OF THE ORIGIN AND DEVELOPMENT OF THE IDEA OF THE "SOCIETY OF NATIONS"

BY

D<small>R</small>. NICHOLAS ROUBAKINE.

SEE FOOT-NOTE PAGE 169.

The idea of uniting all mankind in one great family or society of nations was not born yesterday; it is rooted in the distant past. Its history gives a striking and instructive illustration of the whole of the evolution which, in the course of ages, has sprung from two fundamental ideas, on which are founded the life of every human being: 1) the idea of individuality and 2) that of humanity. This evolution, in spite of certain temporary halts and digressions, has progressed steadily, its final result ever tending towards the highest development of individuality, as well as that of social groupings (societies, states) all striving towards the perfect development of humanity. The highest conception of the thought of a Society of Nations is the one that conceives the term as synonymous with that of "Society of Peoples" meaning in the first place, a Society of the *labouring classes* that form the immense majority of mankind in all countries and states of the world.

This conception of the term is not quite in accordance with what is generally understood by "Society of Nations" for, in its usual sense, the term "people" has not the same meaning as the word "nation." "The people," says Prof. Gumplovitcz, "represent the contents of the State. They are outwardly held together in the whole by merely political bonds, each people being internally divided into sharply defined social classes or clans.

"As the development of the State progresses, the sense of clan-division gradually gives way to the 'feeling of guild, the sense of class' and lastly, to that of national self-consciousness.

"The conglomeration of tribes forms a people, and later on, by gradual development—a nation. The natural diversity of tribes leads thus, first to a cultivated union, and later to a unity based on pure culture.

"The *race* is a natural phenomenon produced by nature (Naturerscheinung) the *tribe* is an ethnical product of life; the *people* is a political fact; the nation however is a product of culture." (Prof. GUMPLOVITCZ. *Allgemeines Staatsrecht.)*

We hardly believe that any people has as yet actually attained to true national self-consciousness in the abovementioned sense. It is generally (and quite erroneously) supposed that this development is attained solely by the upper classes, by those that domineer over the labouring classes, politically and spiritually. It is a grievous error to confound class-consciousness with popular or national consciousness, yet this error is purposely or unwittingly committed by the partisans of the "Society of Nations" who have substituted that idea to that of the "Society of Peoples."

On following the course of the evolution of this idea from the highest to a lower step, we perceive yet another backward move when for the "Society of Nations" the "Society of States" is substituted. The Society of Peoples recognizes the full right of every people to self-determination, by free exercise of will, not merely of every social group of a tribe, but of each *individual*, who is allowed to decide *himself* to what nationality he belongs. The Society of Nations presents that question under the pressure of the domineering classes, whose opinions are declared to be "social" and even "national." The Society of States puts these opinions aside, deciding the question simply by political force, i. e. by the power held by *certain* social groups, classes, etc. In plain speech, by organized violence, as every great modern state, by its very nature, represents an organization of violence, be it in the hands of Nicolas II, or Lenine, of Abdul-Hamid or Clémenceau, of the Pope or of the negro king Mtesa.

We agree with Prof. Gumplovitcz in defining the State as an organized power, created for the defence of certain determined rights of order (Gumplovitcz, Opus cit. § 12). The evolution of the dominion of one empire over another, of one nation over another, of one people over another, of one social class or guild over another, etc. has led, as it did in olden times, to the forming of various allied states (Bundesstaat) and alliances of states, (Staatenbund) which represent a political union of different types of political unities.

The highest type of such unions is the *voluntary* one, the lowest (and most usual) is the union that is *forced*. Such unions or alliances are, as is proved by history, temporary, or perpetual. The Society of Peoples has therefore passed, in this phase of its evolution, through a long series of different sorts of political unions, from prehistoric times to our days. The following are the chief steps in the evolution of the Society of States:

1) *CONFEDERATIONS* (Staatenbunde) i. e. unions formed between a few or many states, for an indefinite period, for certain purposes, such as self-defence, international representation, etc. that create a regularly acting organ, consisting of representatives of the governments of those allied states.

2) *FEDERATIONS* i. e. unions of some or many states, each keeping its own national independence, but uniting for some definite purpose, in a constant common action.

3) *ALLIANCES* between several states, with some definite aim or purpose; they are usually temporary, and do not admit of the existence of any central organ of the interested states that should act regularly or constantly.

History in all countries offers an infinite variety of such alliances, mostly of the third species. Their origin does not date merely from prehistoric times but is found in the animal kingdom, where certain creatures (ants, wasps, bees, wolves, swallows) living in communities or singly, unite for certain purposes.

The history of the Society of Peoples is one with that of mutual help and altruistic action, also with the history of moral instinct and morality. If we go deeper into the subject, we may find that it unites with the history of the Cosmos, in the organization of which, in the mysterious *inconnaissable* or the Noumen, are hidden the roots of all those higher elements of the human soul. We give here a review of the writings on science, thought, altruism and idealism, of men of genius of all countries and nations, containing a collection by the most remarkable thinkers of all times and nations, that is at the same time a most severe judgment of history upon all Societies of Victors and all tigers from those of the Jardin des Plantes to the tigers now lurking in other parts of Paris and who are preparing the way for general violence.

In offering our bibliographical review to the reader, we do not pretend to have exhausted the whole rich fund of literary productivity, treating of the question of the Society of Nations and its evolution. We only point out the most important works that appeared before the year 1914 and some which have appeared since.

1. *The Origin of the impulse of mutual help and of altruism leading to harmony.*

This subject possesses a priceless scientific and scientific-popular literature, that relates however but partly to the subject of this book. We will therefore merely point out some valuable books, that can be of use as a first rate introduction to this question. Such is the remarkable work of P. KRAPOTKINE. *Mutual Aid.* SUTHERLAND. *The Origin of Moral Instinct.* ROMANES. *Animal Intelligence. Mental Evolution in Animals.* ESPINAS. *Sociétés animales.* LETOURNEAU. *Evolution de la Morale.* DARWIN. *Origin of Man.* WUNDT. *Ethik.* WAKE. *Evolution of Morality.* NICOLAI. *Die Biologie des Krieges.*

2. *The Origin of Alliances of primitive and of prehistoric Nations.*

L. MORGAN. *Ancient Societies.* N. SIBER. *Essays on history of economical culture* (in Russian, edited by N. Roubakine). H. SPENCER. *Principles of Sociology.* GIDDINGS. *Outlines of Sociology.* LIPPERT. *Kulturgeschichte der Menschheit.* G. BUSCHAN. *Die Sitten der Erde.* WUNDT. *Völkerpsychologie.* RATZEL. *Völkerkunde.* O. PESCHEL. *Völkerkunde.* LETOURNEAU. *Evolution politique. Evolution juridique.* A. POST. *Der Ursprung des Rechts. Die Anfänge des Staats- und Rechtslebens. Grundriss der ethnologischen Jurisprudenz. Bausteine für allgemeine Rechtswissenschaft.* F. ENGELS. *Der Ursprung der Familie.* MAINE. *Ancient Law. The early history of Institutions. Early Law and Custom. Popular Government, International Law.* SCHURZ.

Urgeschichte der Kultur. G. WOLTMANN. *Politische Antropologie.* P. LAVROV. *History of Thought in our Time.* E. RECLUS. *La Terre et l'homme,* vol. I. E. BÜCHER. *Die Entstehung der Volkswirtschaft.* VIERKANDT. *Naturvölker und Kulturvölker.* GUMPLOVITCZ. *Grundriss der Soziologie.*

3. *History of the Idea of the Society of Nations.*

A first rate introduction to its study (aside from general works, on history, international law, philosophy and ethics, that we shall not enumerate here) can be obtained from the following books: Prof. FRIED. *Handbuch der Friedensbewegung.* NICOLAI. *Die Biologie des Krieges* (chap. Die Entwicklung des Begriffs des Weltorganismus, § 3.355). PAUL JANET. *Histoire de la Science politique dans ses rapports avec la Morale.* D. J. TER MEULEN. *Der Gedanke der Internationalen Organisation in seiner Entwicklung (1300—1800).* LORENT. *Etudes sur l'histoire de l'humanité. Histoire du droit des gens.* 18 vol. Prof. KAREFF. *Typologic course of study of the History of the Régime of State.* 5 vol. (in Russian) (a capital work in which a rightful place is given to the history of federations and confederations in relation to the general history of culture). Edited in the collective work under the dir. of Prof. HOLTZENDORF. *Handbuch des Völkerrechts,* is given the History of international right (vol. I. up to the year 1818). In this edition Rivier gives a valuable essay on international right. WALKER. *History of the Law of Nations,* vol. I. PIERANTONI. *Storia degli Studi del Diritto internazionale in Italia.* Also in a collective work, *Les Fondateurs du Droit international, leurs oeuvres, leurs doctrines, avec une introduction de* A. PILLET. (Collection of monographs relating to Vittorio, Gentile, Suarez, Grotius, Puffendorf, Wolf, Wattel, T. von Martens). NYS. *Les Origines du Droit international.* BAR. TAUBE. *History of the birth of actual international right* (in Russian) vol. I—II, middle Ages.

4. *A Detailed bibliographic index* of literature on international right and history, giving valuable material for the history of the idea of the Society of Nations, such as OMPTEDA. *Literatur des Völkerrechts,* 1789. KAMPTZ. *Neue Literatur des Völkerrechts,* 1817 (sequel to Ompteda's work.) R. MOHL. *Die neue Literatur des Völkerrechts* (2[d] quarter of XIX cent.) vol. of collective work *Geschichte*

und Literatur der Staatswissenschaften, 1855, p. 335—470. A. BUSHNELL-HART. *Introduction to the study of federal government.* Boston, 1891, p. 178—192 (here is indicated literature on the Bundesstaat and Staatenbund.)

5. *Antiquity. The East. Greece.— Rome* (up to the fall of the western Roman empire in 476 A. D.). In this period begins the conception of a general happiness for all mankind, without distinction as to nationality. This conception is met with in the religious as well as the philosophic literature. Because of the rudimentary development of relations between all the peoples of the earth, the conception of uniting all nations politically could not possibly exist. The uniting mediums appeared to be conquerors or the Messiah: the conquerors chiefly by uniting all neighbouring nations under their power, the Messiah—as a saviour from all future earthly suffering. Both these ideas run through all history of religions, of morals and of right like a white guiding thread. At the same time there exists a law forbidding any communion with strangers (in Egypt, India, Judea, etc.) each nation considering itself to be a "chosen" people. National exclusiveness exists by the side of repudiation of war see CHANTEPY DE LA SOSSEY. *Histoire des Religions.* The teaching of Zoroaster, on the reign of Ormuzd, is particularly interesting as the faith of Zoroaster unites all men into one family without making any distinction as to their origin or even their nationality. See Prof. HOPKINS. *Elements of the Science of Religion.* DITTO: *Geschichte der Religionen im Altertum bis auf Alexander den Grossen,* 2 vol. PAUL JANET. (op. cit). *On the uniting of mankind in the antique Armenian understanding.* LEIST. *Altarisches Jus gentium.* On the link between the Persian view of the future single kingdom of Ormuzd on earth with the Hindoo teaching of Varuna: OLDENBERG. *Die Religion der Veda.* Compare the teaching of Zoroaster to that of Empedocles also with the literature on the mysteries of Mitra (in the Roman period). Further, on the reign of the Messiah, see the prophet Isaiah, who prophesies the reign of prolonged peace; see also *Revelations,* and BARUCH, *IV book of Esdras,* KAUTZKY. *Judentum und Christentum* etc. On the unifying of all mankind in

the reign of the Messiah (as understood in the Bible
and ancient Jewish national traditions): DRUMMOND.
The jewish Messiah. RICHURE. *Le Messie.* EVERSHEIM.
Prophecy and history in relation to the Messiah. In
absolutely all ancient countries of the East, in the remotest
time we meet with more or less decided pacifists and
antipacifists. For instance, Lao-Tze is an enemy of war
and he insists on the need of substituting ethics to
politics. (CHANTEPY DE LA SOSSEY, op. cit. v. I. § 10) on
Lao-Tze see J. CHALMERS. *Speculations on metaphysical
policy and morality of Lao-Tze.* Most interesting is the
teaching of Men-Tze, as he formulates clearly and definitely
all ethical and political preliminaries to a Society of
Nations. There were many anti-militarists among the ancient Chinese. On the efforts of Buddhism to win over mankind by ethical theories, and its unification, see OLDENBERG.
Buddha. RHYS DAVIDS. *Buddhism.* Buddha teaches the
unification of mankind. For a detailed account see the
general writings on the religious history of the East.
On the destructive influence of Buddhism on the reign of
caste see PAUL JANET, op. cit. I.

Greece and Rome. P. PÖLLMAN in his *Geschichte des
Kommunismus im Altertum* proves that the thought of
a universal State existed in the minds of a great number
of Greek thinkers, and was even related to the communistic
ideas of the period. Prof. KAREFF, op. cit. vol. II.
SOCRATES was asked where he was born. "On earth" he
replied. And in what country? "In the universal one."
ISOCRATES (436—338 B. C.) spoke first of the need of
making peace with all mankind. ARISTOTLE also strove
to determine what political regime should be introduced
into the State, so did PLATO, 427—347 B. C. DIOGENES
the Cynic (414—323) called himself a citizen of the Universe and taught his disciples that the only rightful
State is the one that includes the whole world.

In the dialogues *Timaeus* and *Kritias* PLATO gives
an illustration of the peaceful kingdom of Atlantis. It
is an irrefutable merit of Plato that he raised the ideal
of the State to the everlasting ideals of right and truth.
Prof. E. TROUBETZKOÏ has demonstrated (see *Questions
of Philosophy and Psychology* 1890, n. 4) that Plato's

theory of the State was a precursor of the theocratic ideals of the middle ages, whereas Aristotle, on the contrary preconceived "the ideal of the cultural European State of our times." Nevertheless both Plato and Aristotle conceive the State solely as a national separate unity. See above PÖLLMAN (op. cit.) who explains the ideal State of Plato and Aristotle in its relation to the ideal universal social State of the Stoic ZENO (v. IV 350—264 B. C.) (see *Politeia*). ZENO took his idea of cosmopolitism from the CYNICS, repudiating however individualism. He aims at making all mankind citizens of one State, submitting them to one law. CICERO too speaks of a universal State, so does EPICTETUS (50 A. D.) SENECA (4—65 A. D.), *Membra sumus corporis magni* protests also against war. MARCUS AURELIUS (121—188 A. D.) represents all mankind as one great society or community, and says that all men should live under one law for all are members of one universal State. The STOICS taught the fraternity of all men, and considered the world as the common fatherland of all. The EPICUREANS put treaty over law. See FLORUS (v. II. cent. A. D.) in *Epitome de gestis Romanorum*. One must mark the views of Roman law, Jus municipii, on treaties, alliances, universal monarchy and the situation of the provinces in the latter. See the writings on the history of Roman law of MOMMSEN, ZEHRING, E. MEUS etc. Also the history of the Amphictionian alliances, symmachia, symplelitei etc.

The teaching of Christ may be considered as a further step towards the theoretical confirmation of the teaching of the Society of Peoples. Christ considers all men to be equal in value. They are all brothers in Christ. All those that labour and are troubled are close to Him. For Him there is no Greek, or Jew, neither Barbarian nor Scythian, neither slave nor free man, but all brothers. All men are men. Those that take to the sword shall perish by the sword. All violence of one man against another is wrong. Love your neighbour whoever he be and of whatever race. Anger and hatred must have no place in the soul. All these precepts are precursory to the theory of the society of nations. The teaching of Christ on riches and on that "those that labour alone shall eat" is precursory to the theory of a social organization founded on the labour of all.

As is well known, in the teachings of the official state churches of Christianity (Catholic, Protestant, Orthodox) the ideals of the reign of God on earth have degenerated into ideals of nationalism and violence.

On the other hand, the history of so-called heresies and sects offers rich material to the history of the idea of the Society of Peoples. Want of space hinders our enumerating the latter.

6. *Middle ages (up to the discovery of America, 1492).*

On the union of nations under the authority of the Pope see the works of THOMAS AQUINUS (1227—74). To his school belongs: *De regimine principum;* EGADIO COLONNA (also called AEGIDIO ROMANUS, 1247—1316) who treats of a league of different parties. The most remarkable authors of the Middle Ages are: DANTE (1265—1321) see his *De Monarchia;* PIERRE DUBOIS. *De recuperatione Terrae Sanctae;* On DUBOIS see SCHÜCKING. *Die Organisation der Welt* (1909). MARSILIO OF PADUA. (1324) see his *Defensor Pacis.* HONORÉ BONNOR (1380) see his *Arbre de Bataille.* The king of Hungary, GEORGE PODIERAD (1420—71) was the instigator of Antonius Marius, his chancellor, who, in his work *Friedensbündnis* expounds the plan of this Hussite king. See Dr. E. SCHWITZKY. *Der Europäische Fürstenbund Georgs von Podiebrad* (1907). Also see biography of Pope Leo X. (1475—1521) FRANÇOIS DE LA NOUE see TER MEULEN (op. cit.).

7. *More recent times* (1492—1799, *up to and including the great French Revolution*). In this epoch were determined not only the preliminary steps to the Society of Peoples but also the fundamental traits of its organization. The history of this subject offers one of the most interesting pages of the history of the spiritual life of mankind. It is seen there that in it are fused all the highest strivings of mankind in the sphere of ethics, religion, law, science, social economy and philosophy. These are the men that appeared as the chief representatives of the idea of a single and peaceful organization of humanity. We enumerate these represen-

tatives of one general idea without more exactly classifying them.

The epoch of humanitarianism produced its special pacifist in the person of ERASMUS OF ROTTERDAM (1461—1531). See his *Militis Christiani Encheiridion* (1518); *Colloquien, Instruktionen für Christliche Prinzen* (for Charles V.). See further: FRANCISCUS VICTORIA (1557). In the beginning of the XVIIth century we find the "Grand Dessein," the first plan for a practical realization of a league of nations (by the French king HENRY IV). It is expounded by the DUC DE SULLY in his *Mémoires ou Economies royales d'Etat, domestiques, politiques, européennes de Henry le Grand*, ed. 1604, 2 vol. See *The Arbiter in Councils* (London 1906). ALBÉRIC GENTILE (1552—1608) *De jure belli* (on the rights of nations). In 1612 appeared a treatise of the Spanish Jesuit SUAREZ (1548—1617) *Tractatus de legibus et de legislatore* (Staatengemeinschaft). We must point out too the following authors (placing them in the order of the date of their death): CAMPANELLA (1568—1639) *De monarchia Hispanica* (1613). E. DE LA CROIX (1590—1648). See his project of universal peace: *Le nouveau Cinée, ou discours d'Etat, représentant les occasions et moyens d'establir une paix générale et la liberté de commerce par tout le monde.* The same project is treated by the celebrated HUGO GROTIUS (1583—1645) in his *De jure belli ac pacis* 1625, that treats of the Society of Nations. In 1624 the German jurist NEYMAYR published a treatise *Von Friedenshandlungen*. We mark further the work of the pacifist FRIEDRICH VON LOGAU (1604—55) of the Englishman RICHARD ZOUCHE: *Juris et judicifecialis sive juris inter gentes* (1650). OPPENHEIM. *International Law* I. (included in *Classics of International law*). Further the writings of the German poet JOACHIM RACHEL (1618–1669). See TER MEULEN, op. cit. On the peaceable solving of international relations, see AMOS COMENIUS (1592–1676) *Consultativ Catholica*. The Quakers of the XVIIth century brought forward from their midst a considerable number of authors who treated of the subject of the abolition of war by means of a general organization of nations and states. The founder of this sect GEORGE FOX (1624–96) was a firm believer in Christian pacifism. We draw attention to the Quakers: ROBERT BARCLAY (1649—90), WILLIAM PENN (1644—1718), *Essays on the present and future peace of Europe* (1693). He gives a plan of a constant international congress. RICHARD PRICE (1723—91) *Observation on the nature of civil liberty.* JOHN BELLERS (1710), etc.

Very close to the idea of Henry IV. are those of the duke KARL VON LOTHRINGEN UND VON BAR (1688) exposed in his Testament. On an organizing of a Catholic Fürstenbund see Landgraf ERNST VON HESSEN, RHEINFELS (1623—1693). The famous SAMUEL PUFFENDORF speaks of an international conference and tribunal in his *Jus naturae et gentium* (1632—94). WILLIAM TEMPLE (an English diplomat) in his *Account of the United Provinces* mentions a European federation on the model of the one then existing in Holland. We further mention JOHN LOCKE (1632—1701) as frequently speaking in favour of pacifism. PIERRE BEYLE (1647—1706) *Dictionnaire historique* (1695—1697). We must also mention the well-known FÉNÉLON (1651—1715) who in his *Télémaque* expounds the theory that all nations form one family and must to avoid wars, form a universal league and a single congress. Most akin to the idea of Fénélon is that of PASCAL (1623—62), also LA BRUYÉRE (1645—1696), BOILEAU (1676—1710). CHRISTIAN THOMASUS (1655—1728) *Fundamenta juris naturae et gentium* (1705), the remarkable works of the ABBÉ ST. PIERRE (Charles Iréné CASTEL DE ST-PIERRE (1658—1743) see his *Projet de la paix perpétuelle* (1712—16) (on the federation of all european states) also his *Projet de traité pour rendre la paix perpétuelle* (1712). LEIBNITZ (1646—1716) *De jure suprematus ac ligationis principium Germanicae* (a federation presided over by Emperor and Pope). See on him CAMILLE LEROUX DE AGRINCOURT, *Exposé des projets de St Pierre, de Bentham et de Kant* (1905). An interesting document is the project of an international organization attributed to Cardinal ALBERONI (1664—1752) (see ROUSSET, *vie d'Alberoni et Bessoni, Storia del Cardinale Alberoni*) and the plan of 1745 (see Ter Meulen, op. cit.) one must not omit what was said about peace and war, and how to avoid the latter by SWIFT (1667—1745) in his *Gulliver's travels*. A noteworthy work is that of CHRISTIAN WOLFF *Jus gentium*, (1749) he is seconded by WITTEY.

The subject of universal monarchy is treated by MONTESQUIEU (1689—1755) see *Deux Opuscules de Montesquieu* 1724, ed. in Bordeaux, 1891, also his *Lettres Persanes* and *Esprit des Lois*. We must mention as pacifists DAVID HUME (1701—66) *Treatise upon human nature* 1738, and GOTTSCHED (1700—66) See C. L. SOMMERLING *Joh. Chris. Gottsched, ein Vorläufer des modernen Pazifismus* in the journal *"Es werde Licht"* (1909—12). The Swiss writer EMMERICH DE VATTEL wrote on the subject of a tribunal (1714—67) see his *Lehrbuch des Völkerrechts*. LILIENFELD (1767) *Neues Staatsgebäude*, MAYER (1777) *Tableau politique et litéraire de l'Europe* and LAGORGETTE *Le rôle de la guerre*, (1906). VOLTAIRE (1694—1778) gave much attention to the subjects of pacifism, antimilitarism and the general organization of nations. See his *De la paix perpétuelle*, also *Dictionnaire philosophique* and the paper *War* ed. 1704. ROUSSEAU (1712—78) on a single general federacy with a congress of nations and a tribunal, joins the Abbé de St Pierre. See *Projet de la paix perpétuelle*. TURGOT also wrote on the problem of an international league (1727—1781) see his *Oeuvres complètes*. So did the encyclopedian DIDEROT (1713—84) and others. We mention as pacifists W. LESSING (1729—81), the Abbé MABLY (1709—85) who insisted upon the subordination of politics to ethics (see his *Droit public de l'Europe* 1747 and other works), the German writer GOTTFRIED SCHINLY, who agrees with the idea of St Pierre (see his *Was ist den grossen Fürsten zu rathen, um das Wohl und Glück der Länder zu befördern* 1788). In 1787 appears a curious project of a *Holy League* see Ter Meulen, op. cit. To the pacifist movement and the idea of the league of nations comes also KARL GOTTLOB GÜNTHER (see Ter Meulen op. cit.). HOLBACH (1727—89) *Oeuvres complètes*, CONDORCET (1743—94) *Oeuvres complètes*, ANGO GONDAR (see Ter Meulen, op. cit.) the famous MIRABEAU (1749—91), *On Europe as one family*. ANACHARSIS KLOTZ (1755—1794), see his *Projet de la république universelle ou adresse aux Tyrannicides, Organisation politique uni-*

verselle de toute la planète and lastly the ardent opponent of war, GOTTLIEB HIPPEL (1741—96) *Kreuz- und Querzüge des Ritters* (1793) also his *Lebenslaufen nach aufsteigender Linie* (1778) etc. On the confines of the XVIIIth and XIXth cent. we must place EMANUEL KANT (1724—1804) whose name is written in the history of the fraternity of nations in indelible characters. Here is the list of the chief works of Kant in which he treats of the subject that interests us: *Zum ewigen Frieden* (1795), *Ideen zu einer allgemeinen Geschichte in weltbürgerlicher Ansicht* (1784). *Mutmasslicher Anfang der Menschengeschichte* (1786), *Religion innerhalb der Vernunft* (1793), *Methaphysik der Sitten* (1797), *Der Streit der Fakultäten* (1798), *Metaphysische Anfangsgründe der Rechtslehre* (1798), *Über den Gemeindsspruch: das mag in der Theorie richtig sein, taugt aber nicht für Praxis* (1793), this last essay is most characteristic. *Rechtslehre* (1797). Contemporaneously beside the theorical pacifist Kant must be placed the practical militarist by profession, Napoleon I who, not having succeeded in forming a unified European state, by violence (and having been vanquished by similar violence, and already in exile) wrote too about the Society of nations. See LASCASES. *Mémorial de St-Hélène.*

8. **Latest Period** (1800—1914).—This period presents an epoch of ever increasing striving of the popular masses to realize on earth the reign of labour and peace. The democratic tendency turns more and more towards socialistic principles and these latter diverge ever more widely from the tendencies of the representatives of the long so-called "old régime" that had long outlived itself and of the régime of capitalism that was equally outliving itself. Meanwhile the partisans of the principle of violence and of war, sowing among the people feelings of hatred, anger and vengeance, are ever deepening the abyss that is already dividing the upper from the labouring classes.

The following bibliographic material will help us fully to comprehend the general course of the evolution of the idea of the Society of Peoples in the XIXth and XXth centuries.

A) *The first half of the XIXth cent.* (up to 1848). Over-abundance of material obliges us to be still more

brief here; we point out the following authors: A. SCHLETT-
WEIN (1731—1802). *Natürliche Ordnung in der Politik
überhaupt* and other works. The Swiss J. F. LAHARPE
(1739—1803), develops the ideas of Voltaire; further his
namesake F. C. LAHARPE, was for a time tutor of the
Russian emperor Alexander I. who owed much of his
relative liberality and idyllic reveries on the league of
nations to that same Laharpe. This dream of Alexander
and his autographic text of the *"Holy Alliance"* as well
as the history of that Alliance have become vividly interesting thanks to the present efforts of an apparently
victorious bourgeoisie to establish a *"Holy Alliance."*
The literature treating of the hopes, principles and
practice of the *"Holy Alliance"* of 1815 is immense.
Noteworthy are: MALINOVSKY, *Le raisonnement sur la guerre
et la paix* (1803); AGRICOLE BATAIN, *Einwurf über eine
Weltorganisation* (1804). JOHANN FRANZ VON PLATEN, *Ver-
suche zum Vermögen* (1804) (on which see Lessing, *Briefe, die
neueste Literatur betreffend*, Vth letter). GABRIEL GAILLARD
(1726—1806), ALEXANDER HAMILTON (1757—1809) father
of the American federation; GOUDON D'ASSON (see his works
on public and international law, and on a universal, constitutional monarchy (1808); WIELAND (1733—1813);
the famous J. G. FICHTE (1762—1814) *Grundlage des
Naturrechts* (1796) *Die Rede an die Deutsche Nation* (1808);
MME DE STAEL HOLSTEIN (1766—1817) who in her writings
also expounded the idea of international unification. CT.
PAOLI CHAGNY (1818) who gave a *Sketch of Europe for
the purpose of peace;* VILNEY (1757—1820) *Die Ruinen* 1791;
SAINT-SIMON (1760—1825) *On the necessity of establishing a
unique european parliament, Letters of a native of Geneva to
his contemporaries, Plan of a reorganization of Europe* 1814
(the latter written in colaboration with A. THIERRY);
JEAN PAUL RICHTER (1763—1825) see his antimilitaristic
writings; *Levana* (1807), *Friedenspredigt in Deutschland*
(1808), *Dämmerungen*. His opinions on the possibility
of perpetual peace place JEAN PAUL close to E. KANT.
We must further mention such authors as HEINRICH VON
JACOB (1759—1827) see his *Annalen der Philosophie*
(1796). BENJAMIN CONSTANT DE REBECQUE (1767—1830)
gave in his essay *Of the spirit of conquest and usurpation* a

whole philosophy of the world; ABBÉ GRÉGOIRE (1750–1831) KARL FR. KRAUSE (1781–1832) *Entwurf eines europäischen Staatenbunds als Basis des allgemeinen Friedens* (1840); the celebrated JEREMY BENTHAM (1747—1832) one of the most remarkable theorists of utilitarianism *Principles of international Law* (1786—1789); SCHENDLER and PALIER DE ST-GERMAIN (see Ter Meulen, op. cit.), CHARLES FOURIER (1772—1837) *Théorie des quatre Mouvements*. On the approach of the reign of harmony see: WILLIAM LADD, *Essay on a Congress of nations for the adjustment of international disputes without resort to arms* (1840); W. TRAUGOTT KRUG (1770—1842) *Aphorismen zur Philosophie des Rechts, Kreuz- und Querzüge eines Deutschen auf den Steppen der Staatskunst und Wissenschaft* (1818); P. R. MARCHAND. *Nouveau projet de paix perpétuelle* (1842); A. HEEREN (1760—1842): *Handbuch der Geschichte des Europäischen Staatssystems* (an exposé of the Weltstaatplan); KARL SALOMON ZACHARIA (1769—1843) (chiefly in his *Janus* 1802); GUSTAV HUGO (1764—1844) *Lehrbuch des Naturrechts* (1808). Even CHATEAUBRIAND (1769—1848) in his *Génie du Christianisme* speaks of the possibility of a tribunal for the suppression of war, and what is particularly instructive for our actual militarists, not only for the prevention of war but of revolution. The famous German philosopher SCHELLING (1775—1854) must also be included. *The System des transcendentalen Idealismus* (1800) has its place beside the Kantian ideas of perpetual peace. A. TIERRY. (1795—1856) *Des Nations et de leurs idées mutuelles* (1816) (Idea of the league of nations). ALEXANDER VON HUMBOLDT, the famous naturalist, also wrote in 1850 of a project for a peace-congress (printed in the paper *Die Waffen nieder* 1892, Heft 3). It is evident that the principle of the league of peoples, that is of the league of the labouring classes, which should be the basis of every social regimen, was already a long time ago warmly welcomed in the socialist teaching. All the chief representatives of social thought, even in the oldest times, treated the subject of a universal reign of liberty, labour and general concord. See PÖLLMANN, op. cit.; the collective work: *Die Vorläufer des neuern Socialismus* (K. KAUTZKY, LAVARGUE, etc.).

A. Swientochowski, *History of Utopias* (in Polish); also see the general history of socialistic thought. The anarchist theorists go still farther. Both socialists and anarchists oppose the division of mankind into nationalities and states and a separation into social classes, according to whether they appropriate the product of the labour of others or not. Therefore both socialism and anarchism consider mankind to be one universal family of men, but not of states. In studying socialistic and anarchist theories, as they are progressively worked out, we perceive how their sphere gradually widens and, from being separate illustrations of Utopian states of a socialistic type, they become gradually scientific theories for a regularly planned transformation of the capitalistic regimen into a socialistic and anarchistic one. We refer all those who are interested in the relation of socialist authors to the question of the universal organization of nations, to the special guide-books on socialist literature. In the first place, to the work of J. Stammhammer, *Bibliographie des Socialismus und Kommunismus*, 3 vol.

B. *Second half of the XIXth cent.* (up to 1914). In this part of our historical-bibliographical review, we chiefly introduce: 1) the works that appeared before the beginning of the war and only a few of those that appeared later and that, in our opinion are specially worthy of notice, 2) books of authors of different tendencies in political, national and social study. We assume that, in order to adequately refute ones opponents, it is indispensable first of all to study their opinions at first hand. 3) We have tried to make our review as brief as possible, but feel it should have been still more brief. May our excuse be the great general interest shown by our readers in all countries for the subject of the political organization of mankind. Alas, there are still but few people in the world who understand fully that without a general social and economical reorganization, an international-political one is not possible; without the former, all victors of all times have always turned into the same depredators. 4) We must further call attention to the fact that the study of a union of states is one of the branches of international law that is the least advanced.

Most of the learned specialists refer to this branch only such questions as those of a real union of states, of federacies and confederations, and these subjects have not been fully worked out, still less the question of a union of the states of the whole world. Furthermore all these questions are mostly considered from the standpoint of *public* and not *international* right. But the first point of view, being narrower and more one-sided, is far from being applicable for the organization of mankind. The result obtained is a great theoretical muddle, that increased during the war of 1914—1919, because of the partiality, and even hidden hatred, that was put into their work by the specialists. As an introduction to the study of a union of all states we may mention the following notable works on international law: A. HEFTER, *Das europäische Völkerrecht der Gegenwart*. BLUNTSCHLI. *Das moderne Völkerrecht der civilisierten Staaten als Rechtsbuch dargestellt*. E. ULMANN. *Völkerrecht*. W. HALL. *A Treatise on international law*. H. BONFILS. *Manuel de Droit international public*. P. FIORE. *Il Diritto internazionale codificato* (ed. française, trad. de A. Chrétien). LIST. *Völkerrecht, Handbuch des Völkerrechts*. F. MARTENS. *Völkerrecht* (translated from the Russian). V. MARITZ. *Die Kultur der Gegenwart*. A. ZORN. *Grundrisse des Völkerrechts*. DESPEGNET. *Cours de droit international public*. MÉRIGNHAC. *Traité de Droit public international*. NYS. *Le Droit international*. PRADIER-FODÉRÉ. *Traité de Droit international public européen et américain*, 2 vol. OPPENHEIM. *International Law*. WALKER. *The Science of international Law*. BIGLATTI. *Diritto internazionale e costituzionale*. CT. L. KOMAROFSKY. *International Law* (in Russian). P. KAZANSKY. *Introduction to the course of international law. Schoolbook of international law* (in Russian). Of the confusion that reigns among all these authorities as regards the subject of confederated states, one may gain an idea by seeing how contradictory is their classification of what a union of states actually is. For instance, Hefter divides the states into: 1) Simple ones, 2) complex ones, of which a) those that consist of ruling and of dependent states, b) states united under one supreme dominion (unis civitatum), c) league of states (confederatio civitatum). Hefter includes in unio civitatum the unions, individual, real and allied states. BLUNTSCHLI considers as complex states: allied states, leagues of states, imperial states, leagues of empires, and real unions. ULLMANN considers as independent subjects of international law only the real unions, league of states, allied states etc. In minor questions the divergency is still greater.

A first-rate introduction to the study of the question of the Society of nations will be found in the series of the edition: *Organisation centrale pour une paix durable* (La Haye 1914—17) including 3 vols. of *Recueil de rapports sur les différents points du Programme minimum* edited by those untiring workers Dr. H. DRESSELHUYS and Dr. B. DE JONG VAN BECK EN DONK. Further P. OTLET. *Constitution mondiale de la Société des Nations*, W. GASS. *Geschichte der christlichen Ethik* (1881). G. UHLMANN. *Die christliche Liebesthätigkeit in der alten Kirche* (1882). O.PFLEIDERER. *Das Christentum, seine Schriften und Lehren* (1887). A. GÖFFERT. *History of Christianity in the apostolic age* (1897). Prof. FOREL. *Les Etats unis de la Terre, un programme praticable d'entente pacifique universelle et stable entre les peuples* (Lausanne 1915). OTLET. *Le nouveau Droit des Gens*. JOHN DE KAY. *The League of Nations* (1918) and by the principles of audietur et altera pars. M. ERZBERGER. *Der Völkerbund. Der Weg zum Weltfrieden* (1918.) G. DUPIN. *La guerre infernale* (Genève 1915). N. LÉNINE. *Ein Brief an den Amerikanischen Arbeiter* (1918). BOLCHÉVIK. *La politique extérieure de la Russie des Soviets.* (Bern 1918.) Against the Bolshevist understanding of dictatorship of the proletariat and universal social revolution, see Ch. NAINE. *La Dictature du prolétariat* (Lausanne 1918). E. VANDERVELDE. *Le socialisme contre l'Etat* (Paris 1918). K. KAUTZKY: *Die Diktatur des Proletariats* (1918). N. ROUBAKINE. *Lenin als Mensch und Revolutionär* (Internationale Rundschau, Zürich 1918, März). See too the admirable periodical *Der Völkerbund, Stimme der Vernunft* ed. by Dr. E. TRÜSCH and Dr. DE JONG VAN BEEK EN DONK. Also the journal of Prof. FRIED. *Friedenswarte* (Bern), *Wissen und Leben*, (Zürich). *Die Menschheit*, a journal, *Les Annales du Progrès* ed. by Dr. BRODA. PHILIPS B. ALISON, *The Confederation*

of Europe (An account of the attempt of the powers
to regulate European affairs after the fall of Napoleon).
W. ANEURIN. Une ligue des Etats pour la Paix (Contem.
Rev.). A. ALVAREZ. Le droit international de l'avenir.
R. W. BABSON. The future of the nations, (Boston).
E. BAYER. Pacigérance (1908). L. BARA. La science de
la paix, (1873). BIGNANI. Projet de ligue des Neutres.
BLUNTSCHLI, Die Grundzüge für einen Europäischen
Staatenverein. P. BONFANTE. Vers le Confédération européenne (Scientia, i, XIII, 1915). BRAILSFORD. Society of
Nations. BLOCH, Der Krieg (1899), Der Zukunftskrieg,
nach den Theorien T. v. BLOCH. L. BOURGEOIS. Pour la
Société des Nations (1910). PH. BOURGEON. La Guerre
allemande et la justice entre les nations (Rome 1917).
BRANDT, Les Etats confédérés d'Europe. Rev. droit intern.
p. 154. R. BRANT, A. GREENWOOD HUGUES. P. H. KERR.
Introduction to the study of international relations. R.
BROWN. International arbitration (1915). BOYLE. Z. HOMMER. History of peace. BRIDGEMAN. First book of World
Law (Boston). BRIE. Theorie der Staatenverbindungen
(1886). E. BRIOUX. L'idée de la Paix perpétuelle de
Jérémie Bentham (1905). VISCOUNT BRYCE and others:
Proposal for the prevention of future wars (London
1916). M. BUTLER. Project for United States of Europe.
A. CAPEL. Reflection on victory and Project for Federation of government, London. G. L. DICKINSON. After
the War. Proposals for the formation of a Council of
Nations (Boston, 1915). G. DUPLESSIS. La Loi des
Nations (Paris, 1916). L'Organisation internationale
(Paris, 1909). CH. DUPIN. Institut américain de Droit
international (Rev. des Sciences polit. 1917). ST. E.
EDMUNDS. Historic proposals for league of Peace (1917).
EIJKMAN. L'internationalisme scientifique (La Haye, 1911).
W. FÖRSTER. Weltpolitik und Weltgewissen. (1919).
FRAMGULIS. Une ligue des Nations (Paris 1917). K. FROME.
Monarchie oder Republik. FOLLIN. L'idolatrie politique.
GOLDSCHMIDT. A league to enforce peace. R. GOLDSCHEID.
Höhere Entwicklung und Menschenökonomie. I, Vol. 1912.
Friedensbewegung und Menschenökonomie. 1917.
B. HARMS. Volkswirtschaft und Weltwirtschaft (1912).
W. HAYS. The united nations of the world. D. HILL.

Völkerorganisation und der moderne Staat (1911). Dr. A.
Hommerich. Deutschtum und Schiedsgerichtbarkeit, (Freiburg, 1917). M. Hornberg. Theory of an allied state
(1891, Russian). M. Huber. Beiträge zur Kenntnis der
sociologischen Grundlagen des Völkerrechts und der Staatengesellschaft (1910). Die soziologische Grundlage des Völkerrechts (Berlin, 1910). Victor Hugo. Les Etats unis
d'Europe (1802—1885). Humani. Essai sur la Constitution
internationale. M. Hyndman. On Federation. 6 vol. D.
Jayne Hill. World organization and the modern States.
L. Jacque. Quelques considérations sur la "Respublica"
européenne. Jellinek. Lehre von den Staatenverbindungen.
Juraschek. Personalunion (1878). K. Kautzky. The
ancient world, Judaism and Christianity (in German).
Kazanski. Les premiers éléments de l'organisation universelle (1877, trans. from the Russ.). Lamasch. Christentum und Völkerrecht (Hochland, 1914—1915, 2. Heft).
Handbuch des Völkerrechts (1914). Europa's elfte Stunde
(1918). Le-Fur. Etat fédéral et Confédération d'Etats
(1898). Posener Bundesstaat und Staatenbund (1912).
H. Lafontaine, Maxima Charta (1910). Lepert. Projet
de justice internat. avec pouvoir législatif et transformation
des forces militaires (1907). F. Liszt. Ein europäischer
Staatenverband (1915). Vom Völkerbund zur Staatengemeinschaft (1918). Lawrence. The peaceful settlement of international disputes. T. Lorimmer. Le problème final du
Droit international. (Rev. Droit international IX, 1877.)
Proposition d'un Congrès international basé sur le principe
de facto, 1870. A. Lubniske. La Charte de l'humanité.
Merignhac. Le Problème final du Droit international.
J. Maxwell. La Philosophie sociale et la guerre. H.
Meyer. Die Staats- und Völkerrechtlichen Ideen von Peter
Dubois. (Marburg, 1908.) D. Mead-Edwin. 1) Organize
the world. 2) The great design of Henry IV. Fr. Meniecke.
Weltbürgertum und Nationalstaat. Gaston Moch. La
garantie de la Société des Nations. De Molinari. Le
Congrès européen. K. Naumann. Der Römische Staat
und die Allgemeine Kirche (1892). N. A. Nilsson. Fédération internationale. Th. Niemeyer. Internationales
Recht und nationales Interesse (1907). Nivion. La
Fédération de l'Europe (1901). Prof. Novgorodtzeff.

Kant and Hegel in their teaching on right and state.
Crisis of contemporary consciousness of right (in Russian).
J. NOVICOV. Fédération Européenne (1902). Prof. OPPEN-
HEIM. Die Zukunft des Völkerrechts (1911). W. OSTWALD.
Die Organisation der Welt, (1910.) PAUL OTLET. Les
problèmes de la guerre (1916). La Loi d'ampliation et
l'internationalisme (1907) and La Société des Nations
(1919). BENJAMIN PANDOLFI. Projet de Société des Nations
(1892). R. OCTAVION. L'Union juridique des nations-con-
fédérations. ETTORE PONTI. La guerra dei populi e la futura
confederazion europea(1915). PROATO. La teoria della pace
perpetua nelle sue derivazioni e nel suo svolgimento (1905).
P. J. PROUDHON, La guerre et la paix (1881). A. RAEDER,
L'Arbitrage intern. chez les Hélènes (1912). REHM. Geschichte der Staatsrechtswissenschaft. Allgemeine Staatslehre.
CH. RICHET. Le Passé de la guerre et l'avenir de la
paix. E. SCHLIÉSS. Der Friede Europas (1892). W. SCHÜKING.
Der Staatenverband der Haager Conferenzen. The work of
the Hague Conference. L'Organisation du Monde (Rev.
du droit intern. public, XV, Paris). Die Organisation
der Welt (Leipzig 1909). Das Werk von Haag and Der
Dauerfriede (1917). Further Der Weltfriedensbund (1917)
and Internationale Rechtsgarantien (1918). Die völker-
rechtliche Lehre des Weltkrieges (1918). SCHWARZ. Les
bases d'une paix durable. SPILLER. The supreme issue,
Law versus anarchy in intern. affairs. WILLIAM STEAD.
The united states of Europe. STEIN. L'idée de la paix
perpétuelle et de la guerre sociale (1907). VON STENGEL.
Weltstaat und Friedensproblem (1909). SCHWANN. Les
bases d'une paix durable (Paris 1917). SUCHTELEN. The
only solution; A European confederation. B. F. TRUEBLOOD.
1) A periodic Congress of nations 2) The Federation of the
World. 3) Parliament of Men. VERDIER WINTELER DE
WEINDECK. De la paix, du désarmement et de la solution
du problème social (1904). GRAHAM WALLACE. The great
Society (1909). JOSE WEISS. L'Alternative: Paix armée ou
Fédération. WESTERKAMP. Staatenbund und Bundesstaat
(1892). F. WRANGEL. Internationale Anarchie oder Verfassung.
L. S. WOOLF. International government; an intern. authority
for the prevention of war, by Woolf and a Committee of
the Fabian Society, with an introd. by G. B. SHAW.

PRINTED BY
C.-A. JUNGER
BASLE